Janner's Handbook of Draft
Letters of Employment Law for
Employers and Personnel Managers

GREVILLE JANNER

Janner's Handbook of Draft Letters of Employment Law for Employers and Personnel Managers

SECOND EDITION

Illustrations by Tobi

BUSINESS BOOKS

London Melbourne Sydney Auckland Johannesburg

Business Books Ltd
An imprint of the Hutchinson Publishing Group
17-21 Conway Street, London, W1P 6BS

Hutchinson Group (Australia) Pty Ltd
30-32 Cremorne Street, Richmond South, Victoria 3121
PO Box 151, Broadway, New South Wales 2007

Hutchinson Group (NZ) Ltd
32-34 View Road, PO Box 40-086, Glenfield, Auckland 10

Hutchinson Group (SA) (Pty) Ltd
PO Box 337, Bergvlei 2012, South Africa

First published 1977 under the title:
The Employer's and Personnel Manager's
Handbook of Draft Letters of Employment Law
Second impression 1977
Third impression 1978
Second edition under new title 1981

© GREVILLE JANNER, 1977, 1981

Set in IBM Press Roman

Printed in Great Britain by The Anchor Press Ltd
and bound by Wm Brendon & Son Ltd
both of Tiptree, Essex

British Library Cataloguing in Publication Data
Janner, Greville
    Janner's handbook of draught letters
    of employment law for employers
    and personnel managers.
    I. Title
    808'.066651   KD1634

ISBN 0 09 145730 0

Again – for
Mrs Pat Garner
with my thanks for
all her help and kindness

Contents

vii

Introduction to the First Edition

Every modern employer and personnel manager must write letters. Thanks to the Trade Union and Labour Relations Act, the Health and Safety at Work Act and the Employment Protection Act, these letters have become increasingly complicated. This book provides nearly five hundred drafts of the sort of letter that must be written with care and precision, for the sake of the company or firm — and also for the satisfaction of the writer himself.

Take 'unfair dismissal'. Failure to follow the correct procedures and to put them into writing may now cost employers up to £11,760 for each mistake. The burden of proving that a dismissal is 'fair' rests on them. Conversely, the executive who is dismissed 'unfairly' may win a small and probably tax-free fortune from the law. The better his documentation, the greater his prospects of success before the Industrial Tribunal.

There are (literally) masses of letters of appointment and dismissal which the employer or personnel manager may have to write — many of which, in the past, were better left unwritten. Today, if you wish to protect the company's position or your own (as employer's representative or as employee) writing the correct letter at the right time may prove crucial. This book starts with a wide selection of the right letters.

Or consider the new rules introduced by the Employment Protection Act, providing for maternity rights and benefits, redundancy consultations and warnings, insolvency rights, guarantee payments, the disclosure of information to trade unions and written reasons for dismissal. The employer or personnel manager who can produce the correct letter will do justice to his company or firm — and to himself. But the executive who makes a mess of his documents will destroy his own case or that of the business, long before it gets to the court or tribunal.

Above all, letters of appointment and written particulars of contracts of employment must be accurate; must follow all the statutory rules; and must contain all necessary terms. Restraint clauses; search clauses; requirements that a mother states *in writing* any intention to return; the duty of employees to follow the health and safety rules, on pain of possible dismissal . . . . This book explains them all, and provides sample clauses.

Then there are collective bargains . . . closed shop agreements . . .

negotiations over disputes, actual or threatened . . . . You may, of course, concoct your own series of letters dealing with these and other employment problems. But precedents, carefully prepared and adapted to your own use, should provide you with an invaluable guide, saving you time and anxiety – and your company's money.

Still, just as no two employees – or legal cases, for that matter – are identical, so it is unlikely that you will be able to use a precedent letter without translating it to your needs. By all means help yourself to letters in this book and use them as standard documents. But mind how you adapt.

In order to explain the use of letters, you have to understand why they are drafted in the particular form used. So I have included explanatory notes with each part and chapter and with most individual letters. These of themselves amount to unique 'potted' versions of labour law and of the rules on dismissals, employee protection, and health, safety and welfare at work.

This book is entirely concerned with employment law. You will find more general letters in my companion volumes: legal letters in *The Director's and Company Secretary's Handbook of Draft Legal Letters,* and contract letters in *The Director's and Company Secretary's Handbook of Draft Contract Letters.* This new book replaces *Letters of Industrial Law: An Executive's Practical Guide to the Industrial Relations Act* which died, along with that unlamented legislation.

Finally, *The Health and Safety at Work etc. Act, 1974* – which is a permanent and very powerful addition to the statute book – has created new perils for employers and managers at every level. Any executive or manager who breaks the rules through his 'consent', 'connivance' or 'neglect' may (at worst) be sentenced to up to two **years' imprisonment and/or to an unlimited fine. In broad terms, the** whole of the civil law on industrial safety has been codified and transferred to the realm of crime.

Once again, to keep out of trouble you need the right letters. These include not only letters to employees, inspectors, the Health and Safety Commission and Executive and to visitors or neighbours affected by your work. But they also involve letters to employees who do not make use of the safety procedures or protective clothing or guards which you provide for their safety. You must not only 'persuade' and 'propagandise' your workers to induce them to take care – you must also, if necessary, be able to prove that you did so. Under the 1974 Act, if you maintain that you took 'reasonably practicable' steps to comply with the rules, then the burden of proving that allegation rests on you.

The Part devoted to letters of health and safety should do as much to keep you out of the criminal courts as those dealing with unfair dismissal should ensure that you dismiss 'fairly' – and provably so. Equally, they should protect your own position as an employee – however mighty.

Finally, some notes on the use of this book. While every care has been taken in the preparation of these precedents and of the chapters and notes which accompany them, the author and publishers wish to emphasise the following:

1   The precedents are guides, to be used or adapted to suit particular circumstances; care must be taken by the writer in so doing.

2   The law (both as laid down by Parliament and as interpreted by the Courts) is subject to change – not least in the interpretation of words. It is confidently expected that judicious use of this book will save many unnecessary visits to lawyers – and, indeed, that the precedents may prove useful to solicitors themselves. But in the event of legal disputes arising or coming into prospect for the non-lawyer there is no substitute for the advice and assistance of an experienced solicitor, in possession of all the facts and knowing the new interpretations placed by courts on the statutes – and knowing also of any changes which may have been made by Parliament or the Courts in the rules themselves.

3   You may find that certain precedents in the book are of particular use and you wish to use or adapt them on a regular basis. In that case, it may be advisable to invite your solicitor to cast a careful eye over your revised draft.

4   Because of the foregoing – and as a further encouragement to care in the use of these drafts – it must be emphasised that **no legal responsibility can be accepted by the author or by the publishers in respect thereof, or arising in any way whatsoever from the use or adaptation thereof, in whole or in part, in any circumstances whatsoever.** (The above statement is known, in law, as a 'disclaimer' – and is a form of 'contracting out' – a subject fully dealt with in the book. The use of disclaimers is particularly important in connection with references – Chapter 19.)

5   In order that each chapter may be as comprehensive as possible, some repetition of the more important points and Sections of the Act is inevitable.

So here – fully annotated – are hundreds of precedents, which I hope will save you time, effort, worry and expense. With them, and with extracts from the relevant Acts of Parliament as Appendices, I wish you good luck!

*   *   *

I am very grateful indeed to His Honour, Judge Brian Clapham, to Mr Desmond Sturman, to Mr Howard Gaventa and to my wife for their encouragement, help and guidance, and to Paul Tobias (Tobi) for his brilliant illustrations.

The Temple   GREVILLE JANNER
London EC4
December 1976

Introduction to the Second Edition

Since 1977, when the first edition of this book was published, substantial areas of law have been changed — some considerably, others enough to require important alterations in both the draft letters and in their explanations and notes. So I have updated the entire book and added special new chapters on trade union rights and remedies; maternity notices and procedures; redundancy, lay off and short time; small businesses; defences to safety prosecutions; and product liability.

I have also removed the somewhat contrived 'Dear Mr Jones' (or as the case may be) from the start of each letter, and 'Yours sincerely' or 'Yours faithfully' from the end.

'Topping' creates few difficulties. Sometimes you may wonder whether to address the recipient by his Christian (or fore) name. Otherwise you have the choice between 'Dear' or (for very good friends) 'My dear'. 'Dear Sir' or 'Sirs' are (of course) reserved for formalities or strangers.

The choice for 'tailing' lies between 'Yours sincerely' for people whom you know and (in general) like. Otherwise use 'Yours faithfully'.

For further and more general advice on letter-writing, please see the companion volume to this work, *The Businessman's Guide to Letter-writing and to the Law on Letters*. Waterlows Ltd have also produced a series of my cassettes on these and other similar topics.

My companion volume to this one, *Janner's Employment Forms*, provides most other employment documents which are better as forms than as letters — although in some cases they provide the employer or personnel manager with a choice.

Details of public and in-company lectures or seminars on employment and personnel law are available on request (see page vi).

I am grateful to the following for their help in producing this second edition: Sam Organ, BA, and Paul Secher, LLB, to my son, Daniel Janner, BA (Cantab), barrister, and, as always to my wife.

April 1981   GREVILLE JANNER

Scotland, Wales and Northern Ireland

All the employment law explained and illustrated in this book applies to England and to Wales; and all the relevant statutes (including the Trade Union and Labour Relations Act, the Employment Protection Act, the Health and Safety at Work Act, the Equal Pay Act, the Sex Discrimination Act and the Race Relations Act) also apply to Scotland. Scottish readers should check terminology and contents of precedents with local lawyers, if in doubt.

In the main, Northern Ireland employment laws are the same as those applied in the rest of the United Kingdom – supplemented by *The Fair Employment (Northern Ireland) Act, 1976* (which covers religious discrimination). The Labour Relations Agency has similar functions to ACAS. *The Employment Act, 1980,* does not at present extend to Northern Ireland, but in due course similar provisions are likely to be brought into effect.

The rules of redundancy consultation are the same. Additional claims from the Redundancy Fund on insolvency apply, e.g. wages and holiday pay, but not the new priority rules. Equal pay and sex discrimination provisions are the same. It is unlawful to discriminate in employment on grounds of religion and the Fair Employment Agency enforces the rules. Details (once again) from local lawyers.

Like the laws themselves, the precedents in this book will serve employers and their representatives throughout the United Kingdom – with rare and usually minor exceptions which can easily be checked and adapted with the help of Scots or Northern Ireland lawyers (as the case may be).

Part One

APPOINTMENT
AND HIRING

Chapter 1

Contracts of Employment — written particulars

A contract of employment is merely an agreement between employer and employee under which the employee agrees to give service to the employer and the employer to engage the employee. Like most contracts (with the exception of hire purchase, insurance, share transfer, transfer of interests in land and contracts of guarantee), contracts of employment are just as binding if made orally as if every term is set out in writing. I repeat: There is no law which requires a contract of employment to be in writing in order to have binding legal effect.

However, *The Employment Protection (Consolidation) Act, 1978,* requires the main terms of a contract of employment to be put into writing. The employee is entitled to receive his written particulars within 13 weeks of the start of the employment — and if there is any variation in the terms, then the employer must put these into writing and deliver them to the employee within 4 weeks.

Failure to provide written particulars will not lead to a prosecution or to a civil action. Theoretically, the employee who has not received his particulars may bring a complaint before an Industrial Tribunal. In practice, when a case involving the employee reaches the tribunal the particulars are asked for and if they are not available the employer starts off on the wrong legal foot.

Anyway, particulars should be provided. Like all useful documentation, they avoid disputes. They enable the employee to know his rights and to prove them. Also, the employer is less likely to act in breach of the employee's rights if they are set out on paper.

At best, written particulars are supplied at the start of the employment — often, in the case of managers or executives, in letters of appointment. Particulars supplied later are not to be used as an excuse for introducing terms which were never agreed. They are intended to confirm and to provide a written record of an agreement.

By all means say to an employee who is not to get his written particulars for a few weeks: 'You will be subject to our works' rules and to our normal terms of service'. Why not let the prospective employee read a copy of your standard terms and works' rules, at the time when you are taking him on?

Parliament has regulated by statute the *miniumum* information to be set out for the employee in writing. There are many other vital terms which *should* be included — ranging, in appropriate cases, from the requirement that a woman who intends to return to work after childbirth should say so in writing to a restraint clause or one entitling the employer to search employees for stolen goods.

Employees who normally work 16 hours or more a week (or 8 hours after 5 years' continuous service) are entitled to written particulars — although you should certainly consider providing written particulars to all employees, however part-time. The threshold for part-timers' rights for this purpose as well as for redundancy payments and unfair dismissal protection was reduced from 21 hours normal weekly working, as from 1 February 1977.

Tribunals and the Employment Appeal Tribunal continue to emphasise the importance of providing full, clear, accurate written particulars. It is rarely 'unfair' to dismiss an employee because he refuses to do something which is required of him by his terms of service. The employer who insists on a change with no provision for change in the contract of service may succeed in showing that this was necessary for the purposes of the business and he is usually the best judge of business needs. But complications are likely and frequent. So provide for maximum flexibility.

Details for inclusion in written particulars of contracts of employment or in letters of appointment

Part 1 — Requirements of law

1   *Name of employer*   In the case of associated companies, be careful to insert correct employing company.
2   *Employee's job title* — his function or position. You are only bound to set out the name of the job so that the employee may know what job he is employed to do. It is often better to be more detailed — although allowing leeway. Thus: 'You will be employed as a driver and to do all other work normally incidental thereto'.
3   *Date of start of employment*   Vital for assessing periods of continuous employment, e.g. for purposes of assessment of period of notice; of continuous employment for unfair dismissal protection; and for redundancy claims — also potentially for pension rights and sick pay.
4   Whether or not current *employment is continuous* with any

(and if so what) previous employment, and if so, when it began.

5   *Remuneration*   Salary or wage, commission or bonus.

6   *Fringe benefits*   For example, use of company car; share options; subsidised canteen facilities; protective or other clothing allowance.

7   *Hours of work*   If you may wish to change the employee's shift, then obtain his agreement at the start of his employment. If you wish hours to be flexible, say so. Also, state whether overtime is guaranteed or compulsory and on what terms.

8   *Holidays and holiday pay*   Remember to include the manner in which holiday entitlement is calculated — especially when employment comes to an end. Is employee entitled, for instance, to a pro rata payment if he leaves during the middle of a year? Will he lose his holiday entitlement if he does not give his agreed notice? And can holidays 'roll over', if not taken when due.

9   *Place of work*   If you may need to shift employee from place to place, so provide. Otherwise, a shift may amount to a dismissal.

10   *Sick pay*   If any. Also, if private health insurance provided, say so.

11   *Pension rights*   Do you contract in or out of the state scheme?

12   *Grievance procedure*   To whom should the employee go if he considers himself unfairly treated?

13   *Disciplinary rules*   Reference may be made to an 'easily accessible' document containing the rules not only in respect of grievance procedures — see above — but the particulars themselves must state to whom the employee can apply 'if he is disatissfied with any disciplinary decision relating to him' — and how the application must be made.

14   *Notice*   How much is the employee entitled to receive — and how much must he give?

Part 2 – Suggested additional items

15   In the case of all women of childbearing age; request that any expected absence due to *pregnancy* or *confinement* and/or intention to return after leaving on that ground be stated in writing to personnel manager (or other named person).

16   *Restraint clause*   Restriction on employee's right to compete after leaving employer's service. A lawyer's help is needed in drafting such a clause, because only if it is 'reasonable' will it be enforceable.

17   Employee to devote full time to employer's business and/or not to engage in other paid employment without employer's consent.

Is *'moonlighting'* a problem in your business? How do part-timers cope?

18   *Accommodation provided (if any)*   Take care: If employee is not to become a 'tenant', and hence protected by the Rent Acts, he must be 'required' to occupy the premises 'for the better performance of his duties'. Again: Professional drafting vital.

19   *Right to search*   The employee agrees to the searching of his person or property at the request of the management. Consent at the time of the search is necessary, even if this clause is inserted – but in those businesses where the inspection of employee's person or property is normal and necessary the contract often includes a search clause.

20   *Employer's secrets*   Do you need a special clause regarding confidential or secret information or documents? Should specific items or processes be referred to? Once again, this is to make explicit what is otherwise only implied into the contract.

21   *Accounts*   Is the employee to keep or render special accounts – perhaps for expenses claims?

22   Employee to disclose *other business interests.*

23   *Health and safety at work* – employee should agree to follow safety procedures. Implied term made explicit – perhaps with warning that failure to comply may – or, in the case of a specially dangerous process, system or operation referred to, *'will'* lead to dismissal.

24   Requirement that employee submit to medical examination at employer's request.

25   Any special terms applicable to the particular employee or employment.

Note: It is both useless and misleading to include a term that the employee will not claim against you for unfair dismissal or redundancy rights, when his employment terminates. He may only contract out of these rights in two circumstances: (1) in fixed-term contracts for one year or more; and (2) where an agreement to settle a claim is recorded by a Conciliation Officer on his form COT3.

Thanks to *The Patents Act, 1977,* and employee normally owns his own inventions – no matter what may be contained in his terms of service. The employer will only own an employee's inventions if *(i)* the employee was employed to invent and the invention was one reasonably expected to emerge from the employment or *(ii)* where the employer has purchased from the employee either the patent or a licence to use it. In either case, the employee may apply to the Court, or to the Comptroller of Patents, for further payment, if he considers that undue advantage has been taken of him. This will not apply where the agreement of purchase was negotiated by a trade union on his behalf.

1   Written particulars

I am happy to confirm your appointment, upon the following terms:
(a)   Employment by: The . . . Company Limited.
(b)   Employment to begin on the . . . , 19. . . . This employment is continuous with your previous employment by . . . which commenced on . . ./This employment is not continuous with any previous employment.
(c)   Your job title to be . . . .
(d)   Your scale or rate of remuneration and the method of calculating remuneration (including bonus and/or commission − if appropriate), to be. . . .
(e)   Payment to be made every . . . , i.e. weekly/monthly on the. . . .
(f)   Your normal working hours to be as follows. . . .
(g)   Overtime. . . .
(h)   You will be entitled to usual public holidays. Your holidays and holiday pay to be calculated as follows:. . . . Your entitlement to accrued holiday pay on the termination of your employment will be . . . .
(i)   In the event of your being absent from work due to sickness or injury, you will receive sick pay as follows . . . .
(j)   We operate the following pension scheme arrangements/ the company has not contracted out of the State Pension Scheme . . . .
(k)   You will be entitled to receive the following periods of notice . . . .
(l)   You will be obliged to give the following notice if you wish to leave the company's employment . . . .
(m)   In the event of your having any grievance relating to your employment, kindly see your supervisor/foreman/ personnel manager/shop steward. Details of grievance procedures are available, if required, from . . ./are in the collective agreement which applies to you and which is available from . . . .
(n)   Disciplinary procedures are as follows . . . . If you are dissatisfied with a disciplinary decision, you should inform Mr/Mrs/Miss/. . ./me.

If you have any questions concerning the above, please do not hesitate to contact me – or Mr . . . , your . . . , who will normally be found in . . . , from . . . a.m. to . . . p.m.

Please sign and return the enclosed copy of this letter to show your agreement to the above terms.

Hoping that this will be the start of a long and happy association between the company and yourself and with my best wishes.

2   Draft contract (alternative)

I confirm that your terms of service are as follows:
1   *Date of employment*   Your employment commenced on . . . , 19 . . and is/is not continuous with other employment by . . . which commenced on . . . , 19 . .
2   *Job title*   You are employed as a . . . .
3   *Place of work*   You will work at . . . and/or at such other of the company's places of business as the management may from time to time require. (In the event of your being required to move, your reasonable removal and/or relocation costs will be paid by the company.)
4   *Remuneration*   Your remuneration will be calculated as follows:
   (a)   . . .
   (b)   . . .
   (c)   . . .
   The company pays the net salary of all monthly paid employees directly into their bank account, one month in arrear, at the end of each month. Weekly and hourly paid employees are paid one week in arrear on the . . . of each week.
5   *Hours of work*   Your normal hours of work will be:
   (a)   . . .
   (b)   . . .
   (c)   . . .
6   *Shift working*   The company does not implement shift working, but if it becomes necessary to do so in the future, it reserves the right to require you to work shifts.
7   *Overtime*   Overtime is not guaranteed. Employees above the level of supervisor or equivalent are not paid for overtime. In other cases, overtime is paid at the following rates:

(a) . . .
(b) . . .
(c) . . .

8   *Holidays*   You will be entitled to the following periods
of holidays:
(a)   All public holidays;
(b)   . . . days/weeks per year after . . . service;
(c)   . . .
(d)   . . .
The holiday year is from . . . to . . . and no payment will
be made (except on termination of employment) for days not
taken. Holiday entitlement may not be carried forward
from one year to another. Any five consecutive working
days constitute one holiday week.
   Your entitlement up to the end of the current holiday year will be . . . days.
   Holiday pay is calculated at your basic hourly/weekly/
monthly rate on a pro rata basis.

9   *Holiday entitlement on leaving*   If the company terminates your employment due to misconduct, holiday pay
may be forfeited at the management's discretion. In all
other cases, payment will be made for all holiday entitlement accrued in the current holiday year but not
taken at the time of the termination of the employment.
In the event of holidays being taken but not earned,
appropriate holiday payment will be deducted by the
company from money owed on termination. In the
event of your being lawfully dismissed for misconduct
or leaving without giving your proper notice, you will
forfeit any accrued holiday entitlement.

10   *Retirement*   The company's normal retirement age is
65 for men, 60 for women.

11   *Pension rights*   All eligible employees will be invited to
join the company's contributory pension scheme which
operates for full time, permanent employees, subject to
the eligibility rules of that scheme and to the discretion
of the trustees.

12   *Absence from work*   If you are absent from work for
any reason, you must inform your departmental manager whenever reasonably practicable by . . . a.m. on the
first day of absence. Where possible, you should obtain
permission for absence from your departmental supervisor or manager; such permission is in any event re-

quired in respect of absence for any reason other than sickness or accident. If the period of absence exceeds two days, then you must forward a medical certificate without delay to your departmental manager; further certificates must be forwarded when previous certificates expire; and a final certificate must be produced before commencing work. If you are admitted to hospital, then you must submit a medical certificate of both entry and discharge. In either and any event, you must yourself write to your departmental manager explaining the circumstances of your absence due to illness and specifying the nature of the illness concerned, otherwise you will forfeit any sick pay to which you would otherwise be entitled.

If you are entitled to claim sickness benefit otherwise than from the company you must do so and the amount equal to the basic sickness benefit will be deducted from sums payable by the company. No deductions will be made while half salary is being paid. The company will pay sick pay on the following scale, according to length of service:

(a)   Up to four weeks' service – nil;
(b)   Four weeks to three months – two weeks' full pay;
(c)   One to two years – three weeks' full pay;
(d)   Three to four years – four weeks' full pay;
(e)   Five to six years – eight weeks' full pay;
(f)   Seven to ten years – twelve weeks' full pay;
(g)   Eleven to fifteen years – eighteen weeks' full pay;
(h)   Over fifteen years – twenty-six weeks' full pay.

In each case, these periods will be followed by similar periods of half pay. (Any day from Monday to Friday counts as one day and one week equals five working days).

The above allowances will apply to each tax year April through March but unused allowances may not be transferred from one year to the next.

13   *Medical examinations*   The company reserves the right to require employees to submit to medical examination by the company doctor or by an independent medical adviser. If you are medically examined and wish a copy of the report to be sent to your own doctor, in addition to being supplied to the management, then the company agrees so to do.

14 *Notice* Your employment will be subject to the statutory minimum periods of notice or to such additional periods as may be given by the management at its discretion. You will be required to give like periods of notice to the company if you wish to terminate your employment. Notice should be given in writing to the departmental manager.

15 *Confidential information* You will not divulge to any individual, firm or company, any confidential information acquired by you in the course of or for the purposes of your employment. Breach of this duty will normally lead to instant dismissal.

16 *Other work* You will not engage in any other form of paid activity, whether during or outside working hours, without having obtained the prior written consent of the company.

17 *Restraint* You will not engage in any branch of the . . . trade/industry within a radius of . . . miles/within the area within which you have been working for a period of . . . months/years after leaving the company's service, without having obtained the prior written consent of the company.

18 *Search* The company reserves the right to search employees or their property while they are at work for the company.

19 *Disciplinary procedures* In the event of disciplinary action being necessary, the normal disciplinary procedure is as follows:
(a) Verbal warning;
(b) Verbal warning, in presence of employee's representative or shop steward;
(c) Written warning;
(d) Final written warning;
(e) Suspension or dismissal.
In the case of serious misconduct, it may not be possible to follow this procedure and the company reserves the right to suspend on full pay at any time for the purpose of carrying out investigations. Offences which may/will lead to summary dismissal include the following: assaulting a supervisor or a fellow employee, removal of property belonging to the company or to any client or customer of the company from the company's premises, without obtaining prior written consent; theft; consuming alcohol or taking

dangerous drugs on the company's premises or in working
hours or during the lunch hour; smoking in prohibited
zones; failing to comply with safety rules (see below);
persistent absenteeism . . . .

If you are dissatisfied with a disciplinary decision, you
should appeal in the first place to the supervisor at the
level above the person who took the disciplinary action.
Alternatively, you may appeal to the personnel manager.

20   *Grievances*   Any grievance relating to your employment should be discussed with your immediate superior.
If you are not satisfied with the result of such discussion,
then you may appeal to your departmental manager or,
in the event of still further dissatisfaction, to the personnel manager or to your director. The person appealed
to will give careful consideration to the grievance and
notify you of his decision.

21   *Health and safety at work*   You are required to comply
with the company's health and safety rules, and with all
rules laid down by the Health and Safety at Work Act,
The Factories Act, the Offices, Shops and Railways
Premises Act and all regulations made under them or
under any other industrial safety statute. Failure to
comply with such rules may lead to dismissal.

The company places paramount importance on the
health, safety and welfare of employees at work and a
copy of the company's written statement of its health
and safety policy, organisation and arrangements is
supplied herewith.

Every employee is further required to take such steps
as are reasonably practicable to ensure the health and
safety of himself and of others affected by his work; he
must make use of all protective clothing and equipment;
and he must co-operate with the management in all
respects for the full implementation of the health and
safety policy. Failure to do so may lead to summary
dismissal.

22   *Fire alarm*   If the fire alarm bell sounds, all employees
must walk to the nearest fire exit door and assemble at
their allocated area. You must familiarise yourself with
your fire drill.

23   *Accidents*   If you are in any way involved in any
accident, however minor, you must report this to your
departmental manager as soon as possible thereafter.

You should also report to your supervisor any accident involving any other employee.

24 *Company property including purchases by staff* Employees may purchase company products from the company's shop, which is normally open on working days from . . . to . . . . The receipt for payment must be retained by the employee and shown at the gate when the products are taken from the company's premises. All such purchases must be taken off the company's premises within 24 hours.

I have read and understood the above terms of service and I accept them.

Signed . . . .

Date . . . .

NOTE:
An employee is not bound to sign terms of service. But wise employers invite employees to do so – having read them and had any doubtful points explained.

3   Staff appointment

I am happy to confirm your terms of appointment as follows:

1   This offer is made subject to the obtaining of satisfactory references. Where an employee commences work before references have been obtained and approved, the management reserves the right to terminate the employment by the giving of minimum statutory notice or equivalent pay in lieu, notwithstanding periods of notice which would otherwise apply.

2   Staff are appointed on an initial trial period of sixteen weeks.* On satisfactory completion of that period, an employee will (if eligible) be offered the opportunity of inclusion in the staff pension scheme, subject to proof of age, medical examination and such other documents as may be required by the rules of the pension scheme. Particulars of the scheme are available on request.

* For problems of trial periods, see Chapter 3.

3   Medical examination. Medical examination will be required for all those eligible employees who wish to join the pension scheme. Other employees may be required to undergo medical examination by the company doctor at any time.

4   You will be employed by . . . Ltd and will normally work at its premises at . . . . The company reserves the right to require members of staff to move to branches within the UK. The company will meet all reasonable removal expenses; the company's decision on what expense is reasonable in the particular circumstances shall be final.

5   Your employment will begin on the . . . , 19. . This employment is not continuous with any previous employment/ is continuous with your employment by . . . , which commenced on the . . . .

6   Your normal working hours will be from 9 a.m. to 5.30 p.m., Mondays to Fridays inclusive, but you may be required to work overtime if the exigencies of the business render this necessary. You will then be paid time and a half during the week or double time at weekends. [*Or:* You will work such hours as are necessary for the proper performance of your duties.]

7   You will be entitled to . . . weeks holiday per annum. The company's holiday year is from the 1st April until the following 31 March and completed years of service are counted at the 31 March preceding the holiday year concerned. In the event of your leaving the company's service, you will be entitled to pro rata holiday pay, unless you are dismissed for misconduct in which case any accumulated holiday pay will be forfeited.

8   You will be employed as a . . . . , and do all work reasonably incidental thereto.

9   Your rate of pay will be as follows . . . .

10   In addition, you will be entitled to the following benefits:

   (i)   Christmas bonus of . . . per cent up to a maximum of

£ . . . . This bonus qualifies for pension payments and is also subject to tax. It will be paid pro rata to staff joining in the current year but for those joining after 30 September, it will be added to the bonus for the following year. Staff who leave for whatever reason before payment or who are at that time under notice, given or received, are not entitled to this bonus.

(ii)   Free canteen lunches provided at headquarters/canteen lunches are subsidised.

11   Any employee who is absent through illness is required to notify (or to ensure the notification of) his immediate supervisor by telephone before noon on the first day of such absence. The management reserves the right not to pay sick pay in respect of any period during which notification of absence has not been given.

12   If an employee is absent due to illness for more than three days, then he must obtain a certificate of absence for this period and for any subsequent week of absence. Subject to the foregoing, and to your writing to explain the reason for your absence, you will be entitled to sick pay as follows . . . .

13   Unless the company is entitled to dismiss summarily, notice will be given upon the following basis:
     After one week's service, 7 days;
     After six month's service, four weeks;
     After five year's service, five weeks;
Thereafter, an additional week's notice for each year of service up to twelve years.

14   Any employee who wishes to seek redress of any grievance relating to his employment should discuss the matter with his immediate superior; if the matter is not satisfactorily resolved, then he should explain the grievance in writing and both the employee and the supervisor concerned must together and as soon as possible submit the grievance for a ruling at an interview with their departmental or branch manager. The manager concerned may refer the matter further in writing to the general manager and will supply both employee and supervisor with copies of his report within two working days of the interview.

15   If the cause for the complaint is not resolved satisfac-

torily, the employee may appeal to the chief general manager.

16   Details of the company's disciplinary procedures are contained in the head office rules, a copy of which is supplied herewith. Note: An employee may at any time be suspended on full pay during investigation of any alleged breach of the disciplinary rules. The employee will always have a right of appeal against a disciplinary decision to his department or branch manager and in the event of a dismissal to the chief general manager.

4   Representative, traveller or agent

We are pleased to confirm your appointment as (sole) representative for the above Company within the area of . . . , with effect from . . . . This employment is not continuous with any previous employment.

It is agreed that you will be paid a salary of £ . . . per annum. You will be provided with a car, to the extent that it is used for the purpose of the Company's business. The running and maintenance expenses will be paid by the company. All expenses claimed must be supported by receipts and dockets. (Alternatively: The company will pay £ . . . per week towards your car expenses.)

In addition, you are to be paid a commission of . . . per cent on the value of goods delivered and invoiced in your area, such value to be calculated after deduction of the average cash discount of . . . per cent. Payment of such commission will be made to you during the month following delivery of such orders as are accepted by the Company.

Please note that any business connected with . . . will be excluded from your area and no commission will be paid in respect of orders taken therefrom.

After one calendar year's employment, you will be entitled to (. . . week's) holiday with pay. After two years' service your entitlement will rise to (. . . weeks). After three years, you will get (. . . weeks') paid holiday. This will be the maximum. In the event of your employment being terminated for whatever reason during the course of a calendar year, holiday pay will be reckoned pro rata.

While in the employment of the Company, it is specifically

agreed that you shall not represent any other company, in
respect of any goods or services whatsoever. You will devote
yourself full time to the Company's affairs. In the event of
this agreement being terminated by either party, you will not
deal in any products in which the Company trades during
your period of employment, within the area in respect of
which this agency is given, for a period of twelve calendar
months.

   This agreement may be terminated by . . . weeks notice, in
writing, on either side to be increased to . . . weeks after . . .
years service. This may be given to you by the Company at
your last known address or by you to the Company at its
registered office or main place of business. After the termination of your employment, you will be entitled to commission
in respect of orders introduced by you which are received
and accepted (and delivered) by the Company during the
period of your employment, but not thereafter.

   In the event of any grievance or dissatisfaction with a
disciplinary decision arising, please consult with me person-
ally/with Mr . . . . Details of the Company's disciplinary procedures are attached.

   Kindly sign the carbon copy sent with this letter and initial
the first page thereof, to indicate that the above terms
correctly represent the agreement come to between us, and
that you are prepared to serve the Company upon that basis.

   We hope that this will be the start of a long and happy
association between the Company and yourself and wish you
every success in your efforts.

NOTE:
The above draft is for employed (and not *self-employed) representatives
etc.*

5   Appointing scientist, researcher or technician

   I am pleased to inform you that you have been selected
from many applicants, for the post of (research . . .). Full
particulars of your terms of service are enclosed herewith. If
any queries arise thereon, kindly inform me at once.

   I confirm that you informed me that you have for some
time been working on developments in . . . . We agreed that if
this work produced results which would be of use to the Com-

pany, you would license the Company to use the same, during your period of service or for fifteen years from the date when application is made for the appropriate patent, whichever is the longer. Save as above, the terms of the licence shall be as agreed or failing agreement, as settled by an arbitrator to be appointed by . . . .

No other licences shall be issued by you to anyone else during this period, without the Company's prior written consent. It is further confirmed that the Company will not object to the patent being issued in your name.

Hoping that you will have a long and happy period of service with the Company, and looking forward to meeting you again.

NOTE:
Even today, there is no objection to an agreement under which an employee who is employed to invent agrees to accept licensing arrangements. Remember, too, that the Patents Act rules, which give employees in general the right to inventions made by them even in their employer's time and which cannot be overruled by a term in a contract of employment, only apply to patentable inventions. They do not cover, for example, ideas or suggestions schemes.

6   Employee retains rights

I confirm that if you are prepared to accept the appointment offered to you, the Company will not object to your retaining or obtaining *(as the case may be)* all patent rights in respect of your inventions, whenever and however made.

7   Employee writes

Thank you for your letter concerning my proposed appointment. Perhaps you would arrange for your solicitor to draw up the appropriate agreement as discussed, concerning rights to inventions — it would be as well, I think, to have the entire matter clarified before I finally agree to take up an appointment with the Company.

8   Reference to other document

I am delighted to confirm your appointment as . . . of the above Company. Full particulars of your terms of service are contained in the Company's standard contract of service, which is enclosed herewith, including our agreed arrangement as to your probationary period. This has, of course, been completed and amended so as to comply with the arrangement reached between us, when we discussed the matter yesterday morning. Kindly detach and sign the portion at the foot of the contract, to confirm that the same correctly sets out your terms of service.

On behalf of our board, I am delighted to welcome you into the Company's service, and look forward to a long and happy collaboration with you.

NOTE:

1   When checking your own terms of employment (actual or prospective), if you run swiftly through the notes of the letters which follow you will find pointers to the main traps to avoid.

In any event, do not regard a standard letter as immutable. Negotiating alterations (for yourself or for others) is an important art.

2   There is no legal necessity for the employee to confirm his agreement with the terms set out in the employer's letter – but once he has done so, he will have little joy if he later maintains that the terms of service are not set out correctly. Confirmation is particularly advisable where there is a restraint clause or some other term which may prove disadvantageous to the employee. Silence from the employee after receipt of the written particulars may be taken to imply consent.

9   Company Secretary

I am pleased to confirm your appointment as Company Secretary of the above company, commencing on the first of next month. Your employment is not continuous with any previous employment. Your salary will be . . . payable on the . . . of each month by Banker's Order. Your office will be at the Company Head Office at the above address and you have agreed to devote yourself full-time to the business and not to engage in any other form of remunerative work, either on your own behalf or otherwise, without the company's prior consent.

You will be entitled to six weeks' paid leave per annum, such entitlement to accrue at the completion of a year's service and thereafter in the event of your employment being terminated for any reason other than your own departure without giving proper notice, you will be entitled to holiday remuneration pro rata.

Your employment will be terminable by three month's notice, on either side. Such notice must be in writing. Details of the Pension Scheme will be sent to you under separate cover. Senior staff such as yourself will be enrolled into the BUPA Scheme, at the company's expense.

In the event of illness, you will be entitled to your full remuneration, less National Insurance or other benefits to which you would be entitled on the basis that you have paid full contribution and subject to provision of a Medical Certificate and of a letter from you, explaining your absence.

You will be responsible directly to the Managing Director, to whom any grievance should be directed and who will take any necessary disciplinary action. Details of grievance and disciplinary procedure are available from our personnel manager.

If you have any queries regarding the foregoing, please inform me at your earliest convenience.

NOTE:
If you wish to insert a restraint clause, see Chapter 2.

10 Holidays and holiday pay – as amended

To avoid misunderstanding, I am happy to confirm that employees such as yourself who have been with us for over . . . years are entitled to . . . weeks holiday in each calendar year – in addition, of course, to the usual public holidays. If your employment is terminated during the course of a year, then you will be entitled to accrued holiday pay on a pro rata basis – that is, the appropriate proportion having regard to the part of the year which you have actually been with us since the date of your last holiday.

11   No holidays until full year served

As appears from the written particulars of your contract of employment which we supplied to you, you are only entitled to the equivalent accrued holiday pay, after the completion of a full year's service with the company. Equally, on the termination of your employment, there is no pro rata entitlement — only those who leave at the end of a full year's service are entitled to their holiday money.

NOTE:
The absence of a pro rata payment is lawful but undesirable

12   Mobility clause

I have discussed your place of employment with the Board. They are agreeable to your being stationed at . . . for a minimum period of . . .years. But bearing in mind the nature of the company's business, it must be understood that you will if necessary accept transfer to any of our factories/shops/branches/offices in the . . . area, if given . . . weeks/months notice of such transfer. The company will pay all reasonable moving expenses.

I hope that the above suggestion will be acceptable to you. Please inform me at your earliest convenience.

13   Right to search

Please note that, as I explained to you when we met, all employees are required to agree to submit to their person or property being searched, while on the company's premises, at any time at the request of . . . . This is, of course, essential having regard to the nature of the company's business.

NOTE:
To search an employee's person without his permission is an assault. To search his property without consent is a trespass. Permission may be obtained in advance — but should be confirmed at the time of the search. If you are satisfied that a theft has occurred and a suspect refuses to be searched, then the police should be called.

14   Promotional prospect

Thank you for your letter, applying for the post of. . . .
Those who serve the company in senior positions on a permanent basis work their way up through the ranks. We are,
however, an expanding organisation and if you are prepared
to start as . . . we hope that you would soon be promoted
to . . . .

If you are interested in joining our company on the above
conditions, we would be pleased to see you, and we could
then go into the matter more fully. Would you please let us
have two or three alternative dates and times when you could
call here, and we would then make arrangements accordingly.

15   Food – requirement to inform of illness

As your job involves the handling of food, the company
requires that immediately you (to your knowledge) contract
any contagious or infectious disease, you will at once inform
your immediate supervisor. You are also required to attend
at our sick room if you have any cut or other accident to
your hands, arms, neck or face, however minor. As hygiene
is vital in your work, failure to comply with these rules may
lead to instant dismissal.

16   Disagreement over written particulars

Thank you for your letter of today's date, enclosing pur-
ported written particulars of my terms of service.

I regret that I cannot agree that the form of particulars
sent to me correctly sets out the terms of my appointment.
In particular, I have at no time even discussed with you or
anyone else on the company's behalf the question of a
restraint clause. I reread our detailed correspondence, prior
to my taking up my appointment with the company and this
confirms my recollection that there was no such clause to be
included in my contract.

Apart from the foregoing, I agree that the written particulars are correct. Would you like me to strike out the clause in
question, sign the slip and return the document? Or would
you prefer to send me different particulars?

Incidentally, I would like to point out that I sincerely hope in any event that the question I raise will remain purely theoretical – you were good enough to indicate that the Board are satisfied with my services, and I am very happy in my position and look forward to a long period of service with the company.

NOTE:
The contents of this letter may be put into an inter-office memorandum – and if you wish to make it appear informal, by all means write the letter by hand – but be careful to retain a copy.

17   Approval of variation

Thank you for your letter, confirming that my salary is to be increased. I am much obliged – and in the circumstances I agree to my terms of service being varied by the inclusion of the proposed restraint clause.

NOTE:
Employers who wish to insert restraint clauses or other new terms which will act to the employee's detriment should choose their time – the best being, of course, when the terms of service are being improved in other respects. The employee who is getting a rise should be in a very amenable frame of mind. But he should ensure that his employer does not attempt to insert new terms under the guise of giving written particulars – or of confirming terms previously agreed. Trade unions, professional associations and even individual employees are generally on to that one. See Chapter 5 for rules on varying contracts of service.

18   Acceptance of agreed terms

Thank you for your letter. I confirm that it correctly sets out the terms upon which I have agreed to be employed by the company as its . . . . I look forward to starting work on the . . . .

19   Brief acceptance

I happily acknowledge receipt of your letter of . . . and

confirm that I agree to serve the company on the terms set out therein/in memorandum attached thereto.

NOTE:
One object of a swift and unequivocal reply is to prevent the offer from being withdrawn until you have had time to say 'yes'.

20   Contract accepted – but terms queried

I am obliged to you for your letter of . . . . In general, I agree that it sets out very fairly the arrangements arrived at between us when I saw you last Thursday. However, I would like clarification of the following matters please:

1   . . . .
2   . . . .

I would be grateful if I could hear from you concerning the above, at your early convenience.

21   Record of reasons for non-appointment of applicant

Name . . . .   Age . . . .
Address . . . .   Job applied for . . . .
Reason/s for non-appointment:
1   Inadequate experience of job/trade/generally.
2   Lack of skill in job/generally.
3   Age.
4   Personality.
5   Sex *(only where 'essential qualification for job').*
6   Colour, national origin, nationality, race or ethnic origin *(only where 'essential qualification for job').*
7   Non-union member *(where closed shop –* and no genuine objection based on conscience or other 'deeply held personal objection').
8   Other.

NOTE:
All those who appoint should be warned to beware of (5) to (7) above. If in doubt, these should not be (or, of course, be shown as) *a reason for rejection. Omit (5) and (6) if you have no jobs where sex, etc., is an 'essential qualification', and (7) if you have no Union Membership Agreement.*

Chapter 2

In restraint of trade

Everyone is entitled to use his talents, knowledge, contacts and know-how to his own best advantage or as he sees fit. If an employee – however senior or junior – leaves your service, he may enter into competition with you, in your own immediate territory.

Exception – where there is a valid, binding restraint clause in the employee's contract of service. These clauses (by definition) restrain a person's freedom to earn his living as, where and when he sees fit. They are therefore '*prima facie* void' as 'contrary to public policy'. They will only be upheld by a court if they are 'reasonable' – in every respect.

A valid restraint clause must not be wider than is reasonably necessary for the protection of the employer's business. It must not place an unreasonable restraint on the employee's freedom to earn his living; and it must not be unreasonable from the public viewpoint. A clause that is too wide in time or space is normally a dead letter.

It is a grave error to draft your own restraint clauses. Only a lawyer who knows what clauses have been upheld by courts in similar cases, can hope to create an enforceable obligation. For that reason, the restraint clauses embedded in the letters which now follow are not precisely stated. To make a will; to convey property – or to draft restraint clauses – you need in each case the help of a lawyer.

Naturally, the converse applies. If you wish to compete with your present company when you leave its service, check your contract of service or the written particulars of your terms. If there is no restraint clause, worry not. You may compete to your heart's content. If there is a clause, do not panic – with any luck, it will not be enforceable. If in doubt, consult your solicitor.

*   *   *

22   Standard restraint

I confirm that if you join this company, it must be a term of your employment that you will not engage in . . . for a period of . . . years after leaving the company's service, anywhere in . . ./within a radius of . . . from the company's works.

23   Representative's restraint

I confirm our conversation – that in consideration of the Company agreeing to employ no one else in the counties of . . . and . . . , you undertake as follows:

1   That within . . . years of leaving the Company's service, you will not engage directly or indirectly, whether for yourself or for others and where there is principal or agent in the sale of . . . , in the counties of . . . and . . . .

2   That you will not during the above period solicit orders from any person, firm or company who or which was a customer of the Company during the subsistence of your service/ agency.

3   That you will not during the above period employ, directly or indirectly, whether for yourself or for others, any person who was in the Company's employment or employed by the Company as an agent, during the subsistence of your service/ agency.

24   Breach of restraint – complaint

I have been informed that you are employed by the . . . Company at . . . , in the capacity of . . . . Is this correct? If so, you are acting in direct contravention of the restraint clause contained in paragraph . . . of your terms of service/ set out in our agreement contained in our exchange of letters dated . . . and . . . ; and if the breach continues, the Company will instruct its solicitors to commence proceedings against you and against your present company for an injunction and damages, without further warning.

I am sending copies of this letter to the Chairman of your company and also to my Company's solicitors, Messrs . . . of . . . .

NOTE:
With luck, the threat of action will suffice – particularly as the current employers may be unwilling to keep on the man if it could lead to legal proceedings. They may also contend that they would not have taken him on, had he told them of the existence of the restraint clause.

25   Denial of breach

I was sorry to receive your letter dated . . . , alleging breach of the restraint clause in my contract of service. I am advised that this clause is too wide to be enforceable. I was employed only in the . . . area/operated only from the . . . branch. The restraint covers the whole of the United Kingdom. In the circumstances, I respectfully suggest that you might care to consult your solicitors – who no doubt will give you the same advice about the restraint as have mine to me.

Any proceedings which you may see fit to institute will be vigorously defended.

NOTE:

1   The danger of including a restraint clause in your contract of service is that you may have to 'put up or shut up'. You should not wield the sabre unless you are prepared to strike with it, if necessary. Better to have no restraint clause than one which you are not prepared to enforce.

2   On receipt of a letter such as the above, you are in a real dilemma. On the one hand, if you attempt to enforce the restraint and succeed, all is well – on the other, if your attempt fails, everyone will know that the clause is worthless. If you do not sue, then (equally) you will have revealed your weakness. Still, you could try the following:

26   Without prejudice – suggested compromise

Without Prejudice

Thank you for your letter. I do not accept – and nor do the company's solicitors – that the restraint clause is unenforceable. However, without prejudice to the company's rights, I will be prepared to see you to discuss whether we can come to some reasonable arrangement which would result in the company's interests being moderately protected while you do not risk being thrown out of work. We are prepared to see whether it is possible to find some sensible common ground.

I look forward to hearing from you.

NOTE:

1   'Without prejudice' letters are used in the course of efforts to negotiate compromise settlements. They cannot be placed before a Court unless and until the negotiations reach fruition. In that case, the letters may be produced if they contain the concluded agreement between the parties.

2   Compare the use of the term 'without legal responsibility' in connection with references (Chapter 19).

3   Remember that if you reach a compromise settlement of an unfair dismissal or redundancy claim, it is not binding on the employee – whether or not it is made 'without prejudice' – unless and until it is recorded by a Conciliation Officer on his form COT3.

27   Personal assistant

I am happy to appoint you as my personal assistant at a salary of £ . . . per annum, payable monthly. Your employment will be continuous with your previous employment by the firm, which began on . . . .

You will work with me at the above address and your normal hours will be from . . . a.m. to . . . p.m., Monday to Friday, with one hour break for lunch. You will have three weeks' paid holiday, your entitlement to arise after a full twelve months of service. Your appointment shall be subject to four weeks' notice on either side for the initial twelve months and thereafter to three months' notice on either side.

In the event of your leaving our employment, for whatever cause, you must not under any circumstances for a period of six months – whether on your own behalf on or behalf of others – solicit custom from any individual, firm or company who was a customer of ours during your period of employment, other than those on the list attached, who you are now introducing to the firm. Nor must you for . . . months after leaving, employ or seek to employ any person employed by the firm during your period of employment.

If you are ill you will be paid full salary for a period not exceeding three months in any calendar year, minus any sick benefits receivable on the basis of full contributions paid. All applications for sick pay must be accompanied by a doctor's certificate. Remittances will be made to you with deductions in respect of your National Insurance benefits received – so that you will receive exactly the same pay while ill as when

you are well. Details of our grievance and disciplinary procedures are enclosed herewith.

With all best wishes.

NOTE:
*It is vital to confine any restraint against soliciting custom to customers
(or clients) who dealt with the employers during the employee's period
of service. Any attempt to prevent the soliciting of those who started
to deal with the employers after the employment ended will fail and
will probably invalidate the entire clause.*

28   Manager's restraint – alternative

I was pleased to meet you and to appoint you as manager
of our . . . branch, upon the terms set out in your letter to
me of the . . . . You did omit one clause – namely that you
agreed that upon leaving our service you would not engage
in . . . within a . . . mile radius of our branch, for a period of
. . . years, either on your own account or as an employee of
any other agency/business. As I explained to you, this restraint is one upon which we must insist, due to the high
degree of trust which we place in our senior staff and the very
considerable measure of responsibility and independence
which we give to them in their work.

Please confirm your understanding of the above – and that
you will commence work on . . . .

Looking forward to a long and happy period of co-operation with you and with kindest regards.

29   Restraint on executive – alternative

I am pleased to confirm your appointment as . . . , upon
the terms attached hereto.

Kindly note that you are restrained from engaging in the
. . . trade/industry for a period of . . . months/years after
leaving the company's service, within a radius of . . . from the
company's headquarters/works/office where you are employed.

You are also restrained from employing (whether for yourself or others) any persons who were employed by the company at the date when your employment ceases or within six

months prior thereto — this restraint likewise to apply for a period of . . . months/years after leaving the company's service.

Please acknowledge receipt of this letter and your agreement to the terms offered. And kindly confirm that you will see Mr . . . in his office by not later than . . . on . . . .

With kind regards and wishing you every success in your new position.

30   Company Secretary — alternative

The Board is pleased to accept your application for the post of Company Secretary of . . . Ltd, but this must be on the strict understanding that you will not accept employment in the field in which the Company is engaged, anywhere in . . . , for a period of . . . months/years after leaving the company's service.

The work you will be doing will be highly confidential and it is essential for the protection of the Company's business that this restraint should be acceptable to you. If you will be good enough to confirm that you agree thereto, I will then confirm in writing all details of your proposed contract. I would be most obliged for an immediate reply.

NOTE:
The more responsible the post . . . the more confidential the information entrusted to the employee . . . the greater the area covered by the company's business — the wider the restraint which would be enforceable by law. Once again, I repeat — these precedents are skeletons which should be fleshed out by the lawyers. Restraints accepted by vendors of businesses will be enforced far more readily than those imposed upon employees.

31   Letter before action — to new employers

We understand that you are employing Mr . . . , who was previously employed by this company under a contract of service which contained a restraint clause, a copy of which is attached hereto. His current employment by you is in clear and blatant breach of his agreement with the company. I have instructed the company's solicitors, Messrs . . . of . . . , that unless we receive from you not later than . . . a clear assurance that the employment of Mr . . . by you has been terminated forthwith, legal proceedings are to be commenced against you forthwith. I trust that this will not be necessary.

NOTE:

The proceedings would be for an injunction – an order, restraining the employer from employing the person concerned in breach of his agreement. A claim may also be made for damages – and (if appropriate) for the return of any of the company's documents, e.g. mailing lists.

Chapter 3

Trial and probationary periods

The law provides what amounts to a 52-week* probationary or trial period, during which you may dispense with the services of any employee — fairly or unfairly and for any reason or for none. So the need for trial or probationary periods has diminished, except where you promote someone and wish to reserve the right to move him back down if your hopes for his success at a higher level do not mature into good results. Still: many employers do still provide for these periods — and the following drafts cover the ground.

Remember, above all, that if you promise an employee a trial period of (say) three months, believing that during that period you can dismiss him without notice if you are dissatisfied with his performance, you are wrong. You have given him three months' security of tenure in his job, which he would certainly not have had in other circumstances. What you should have said was: 'During the first three months, your employment will be subject to . . . period of notice. Afterwards, if all goes well, we will reconsider this and other terms . . . '.

32   Trial period — no notice

I confirm that we shall be pleased to employ you as . . . , on the terms set out in the attached sheet. This appointment is, as discussed, subject to a four-week trial period, during which notice will not be required.

With best wishes,

NOTE:
Compare Chapter 6, Trial Periods for Promotion.

33   Probationary period — three months

I am pleased to confirm your appointment as . . . , on the terms set out at the foot of this letter — kindly sign the

* For the smallest firms, 104 weeks; see Chapter 15.

attached sheet to confirm that you are in agreement with the arrangements. I also confirm that this appointment will be subject to a three month probationary period, during which it will be subject to seven days' notice on either side.

I hope that this will be the start of a long and happy association between us and send you my best wishes.

34 Trial period – followed by reassessment

I enclose herewith, as promised, a statement of your terms of service – and am pleased to confirm that you will start work for the company on the . . . .

I also confirm that after a six-month trial period, we will be pleased to reassess your term of service, with a view – all being well – to arranging an increase in salary.

35 Trial period terminates

Your trial period of service with the Company being due to expire on the . . . , I am now instructed to inform you that the Board is very pleased indeed with your efforts on the Company's behalf and I am to offer you service with the Company on a long-term basis. The terms to this offer are set out in detail upon the enclosed contract. Will you kindly confirm at your earliest possible convenience that these terms are acceptable to you.

NOTE:

1   The wording of the final sentence is important. It presupposes that the employee will accept the terms – and provides a positive approach, much better than the alternative: 'If any of these terms are not satisfactory to you, please let us know'. By taking it for granted that the terms will be satisfactory, you are creating a psychological atmosphere in which the employee will find it harder to challenge them.

2   The same effect is achieved by referring to 'our usual terms'. Of course, if you are at the receiving end of such a letter, beware – check each term with great care to make certain that it really does suit your purpose. If it does not, never mind the fact that it may be 'normal' or 'usual' – the time to challenge it is now – once you have signed up, it will be too late.

36   Confirmation – trial satisfactory (alternative)

We are pleased with the manner in which your trial period
has worked out. I am happy to confirm that we shall be
pleased to employ you on a more permanent footing, upon
the same basis as at present – but subject to four weeks'
notice on either side. Kindly confirm that this is satisfactory
to you.

37   Trial unsatisfactory

I am instructed to inform you that the Company will not
wish to retain your services when your trial period comes to
an end.

NOTE:

*1   Many companies prefer to pay the employee his full entitlement,
up to the end of his trial period, and tell him at the same time that they
will no longer require his services. An employee who knows that he is
on his way out is unlikely to be the company's star turn during his
remaining period of service.*

*2   But note: if the trial period is sufficiently long (four weeks or
over), at least seven days' notice will be required. So the above letter
must be sent in due time.*

38   With short notice

I confirm that the company will employ you in the capacity of . . . as from the . . . . For a trial period of . . . your
employment will be terminable by the giving of . . . week's
notice on either side. Thereafter, the period will be . . . .

I trust that the trial will prove satisfactory both for us and
for you and look forward to your employment being put on
a long-term basis thereafter. I hope that you will have a long
and happy period of service with the company.

39   Offer of trial period

I am pleased to confirm our conversation. The company

will employ you for an initial period of . . . at a salary of
£ . . . . At the end of that period, we will assess the situation.
If all goes well you will then be offered an appointment on a
long-term basis.

Kindly confirm that you will be prepared to serve the company upon this basis. I would like you to commence work on
the . . . .

Hoping that this will be the start of a long and happy
association between us, and with my kindest regards,

NOTE:

*It is wrong to regard the trial period as one during which the employer
can sack without notice, whenever he sees fit. The above letter confers a
fixed term during which the employee is entitled (unless he has earned a
summary dismissal) to be kept on. If you wish a trial period to have
some other meaning, then use the previous form of letter.*

Chapter 4

Fixed-term contracts

A fixed-term contract is one that will automatically expire when the term comes to an end. If the employee is not then kept on, he is *deemed* to have been dismissed. And if the contract lasted for 12 months or more, he will generally be qualified for protection against unfair dismissal.

However: a fixed-term contract for 12 months or more may now contain a valid contracting-out clause, under which the employee effectively gives away his right to claim unfair dismissal or redundancy protection.

A recent High Court decision contrasted 'fixed term' with 'fixed job' contracts. If you take on someone to do a job, he is not protected when that work is completed. When the contract expires, so do his rights.

The law on fixed-term contracts is extremely complicated and subject to change through judicial interpretation. If in doubt about a particular case — especially your own — consult a solicitor.

40   Executive — fixed-term contract

Your contract of service expires on the . . . . I regret that I am unable to offer you further employment with the company, for the following reasons:

    1 . . .
    2 . . .
    3 . . .

NOTE:
The employee whose term is not renewed or extended is in precisely the same position as any other employee who has been dismissed — with or without notice. His dismissal may or may not be 'fair'. If his employment was for 52 weeks and his contract contained no 'contracting out clause', he may claim compensation for 'unfair dismissal'. You should therefore consult Part 2, and adapt the appropriate letter to your needs.

41   To apprentice – who has not contracted out

I write to remind you that you will have completed your apprenticeship with this company on the . . . . As you know, the journeyman principle applies in this industry and it is not normal for apprentices to stay on with the company with whom they served their apprenticeship. In the circumstances, it is presumed that you would wish to seek employment elsewhere. Please let us know if you have any difficulty in finding a place and we will do whatever we can to help you. (We would also be prepared to consider an application for further employment with the company.)

NOTE:

1   This letter leaves the door open for the apprentice to ask for further employment. If you receive such a request, you turn it down at your risk.

2   On the other hand, if there is no other work, available for the apprentice, he (like any other employee) must 'mitigate his loss'. He must keep it to the minimum (see Part 2 for the principles on which compensation is assessed). So if other work is available, even if the dismissal is technically 'unfair', it will not give the apprentice any rights against you. Alternatively, you may be able to make the youngster redundant, 'fairly'.

42   Offer of fixed term to executive – provided he contracts out

We appreciate that you would like a lengthy period of security, if you are to pull up your roots and to join the company in London. In the circumstances, we are prepared to offer you a one-year contract. But you will appreciate that any continuation of your service when that contract concludes would have to depend upon the current facts which cannot be anticipated at the present time. In the circumstances, will you please confirm that you are prepared to accept an engagement on the above basis, and in particular that you are agreeable that you will not exercise such right (if any) as you might otherwise have, in respect of redundancy or unfair dismissal.

43   Rights excluded

I refer you to your contract of service in which it was agreed that as the company was prepared to grant you a fixed-term contract of one year or more, any rights to claim compensation for unfair dismissal were excluded.

In any event and without prejudice to the above, it is denied that your dismissal was 'unfair'. As you well know circumstances were such that it was not possible to re-engage you.

44   Offer of apprenticeship – term excluding unfair dismissal rights to be included

I have considered your application for an apprenticeship with our company, and am pleased to say that we are prepared to take you on. I enclose herewith the proposed indenture. Would you please read it through very carefully; discuss it with your parents – and if there are any points you would like to raise with me, please do so. If you and your parents are satisfied with the proposed arrangement, would you and they please sign, where indicated.

As you know, this agreement will last for four/five years – and we hope that you will have a very happy time here. If at the end of your apprenticeship we have a place for you and we are satisfied in every way with your work, we shall be pleased to offer you further engagement. However, the contract contains our usual term excluding any claim in respect of rights which you might otherwise have, if it is decided not to offer you further employment after your apprenticeship terminates.

I look forward to hearing from you.

NOTE:

1   It is sensible to draw the attention of the proposed apprentice to the 'contracting out' clause. It is also fair. The law would not require you to do so.

2   There is no law which says that parents must guarantee that a apprentice will carry out his duties – and, in practice, it is very rare that such an agreement is enforced against a parent. However, it is a well to let the parents feel that they do owe you some responsibility

They may well, in the circumstances, feel it right to induce their son to carry out his obligations under his agreement.

45 Variation of executive's fixed-term contract, subject to contracting-out clause

I am pleased to inform you that we are prepared to increase your pay from £ . . . , to £ . . . per week/month. However, this is conditional upon your agreeing that in the (I hope, unlikely) event of the company not wishing to renew your contract after the present term expires, your contract will contain a clause excluding any possible claim for compensation for 'unfair dismissal'.

I look forward to hearing from you.

NOTE:

1 You cannot force any employee, of whatever status, to vary his contract of service so as to include a contracting-out clause – which, after all, is against his interest.

2 On the other hand, any contract of service may be varied, by agreement between the parties. You are fully entitled to invite your employee to accept a variation.

3 Employees are far more likely to agree willingly to variations, if you put the matter to them at the time when you are increasing their pay. Hence the above letter. You may even want to serve written particulars (see Chapter 1) – and to revamp many of the employee's terms (including, for example, restraint clauses). By all means do so in one go – which includes contracting out.

If the employee is not prepared to contract out, then you certainly have no right to dismiss him for that reason, however early or late in his 'fixed term' it may be.

If you are asked to contract out of a possible right to compensation for unfair dismissal, think carefully before you agree. You are giving up a potentially extremely important claim. Before you invite your employees to do so, you may well wish to refer them to their unions – or at least to include the arrangement as part of a package deal, which when looked at as a whole, will be to the employee's considerable benefit.

46   Effort to obtain another job for apprentice

George Smith has been apprenticed to this Company for
... years, and on the ... , his apprenticeship will come to an
end. In this Company, we feel strongly that it is best for
apprentices to move on and not to serve their entire time
with the same outfit – and we understand that you agree.
In the circumstances, I was wondering whether you would
have a vacancy for George? He is an excellent young man –
and I am sure would be useful to your Company.

For our own part, if there are apprentices whom you
would recommend, we would be pleased to consider taking
them on to our books, when their training by and with you
terminates.

With best wishes.

NOTE:
*If you dismiss your apprentice by not re-employing him, then the dis-
missal (as we have seen) may be 'unfair'. But if he immediately obtains
other work, he will have suffered no loss as a result of his dismissal and
will therefore obtain no compensation under the Act. Hence it is now
not only an act of kindness to your apprentice but also of good sense
and even necessity from the company's viewpoint, to use your best
endeavours to obtain other work for him. There are, however, occasions
when you have to provide an unhappy reference, thus:*

47   Poor reference for ex-apprentice

I note that George Smith has applied for a post with your
Company, upon the termination of his apprenticeship with
us. You ask for a reference.

If you would care to speak to me by telephone, I will be
pleased to discuss Mr Smith with you.

NOTE:
*1   You are not bound to give a reference. If you give a bad one, then
it is defamatory. Put it into writing, and it is a libel. Say it orally and it
is a slander.*

*2   Slanders are much more difficult to prove than libels – hence if
you feel bound to give a poor reference, it is normally best to do so by
telephone. But in practice you have little to worry about because the*

honest givers of even poor references are protected by law. Apart from 'justification' – the defence that the statement made was substantially true – you would plead that the occasion was one of 'qualified privilege'. You were under a moral obligation to give the reference and the recipient had a direct interest in its contents.

3 Note that no 'disclaimer' will avoid defamation perils. But in case you give a good reference to the wrong person – and this does happen – particularly in large outfits – you should in fact disclaim – as in the next letter. (See Chapter 19 for law and precedents.)

48 Satisfactory reference for ex-apprentice

I am pleased to say that George Smith has proved a very good apprentice. He is reliable and hard working and I am sure would be a credit to your company.

While we are pleased to supply references for ex-employees, this is done on the basis that no legal responsibility therefore is accepted by the Company or any of the employees.

With best wishes.

49 Redundant ex-apprentice

I accept that by not re-engaging you at the end of your term as an apprentice with the company, you were in law 'dismissed'. However, I regret that there is no job available for you and the reason for your dismissal was on the grounds of redundancy.

Unfortunately, you are not entitled to redundancy pay because you have not been with the company for two years or more since reaching the age of 18. (*Alternatively:* You will be receiving your appropriate redundancy pay because you have served the company for over two years since reaching the age of 18.)

Chapter 5

Varying a contract

Any contract may be changed – with the consent of the parties. You may agree to alter your own terms of service or you may change those of your employees – with consent. Your supplier or contractor may induce you to allow him to put up his rates, if only to keep his business alive and to enable him to complete the work. Or you may induce your customer to accept a variation, to help you – or possibly, to assist him by enabling you to do the work or supply the materials quicker or better.

However: you have no legal right to impose a variation, without consent. To do that is a breach of contract.

Examples: Reducing an employee's pay or status – perhaps because he is old or ill or because your business is being run down or 'rationalised' . . . introducing a restraint clause . . . a clause allowing you to make deductions . . . an agreement that the employee will submit to medical examination or to search, at the request of the management . . . .

Vary, by all means – but get consent first. Conversely, recognise that 'unilateral variation' is a breach of the contract concerned, and if you are faced with a change in your own terms and do not agree to it, protest – loud and clear.

* * *

50   Changing employee's terms of service

I am happy to inform you that as from . . . , your salary/ wage will be increased to £ . . . per week/month/annum. We are taking this opportunity to revise the company's terms of service, as a result of recent statutes and regulations, and Court and tribunal decisions. Please read the enclosed document, if you have any questions about it by all means contact me, and please sign the duplicate and return it to me, to show that you have received, read, understood and accepted these revised particulars.

We are very pleased to be able to make such a substantial increase in your wage/salary − and thank you for the service which you have given and are giving to the company.

With best wishes.

NOTE:
1 Always try to tie changes which may not be to the employee's benefit to those which undoubtedly are − in particular, increases in pay.

2 Conversely, do not try to sneak in adverse changes, without giving the employee full notice of them.

3 As usual, a signature is not vital − but it is certainly advisable, so that the employee cannot afterwards say that he has not received, understood nor agreed to the new terms.

51   Restraint clause − added

In view of . . . , it has been decided to request all employees to agree that they will not compete with the company for . . . months/years after leaving its employment, by engaging in the manufacture or sale of . . . , whether on their own behalf or on behalf of others, for months/years after leaving the company's service. Please indicate your acceptance that this restraint is reasonable and necessary in the company's interests and in the interests of all those who depend upon the company for their livelihood − by signing the duplicate and returning it to me.

With best wishes.

NOTE:
The employee may refuse to sign. In the event of an unreasonable refusal, it may well be 'fair' to terminate his employment. Everything would depend upon all the circumstances of the particular case. See also, Chapter 2.

52   Refusal to accept variation

Your letter represents an attempt to impose a unilateral variation of the contract upon me/this company. This is unreasonable and cannot be accepted. I am sure that on reflection you will understand that it would not be fair to expect me/my company to agree to such a potentially substantial deterioration in its terms of service/contractual terms.

53   Variation essential if contract is to survive

I am entirely in your hands. If you are prepared to increase my pay by £ . . . , I will gladly stay on. If, on the other hand, I am not to receive an increase in spite of my increased responsibilities, then I will have to leave your service. Please do give this matter your most serious consideration and let me know at your earliest possible convenience.

54   Denial of variation

The clause which requires you to comply with the health and safety requirements is not a variation of your contract of service. It is merely making express a term which would in any event have been implied by law.

NOTE:
Every contract has express and implied terms. In a contract of service, for instance, express terms invariably include the employee's pay – implied terms include: 'You shall not steal from the company . . . give away its secrets . . . ' and 'You will not engage in dangerous practices'. Hence the above letter. That which appears to be a variation may not be one after all.

Chapter 6

Promotion and demotion

Few employees mind being promoted — trouble comes when they cannot cope with their new responsibilities. To return an employee to his old status and pay is almost always a dismissal. You are reducing the man's current and future earning ability, and that is a very serious breach of his contract of service.

Promotions must be undertaken with care, not only for the sake of the business (and, for that matter, for that of the employee promoted) but also so as to protect the promoter against a potentially successful claim for unfair dismissal remedies.

Equally, you may demote in law even if you do not intend to do so in fact. Any change of status which acts to the employee's detriment may amount to a demotion. A transfer to a job with less responsibility . . . a reduction in status . . . a lowering of total remuneration . . . . All these involve a major variation in the contract of service — as does, for that matter, the movement of an outdoor worker into an inside job or the shifting of a headmaster from a permanent to a relief position, constantly on the move.

It is, of course, always possible to vary a person's contract with his consent (see preceding chapter) or to arrange the change in the contract so as to give scope for reversal, if all does not go as well as the parties have intended. As these letters will show.

*   *   *

55   Promotion — for trial period

I am delighted to confirm that my recommendation to the Board that you be promoted to . . . has been accepted. But as explained to you, we felt that this change ought to be for an initial trial period of . . . months, so as to ensure that you are successful in coping with the new responsibilities as both we and you hope.

For the trial period, your salary will be increased to £ . . . per annum, payable monthly as before. Remaining terms of your contract will remain unaffected.

It must be clearly understood that if for any reason the management considers that the trial has proved unsuccessful, you will revert to your former position with the company, at the same pay as previously. But, of course, we hope that this will not arise.

Wishing you good fortune – and with my renewed congratulations.

NOTE:

1 The word 'trial period' is often misleading – see Chapter 3. It is essential to set out the terms during that period – even if these are to remain the same as before.

2 The above letter gives a fixed trial period, during which it will not be possible to reduce the employee's (increased) pay, even if he is totally incapable of coping with his new responsibilities. The alternative is to provide for a return to the status quo during the trial period – thus:

56   Promotion for trial period – subject to immediate return

Many congratulations on the Board's decision to promote you to the position of . . . for a trial period of . . . months. As is normal custom in this company, this promotion is for an initial period of . . . months, during which time if either you or the management considers that it would be in the company's interests for you to revert to your former post, this may be effected by the giving of seven days' notice on either side.

Your new remuneration will be . . . .

In all other respects, you will serve on the same basis as before.

Wishing you the best of luck in your new and important post and with my very best wishes.

NOTE:

Obviously, the provision of a line of retreat means that the promoted employee's position has to be held open for him, or at least covered by someone else who can be moved out again, during the trial period. The alternative is to promote and to hope for the best. What matters then is to ensure that you can if necessary prove that you – and the employee – entered into the revised arrangement after adequate thought, training

and that the employee's failure to cope with his new burdens was not
due to any lack of backing from his superiors. Thus:

57   Full backing of Board with new responsibilities

I congratulate you on your promotion to . . . – which I
am happy to confirm. Your remuneration will be £ . . . per
week/month, as from . . . . You will be entitled to receive
and expected to give not less than . . . weeks'/months' notice
to terminate your employment. In other respects, your terms
of employment will be as before. We have carefully discussed
the implications of your added responsibilities/and after your
period of special training at/in . . . . You will of course have
my full support and that of the Board/the management/your
colleagues concerned as you will be with . . . , in your new
tasks – and I wish you the very best of luck with them.

58   Executive – accepts promotion – on terms

Thank you for your letter. I shall be pleased to serve the
company in the position of . . . , but I confirm our discussion.
You have agreed that in the event of my not finding the work
as satisfactory and rewarding as we both hope, I shall be entitled to return to my former position at any time within . . .
months, giving you of course sufficient notice (of not less
than . . . weeks nor more than . . . weeks), to enable you to
find a replacement.

I further confirm that I am agreeable to remuneration at
the rate of £ . . . per month/year in my new post – I appreciate that if I return to my former post, it will be at the
former rate of pay.

With all best wishes – and with my thanks to you and to
the Board for your confidence in me.

59   Acceptance of promotion – no reservations

I am happy to confirm that I shall be most pleased to work
for the company in the position of . . . at a salary of £ . . . .

I am concerned, however, at your suggestion that this
should be on a trial period. This was not agreed – once I have

taken the plunge and have moved to different work/and to a different works/office/town, I shall not be willing to go back to square one. I am sure that on reflection you will agree that it would not be reasonable or fair to ask me to do so. Nor was this suggestion agreed or even discussed when we came to terms over my new appointment.

I have now worked for the company for . . . months/years; you certainly know of my devotion to the company and I need not emphasise my determination to make a success of my new position; but equally, both I and those who are working under me must feel that I have your full confidence and backing and that the job is one which I am to have the opportunity to see through to its end.

NOTE:
If you do not agree to the trial period – or, indeed, to any other term of your proposed service – it is crucial that you say so, in writing and at the earliest possible date. Otherwise no court is likely to believe you if you later maintain that the letter from your employers does not correctly set out the agreement between you.

60   Rejection of promotion on suggested terms

I have given the most careful thought to your kind suggestion that I accept the position of . . . . As you know, I am very happily settled into my present post and I was most reluctant to move – even at the generously increased salary which you suggested.

I have, as you asked, carefully considered the position, and I have come, with some reluctance to the conclusion that I would not be justified in accepting your offer. I prefer to have the certainty of serving the company well and happily in my present post, rather than take the risk of failing to cope with the wider responsibilities which you have in mind.

In the circumstances, I was wondering whether you had given thought to the possibility of appointing John Smith to the new position? He is younger than I am; he has shown considerable initiative and perseverance; he is a thoroughly reliable manager – and I for one would be very pleased to work under him.

I hope this letter will not disappoint you. I can assure you that I have not turned down your offer without the most anxious thought — and I greatly appreciate the confidence which you have shown in me by inviting me to accept promotion.

With my best wishes.

NOTE:

In refusing to accept wider responsibilities, it is crucial not to lose existing goodwill. Hence the need for a careful, reasoned turn down — and, if possible, the suggestion of an alternative.

61   Persuasion to accept promotion

My colleagues and I were very sorry to receive your letter and to learn that you are still worried about taking on the added responsibilities which would be involved, were you to accept our invitation to serve the company as . . . at £ . . . .

It occurs to us that you may be worried about . . . . May I assure you that your anxiety on this score is totally unjustified for the following reasons:

    1 . . .
    2 . . .
    3 . . .

Above all, if you do change your mind — as we earnestly hope — you will not only have the full support of the Board but it has been decided to provide you with a further assistant/secretary/deputy, so as to make your task less burdensome and more congenial.

In the circumstances, I hope to hear from you that you will in fact be prepared to accept promotion — and if you have any further doubts, please telephone and we will arrange to meet.

With my warmest good wishes.

Chapter 7

Sickness and health

An employee is entitled to sick pay if there is some express or implied term in his contract of service, giving him that right. Written particulars of contracts of service should set out whether or not there is such a term – and if so, then details should be specified.

In the absence of any express (or rarely – implied) agreement, hourly paid workers generally get no sick pay. But it has been held in a High Court case that there is no such implied term in the contract of a salaried employee who, in the absence of agreement to the contrary, is entitled to his pay, in sickness as in health, unless and until his contract is terminated*.

You may dismiss an employee when he is ill, in the same way as if he were well. Unless the illness is so serious that the employee is never going to be able to return to his job, he will be entitled to his proper notice or pay in lieu, which will be the same as if he were fully fit. If his sick pay entitlement has expired before his notice begins, his right to his normal remuneration will revive for the period of that notice.

In addition, an employee is entitled not to be dismissed 'unfairly'. But lack of capability – which may be caused by ill health – is one of the reasons which may make a dismissal 'fair'.

Whether it is 'fair' to dismiss any particular employee because he has been absent through ill health (actual or alleged) will depend on all the circumstances of the case. The sort of questions which an industrial tribunal would ask are these:

1   How long has the employee worked for you?
2   How many times has he been away through ill health in the past?
3   What is the prospect of his returning to work – or not being absent through ill health in the future?
4   What is his age . . . status . . . responsibility . . . ?
5   Above all, have you fully discussed the problem with him?

Ask yourself, then, would a decent employer in these circumstances dismiss an employee for this reason? If you are sure that the answer is, yes – then you should be all right. If you are certain that it is, no – then restrain yourself. If you are doubtful, then either give the employee the benefit of the doubt or take legal advice.

*The Employment Appeal Tribunal recently ruled that every case must be considered on its own facts.

Assuming that the employee has been with you for at least 52 weeks and is neither a part timer (normally working up to 16 hours a week or 8 hours after five years' service) and that he is not a pensioner, then he is protected against unfair dismissal. This means not only (almost certainly) that you may have to show the reason for the dismissal but a tribunal may have to rule that you acted reasonably in treating that reason as sufficient to deprive the employee of his livelihood. You must also operate a fair system. The ACAS Disciplinary Code requires, in particular, that (where practicable) you give at least one written warning of intended dismissal.

If, then, you intend to dismiss a sick employee, write to him and at least give him the chance of coming back to work.

If you operate a sick pay scheme and you believe that a particular employee is taking advantage of it, then tell him so. If you want to vary his contract of service by removing his sick pay entitlement and he is not willing to agree to that change, you must appreciate that insistence on such removal will itself amount to a termination of employment. You are refusing to employ the man on the agreed terms. This termination may be fair or unfair, depending on the circumstances. If in doubt, take advice.

Recent experience suggests that absenteeism can be substantially reduced by requiring an employee to write a sick note *in his own hand,* explaining why he was away.

Here is a selection of the letters which you may need if your employee is ill.

62   Confirmation – sick pay entitlement

You have been with the company for six months and I am happy to confirm that your sick pay arrangements will in future be as follows:

    1 . . .
    2 . . .
    3 . . .

63   No sick pay

I was extremely sorry to receive your letter and to learn that you are unable to attend for work because of illness. If you will kindly refer to your terms of service, you will see that we have no sick pay arrangements for employees until they have been with us for 12 months, and your employment has lasted only 8 months.

We wish you, however, a speedy recovery and hope that you will soon be fully recovered. Please let me know at your early convenience when you hope to be able to return to work.

64   Written warning to ill employee

I was very sorry to learn that you are still unwell. As you will appreciate, the company cannot continue to keep your job open indefinitely and I must regretfully inform you that unless you return to work by . . . , we shall have to give you notice to terminate your employment. However, even if you cannot return by the above date, do please let me know if you wish to return to the company later on and I shall make every effort to find a position for you.

With best wishes.

65   Notice – while ill

I was very sorry to learn that your illness continues. However, I am afraid that it will not be possible for the company to retain you in its employment because your continued absence is causing/absences have caused considerable difficulty and disruption in the office. I must therefore give you notice to terminate your employment on the . . . . , in accordance with your terms of service. I shall arrange with our accounts department to send you your pay for that period.

With kind regards.

NOTE:
Even if the employee is not entitled to sick pay or if his sick pay entitlement has expired, it revives during the period of notice. Hence, pay in lieu may be given, thus:

66   Pay in lieu – while ill

You have now been off work for the following periods:
    1 . . .

2 . . .
3 . . .

I refer you to my letter of . . . in which I warned you that any further absence could not be tolerated by the company because of the difficulty and disruption which it would cause.

Kindly accept this letter, therefore, as terminating your employment as from today's date. I am asking our accounts department to send to you your pay in lieu of notice for the period of . . . weeks, in accordance with your contract of service.

NOTE:
You will probably use this letter for an employee whose 'illness' is in doubt. Note, however, the need to give written warning of intended dismissal, thus:

67   Warning of intended dismissal – illness

I have been greatly concerned at your frequent (and often unexplained) absence from work. I appreciate that on occasion you have presented medical certificates and that at present you are away as a result of illness. However, I must warn you that unless you are able to return to work by not later than . . . and unless you thereafter attend regularly and without any further absences, whether caused by illness or otherwise, I shall have no alternative other than to terminate your employment.

68   Demand for sick pay – implied term

I appreciate that there is no express term in my letter of appointment concerning sick pay. I am advised, however, that as I am a salaried employee, there is an implied term that I am entitled to payment while absent due to illness. In the circumstances – and especially bearing in mind the difficulties which are being created through the withholding of this money – I would be grateful if I could receive a cheque at your early convenience.

I am pleased to tell you that I am making steady progress towards recovery and I hope to be back at work within . . .

weeks/months/by about . . . .
With kind regards and best wishes.

NOTE:
You could, if you wish, say: 'I am entitled to be paid, in sickness or in health, while my contract of service subsists' – but that is almost an invitation to terminate the contract of service.

69   Denial that sickness warrants dismissal

I was saddened to receive your letter, which I certainly would not have expected from the representative of a company which I have served so loyally and so well and for so long – and which has in the past always prided itself on standing by its employees when they were ill. I am, of course, protected against unfair dismissal – and I would ask you kindly to reconsider your decision to terminate my employment. I have received preliminary advice from my solicitors that the dismissal in my case would be extremely unfair. I have no wish whatever to bring a claim against the company – on the contrary, I look forward to returning to the company's service as soon as I am fit to do so. I shall therefore be glad to hear from you at your early convenience.
With my personal regards to you.

69a   Employee's explanation – absence due to illness

I regret my absence from work, from . . . to . . . , which was due to illness. I was suffering from . . . .

Part Two

DISMISSAL

Chapter 8

Introduction

There are many ways in which a contract of employment may be terminated. Dismissal is a termination by the employer, without the employee's consent. In law, dismissals may be divided into three categories.

1   Actual dismissal

A dismissal is 'actual' if the employee is sacked, fired, discharged . . . if the employer puts an end to the contract of employment, whether with or without notice.

The employer is saying, in effect: 'I refuse to continue to employ you'. He may also say: 'I will not employ you in future on the same terms as in the past'. In that case, there is an actual dismissal, even if he is prepared to keep the employee on the books on different terms. For instance:

1   An employee is engaged to work on a particular shift; the employer seeks to change that shift, without his consent; the employee refuses to move – but the employer insists.

2   An employee is promoted but fails to perform as hoped. Without his agreement, the employer has no right to move him back to his old job. A demotion is a dismissal from the old job – even if a new one is offered at a lower level.

3   An employee's status is important, not merely in his current job but because it affects his employability by others. A reduction in status may well amount to a dismissal, even if the employee works at the same pay and at the same place.

4   An employee who is engaged to work at one place may not be shifted to another, merely because such a transfer suits the management. An attempt at a 'unilateral variation' will produce a dismissal – whether or not the employer is conscious of the legal result of his behaviour.

*   *   *

There is no dismissal, of course, if the employee agrees to the change, however basic that change may be (see Chapter 6 for variations of contracts). You should always attempt to achieve change by agreement. If you fail and you force that change upon your employee, you must recognise that you are 'dismissing'.

2   Constructive dismissal

An employer dismisses 'constructively' if he forces the employee out of his job. The two most common examples:

1   An invitation to resign which the employee cannot refuse. 'If you resign, you will get your severance pay and your reference — if you do not, you will be dismissed.'

2   The 'wearing down' of an employee by his manager or supervisor. Many employees are forced out of their position by being given the dirty jobs; because the foreman picks on them; because they get no favours and many kicks; because they are treated in a way that they do not have to put up with.

Where an employee leaves his job when he is entitled to do so as a result of his employer's conduct, he is dismissed. It is not enough, though that the employer acted unreasonably. He must have done something so serious as to amount to a 'repudiation' of the contract. If the employee then leaves, he is not destroying that contract but merely accepting a position which the employer has himself created.

This is precisely the reverse of the situation in summary dismissal cases. You are entitled to dismiss an employee with neither notice nor pay in lieu when he has done something so serious as to smash the contract and not merely where he has broken it. Where the employee repudiates, his employer may sack him summarily; where the employer repudiates, the employee may leave and regard himself as dismissed 'constructively'.

In practice, the dangers of constructive dismissal are huge and largely unrecognised. Failure to train lower levels of management and supervision in the dangers of constructive dismissal frequently lead to heavy legal penalties.

*   *   *

An employee has to prove that he was 'dismissed' before the burden shifts on to the employer to show the reason for the dismissal. The tribunal must then look at all the circumstances of the case and consider whether the employer acted reasonably in treating that reason as sufficient to warrant taking away the employee's livelihood.

It is simple to prove an actual dismissal and often difficult to prove a constructive dismissal. But, many employees successfully obtain unfair dismissal remedies when their employers have failed to realise that there was a dismissal at all. Every manager and supervisor should be taught to avoid forcing dismissals — which by definition do not go through the normal procedures — including warnings and documentation.

3 Expiry of fixed-term contracts

When a fixed-term contract expires without being renewed, this is treated by law as a 'dismissal'. Details in Chapter 4.

* * *

A dismissal is 'wrongful' if the employee does not get his proper notice. Proper notice means:

1   That period which has been agreed between employer and employee — for details, see written particulars.
2   In the absence of agreement, then 'reasonable' notice — the period which is reasonable will depend upon all the circumstances of the particular case, including the employee's length of service, his status, responsibility and the intervals at which he is paid.
3   In any event, the employee must be given not less than the statutory minimum period which is now: 7 days after 4 weeks and then a week a year from 2 years to 12 years. *Note:* it is incorrect and even fraudulent to include a term in the employee's contract to say that he is entitled to 'statutory notice'. There is no 'statutory notice' — only a statutory *minimum.*

Chapter 9

Constructive dismissal

Constructive dismissal avoids disciplinary procedures altogether. Suddenly you find that a person whom you had thought you still employed was dismissed.

Where an employee leaves when he is entitled to do so because of the employer's conduct, then he is 'dismissed'. If he is forced out of his job, he is entitled to go.

Where one spouse walks out on the other without due cause, that is 'desertion'. Where one spouse pushes the other out of the home, that is normally 'constructive' desertion.

The following conversations should be used with care:

'You have the choice. You may either resign — in which case, you will get your severance pay and a reference; or I would have to dismiss you.'

'OK, so the personnel manager won't dismiss you. I have to put up with you. So you are going to do all the dirty jobs . . . . No favours from me . . . . I'll decide whom you'll work with and you won't like it . . . . You don't like being call 'Taffy'? — that's too bad . . . .

To wear someone down or push him out or force him into resigning at any level is to 'dismiss' — and may lead to precisely the same consequences in law as any other dismissal.

70 Allegation of constructive dismissal

By your actions and those of Mr . . . , you have made it impossible for me to continue to serve the company. I am therefore forced to regard my contract of service as repudiated by the company.

I have worked loyally for the company for over . . . years. The following are the major matters which have driven me out of that service:

1   My . . . transfer to X Department, contrary to my express wishes.

2   The requirement that I must work under Mr Y, whom you know has frequently expressed hostility towards me.
3   The reduction of my staff and in particular the transfer of my secretary, Miss Z.
4   . . .
5   . . .
6   Continual and unnecessary interference with my work.
7   The frequent and totally unwarranted complaints concerning the operation of my department — which has been doing remarkably well, in spite of great difficulties.

I would finally refer you to my letters of . . . and . . . in which I made it plain that the situation was becoming impossible.

The following payments are outstanding to me as at the above date, when my employment terminated, and I shall be pleased to receive the company's cheque at the earliest convenient date.

1   Salary to . . . .
2   Commission to . . . .
3   Agreed bonus . . . .
4   Holiday pay to . . . .

In addition, in the event of my not obtaining other equivalent work without delay, I shall apply to the Industrial Tribunal for compensation for unfair dismissal.

I am indeed sorry that my association with the company should end in this unhappy manner.

NOTE:

1   A previous letter, warning that you cannot carry on, is advisable but not vital. There is no legal requirement — but provable previous warnings are of great help in showing repudiation by the employer as they are when provided for the employee.

2   Reduction in status is a major change in the term of employment, and amounts to dismissal, even if pay remains the same.

3   If you have any doubt as to the proper framing of the matters relied upon as amounting to a repudiation, see your solicitor. If your funds are sufficiently low, you may get his initial advice and help, to the value of £40, at little or no fee if you are short of funds. Ask your solicitor for details. Otherwise, at least make absolutely sure that the reasons are either set out accurately and as fully as possible – or omitted altogether.

4   *Other letters* from *executives are collected in Chapter 17.*

71   Employer's denial of repudiation

I acknowledge receipt of your letter of . . . in which you allege that you have been forced out of your employment with the company and further that you have been constructively dismissed. These allegations are denied. You left the company of your own volition and in no circumstances can the company accept that you were dismissed, unfairly or at all.

You will receive your pay to date and all other money due to you, together with your P45, as soon as possible.

72   Alternative denial – with counter-allegations

Thank you for your letter of . . . , in which you informed the company that you have left its service. You were certainly not forced out of that service, as you allege or at all. The answers to your allegations arc as follows:

  1 . . .
  2 . . .
  3 . . .

73   Alternative denial – alleging repudiation by employee

I am instructed to thank you for your letter of . . . and to inform you that the company denies that you were constructively dismissed, as alleged or at all. You yourself repudiated your contract of service by your actions, and in particular as a result of the following:

1   You failed to comply with lawful instructions given to you by . . . , in particular:
  (a) . . .
  (b) . . .
  (c) . . .
2   . . .

You will receive all money due to you, as soon as this can be arranged.

74 'Constructive dismissal' denied

It is denied that we dismissed Miss . . . as alleged in her claim or at all. The letter dated . . . is admitted. As therein stated, she was warned that if she did not improve in the ways stated, then she would be dismissed. The letter was intended as a warning, not as a dismissal. It was hoped that she would improve her performance so as to retain her job. She left of her own accord.

If it be held contrary to the above contention that the company did dismiss Miss . . . as alleged or at all, then we shall if necessary contend that her own conduct was the sole cause of, or alternatively contributed substantially to, such dismissal (if any) which we deny.

75 Warning by employee

Unfortunately, I am continually being harassed and hampered in the carrying on of my duties for the company. I am doing everything in my power to produce the best results in my department/office – but I am slowly being driven to the conclusion that a concerted effort is being made to force me to resign from my position.

It is right for me to point out that in the event of my being unable to carry on with my work, I shall regard this as a clear case of constructive dismissal. I am sorry to have to write in this way, but it is obviously both fair and proper for me to let you know the situation – in the hope that matters may be corrected before they get any worse.

My specific complaints are as follows:

    (a) . . .
    (b) . . .
    (c) . . .

I shall, of course, be pleased to call upon you to discuss the situation at any time convenient to you.

Chapter 10

Warnings of intended dismissal

Whenever reasonably practicable, an employee shall be given at least one written warning of intended dismissal before he is deprived of his livelihood.

Note:

1   It is not sufficient merely to send a note or a memorandum of dissatisfaction or complaint. The employee must be warned that continued behaviour (or *mis*behaviour) of the kind referred to will (or may) lead to dismissal.

2   If the warning brings the desired result but the employee's behaviour reverts, the warning may have gone stale. The more important the misconduct and the more serious the warning, the longer it will remain effective. Whether and when a further warning is required is a question of fact and of degree. Usually, after six months or so, the procedure should be restarted.

3   These warnings apply at every level. Even a board member is entitled to a written threat. Conversely: Employees at and below board level should protect their own position by replying to such warnings – in writing and keeping copies.

4   If you give proper written warnings, ensuing dismissal will probably be 'fair'. At least the procedure is likely to be so. However, there are circumstances in which it is not reasonably practicable to give a warning – as where the conduct complained of is immediate, serious and such that would make a reasonable employer refuse to keep the employee on his books or to give him another chance.

5   If the written warnings are properly and carefully drafted, then if an employee of at least six months' standing asks for written reasons for his dismissal, the employer should refer the employee to the warnings; repeat their terms; and say (if it be so) that the employee was dismissed for failing to heed the warnings, in the ways stated.

6   Because the written warnings have a double effect — both to make the dismissal potentially fair and to provide the basis of written reasons for dismissal (which are generally sought by an employee who has litigation in mind) — these warnings should be most carefully drafted. They should, in general, specify with precision the conduct complained of. The employee will know then what is required of him if he is to retain his job; and the employer will have documentary evidence of the type, nature and date of the complaint.

*   *   *

76   Warning — misconduct

I must warn you that if you persist in . . . we shall have no alternative other than to give you your notice. I do hope that this will not become necessary.

77   Alternative warning

We have now warned you on many occasions that we are dissatisfied with . . . . Unless the situation improves, we will have no alternative other than to dismiss you. Please take this warning seriously.

NOTE:

1   A warning — or many warnings — may not justify dismissal, either summarily or with notice. The warnings themselves may be unreasonable or insufficient. Everything depends upon the facts of the particular case. However, the more warnings that are given, and the stronger the terms, the more likely it is that the Tribunal would regard the employer's behaviour as 'fair', if he eventually does have to dismiss.

2   As with agreements, so with warnings — there is no law which says that they have to be in writing. But a written warning is not only admissible in evidence but essential, where possible.

78   First warning

Your foreman has now spoken to you several times about . . . . The management take these breaches of the works' rules extremely seriously and I must warn you that if there is any repetition, your employment may be terminated.

Please do not behave in the same way again/again give us cause for complaint in this regard.

79   Second warning

I refer to my letter of . . . , in which I complained to you about your misconduct in respect of . . . .

I regret that I have received a further complaint of the same kind. Bearing in mind that your conduct improved for several months/over six months (*or as the case may be*), it has been decided not to take further disciplinary action on this occasion/not to discharge you from the company's service on this occasion, as we would have been entitled to do.

I understand from your foreman/from the personnel manager that you have promised that there will be no further repetition of the conduct complained of. I hope that this is correct because although we have been lenient on this occasion, it is most unlikely that the company would be willing to tolerate any further repetition of this conduct.

80   Stale warning – renewed

I appreciate that since my letter to you of . . . , you have desisted from . . ./not again offended against the company's rules by . . . .

I was therefore most sorry to learn from Mr . . ./your personnel manager that he had once again found it necessary to complain that you have . . . .

After careful consideration, I have decided not to terminate your employment on this occasion, but I must once again warn you that any repetition is likely to lead to the end of your service with this company.

81   Reply to warning

I was most surprised to receive your letter dated . . . , containing a threat of dismissal.

As I explained to Mr . . . when he saw me, I deny that I

have been guilty of the alleged or any breach of the works'
rules. The situation is as follows:-

    1 . . .
    2 . . .
    3 . . .

I wish to place on record my dismay that you should have
seen fit to write to me in the manner concerned, without
even having discussed the matter with me. I regard this as
most unfair.

I shall be glad to discuss this matter with you, if you wish.
We have always had a most happy relationship in the past
and I can assure you that I shall not allow this apparent
misunderstanding to interfere with my determination to continue to give loyal and vigorous service to the company.

NOTE:
*A warning should be answered, in kind and in writing. And a copy
carefully kept.*

82 Record of warnings

I regret to inform you that I have had to warn Mr . . . on
a number of occasions regarding his behaviour, and the time
has now come for the disciplinary procedure to be put into
action. Details of warnings are as follows:

    1 . . .
    2 . . .

83 Warning of dismissal after refusing alternative job for
age or health

I was very sorry that you have so far turned down the offer
of a job as . . . . I appreciate that the pay is lower than com-
manded by your present position — but unfortunately, as you
know, your health/age is such that I do not feel that you are
able to cope with your present job. The alternative offer is
made because we want to be as helpful as possible and to
avoid the necessity of having to terminate your services.

I must ask you, though, to reconsider your refusal. Failure
to accept the alternative position will leave me with no alternative other than to give you your notice — a step which I

would greatly regret.

Please do call to see me, whenever you wish, so that we can discuss the position.

With best wishes.

84   Technical changes – warning: demotion or dismissal

Unfortunately, you have not been able to cope with the results of our switch to automation/introduction of new techniques/machinery – but we are anxious to help you, if we possibly can. It was for that reason that I was authorised/ instructed to offer you the post of . . . .

It is most regrettable that you have declined to accept our offer because if you persist in that refusal, I shall have no alternative other than to terminate your employment. It is not possible to keep you on at your present job; the new job carries less pay but reduced responsibility; and I do ask you to reconsider the position very carefully and to let me know your decision as soon as possible.

NOTE:
If you force a person into a lower paid job, you are in effect dismissing him. Are you able to prove that the dismissal was 'fair'?

85   Impending dismissal

As you know, we are affected by the current recession in the trade and are likely to have to cut down our payroll, before long. In the circumstances, we are trying to give our employees the maximum possible warning, in the hope that they may find other jobs in the area. If you find one, then we shall be pleased to provide you with a reference.

We are very sorry that the situation has come to the present pass – but it is not of our making.

With our best wishes to you.

NOTE:
This letter does not amount to a 'dismissal'. If an employee leaves, having been warned of impending dismissal – or, for that matter, that redundancies are on the way – he loses his rights either to redundancy pay or to compensation for unfair dismissal. In the former case, a man

has to prove that he was 'dismissed' — at which stage a redundancy will be presumed. In the latter case, he must also show that he was 'dismissed' before his employer has to show that the dismissal was 'fair'. Any employee who jumps the gun does so at his own risk.

Chapter 11

Fair dismissal with notice

In the past, an employee's only protection against the miseries of dismissal was the length of his period of notice. He now has two further cushions — redundancy pay — and 'unfair dismissal', remedies which he can claim whether or not he has been given notice.

It follows that while there are still occasions when it is advisable to give no reasons in your letter of dismissal, it is often wise to be specific and to indicate your reasons, so that if the employee does make a complaint to an Industrial Tribunal, you will be able to show both reason and consistency and he will not need to request written reasons.

Naturally, if you dismiss an employee summarily you will not say to him: 'If you sue me for damages, this letter indicates the defences which I will raise'. But you should still make those reasons plain in your letter, where possible,

There are circumstances in which you have been told by an employee — or by his union representative — that if you do give notice, you will be taken to the Tribunal. In that case, it becomes all the more important for you to express yourself clearly, concisely and firmly in your letter. This will be read by the Tribunal — unless, of course, the case is settled before reaching that stage. So take care.

86   Dismissal with notice

Please treat this letter as notice to terminate your employment on the . . . , in accordance with your contract of service.

NOTE:
Any employee at any level is entitled to his agreed notice; in the absence of agreement, to reasonable notice; in any event not less than the statutory minimum periods: after four weeks, one week's notice; after two years, two weeks, after three years, three weeks; and so on adding a week a year up to twelve weeks after twelve years.

87 Dismissal of director with reasonable notice

I am instructed to give you notice to terminate your service with the company. As no period of notice was agreed with you when you were appointed to the Board of the company, you are entitled to reasonable notice. As it is the wish of all your colleagues on the Board that the company should act towards you in as generous a manner as possible the period of notice will be . . . .

Please forgive the formality of this letter, but from your viewpoint as well as that of the company, it is as well to give this notice in proper form.

88 No accrued holiday pay where dismissal for misconduct

Thank you for your letter. You have received everything to which you are entitled. I would refer you to the written particulars of your contract of employment, dated . . . . You will see therefrom that where the company dismisses an employee as a result of his misconduct, the employee forfeits any right which he would otherwise have, to accrued holiday money. As you well know, you were dismissed for serious misconduct and we are not prepared to waive our normal rule on this occasion.

89 Lack of 'capability' — insufficient 'skill'

Unfortunately, the series of unhappy accidents in which you have recently been involved have made it plain that you no longer possess the skill necessary for the carrying out of your work. It is therefore with the greatest regret that I must ask you to treat this letter as giving you notice, to terminate your employment on the . . . . You will appreciate that you are entitled under your contract of employment to . . . weeks notice.

I would only add that were it possible to find other work for you within our business, we would have been happy to do so. Unfortunately, no such work is available.

We wish you success in the future.

NOTE:

1   If an employer wishes to show that dismissal was 'fair' he must show one of the specified reasons, or some other 'substantial reason'. The first such reason given is one which 'relates to the capability . . . of the employee for performing work of the kind which he was employed by the employer to do'.

2   'Capability' is defined as meaning 'capability as assessed by reference to skill, aptitude, health or any other physical or mental quality'.

3   When an employee is dismissed because he does not possess the requisite skill, this is very often in no way his fault.

4   Even if you can prove one of the specified reasons, you will still have to pay compensation, if the employee suffers loss as a result of his dismissal, unless the Tribunal considers that the dismissal was 'fair'; and that question is determined in accordance with equity and the substantial merits of the case.

5   In other words, a Tribunal will ask: Was the dismissal fair in all the circumstances? Did the employer act 'reasonably'?

If you dismiss a man because he did not possess the requisite skill, then it may be unreasonable to do so if there is other work available for him – so it is wise in the letter to indicate that such work could not be provided. And in all such cases (as in the ones now following) I advise **the maximum generosity in the periods of notice actually given –** *which (both out of kindness and for tactical reasons) should exceed the minimum required in the circumstances.*

90   Lack of 'qualification'

Unfortunately, due to the introduction of the new machinery/equipment, you are no longer qualified to carry out your duties. We have offered you the opportunity to undergo a training course, at our expense, so as to equip you to do your work in the new circumstances, but you have declined to accept our offer.

In the circumstances, please treat this letter as notice to terminate your contract of employment as at the . . . . By giving you . . . weeks notice – instead of the . . . weeks, as required by your contract of employment – we hope that this will enable you to obtain other work, for which you remain qualified. We thank you for your co-operation during the time that you have been with us.

NOTE:
1   Lack of 'qualification' may be a good reason for 'fair' dismissal – normally with notice. 'Qualifications' are defined as meaning 'any degree, diploma or other academic technical or professional qualification relevant to the position which the employee held'.

2   In industries in which there are frequent technological changes – and even in offices or businesses where computers are introduced – this ground of dismissal is fairly common. It is unlikely that a Tribunal would regard lack of qualifications as forming a reasonable ground for dismissal unless the employee has (where possible) been given the opportunity of acquiring the qualifications he needs. The longer his service with the company, the more important it becomes to allow him to obtain the necessary training – or at least, in the letter of dismissal, to indicate why such training was not undergone.

91   'Capability' and 'qualification' combined

As discussed with you, when you called on me this morning, I regret very much that your health, combined with your lack of technical qualification, have forced us to terminate your services. In the circumstances, please treat this letter as notice, terminating on . . . .

NOTES:
1   If there has been an oral discussion, then by all means refer to it. It shows that you have at least taken the trouble to see the employee – and this sort of opening may be used in all similar circumstances.

2   If you have more than one reason for the dismissal, say so. If you come before a Tribunal and wish to add reasons which were not set out in your original letter, you may find your case disbelieved.

92   Lack of 'aptitude'

I am sorry that you do not possess the aptitude necessary

to deal with the tasks allocated to you. I hope that you will
be successful in finding other work elsewhere, more in your
line. As I told you this morning, the company will not require your services after the . . . of this month.

NOTE:
*You do not need to go into details – but if there are specific, vital tasks
with which your employee could not cope, then you may wish to say
so in your letter.*

93 'Physical or mental quality'

We had all hoped that you would manage to cope with
your job – but this has proved impossible. So I must give
you notice terminating your employment on . . . . If you
would like to discuss this or any other matter with me, please
do not hesitate to call on me in my office.

NOTE:
*It is sometimes kind to say little – and most Tribunals will accept this
as a reason for putting little into a letter. You may not wish to tell an
employee that he is 'getting beyond it' – or that some physical or
mental incapacity prevents him from doing his work properly. Still less
may you wish to put this into writing. But in those circumstances you
should keep a note on your file, attached to the letter. This could be
merely a memo, for yourself – or for those who succeed you. It could
be a note addressed to your superior. Thus:*

94 Note of reasons, to superior

I enclose herewith a copy of a letter which I have today
handed to Harry Smith. The unfortunate chap is still suffering from . . . . He cannot do his job properly. Indeed, his lack
of concentration is proving a danger to other employees. But
I have thought it best not to say too much in this letter. I do
not want to upset him – he is a good man.
I hope that you will also approve of my having given him
a good deal longer notice than is strictly required.

NOTE:
Be sure to keep a copy of all letters, notes and memoranda. Careful

filing now can save both money and worry at a later stage. Documents win cases. Remember – you may be forced to reveal at any hearing nearly any document that is relevant, however private.

95   Misconduct – and 'without prejudice' payment

I have now had to warn you on at least . . . occasions about your carelessness. This not only causes danger to yourself but also to fellow employees. In the circumstances, I feel that I have no alternative other than to terminate your employment forthwith. I enclose herewith your pay in lieu of notice – although I think it right to point out that having regard to the persistent and habitual nature of your misconduct, I take the view that the company would have been entitled to dismiss you summarily. However, it is appreciated that there are mitigating circumstances in your case, and we do in particular know that you have not been in good health. So, *without prejudice to the company's rights,* I am pleased to be able to enclose a cheque herewith in the sum of £ . . . , details of which are contained in the attached slip. You will appreciate that this also includes your accrued holiday pay as at the date when your notice terminates.

NOTE:
1   It is vital to appreciate that where you give notice or pay in lieu, in circumstances in which you would have been entitled to dismiss summarily, this should be stated in your letter – for your own protection.

2   By all means give details of the misconduct, at greater length, if you wish. The letters which now follow briefly indicate the sort of comparatively minor misconduct which may lead to dismissal with notice – and which you must now hope would be sufficiently 'habitual' or 'persistent' to enable you to satisfy a Tribunal, if necessary, that the dismissal was 'fair'.
One reason which may warrant 'fair' dismissal 'relates to the conduct of the employee'. This will not mean any 'misconduct' – we may also have an occasional 'off day' – and any employee may be guilty of a momentary slip or an occasional misdemeanour. To warrant 'summary dismissal' – with neither notice nor pay in lieu – misconduct must be sufficiently serious as to amount to a 'repudiation by the employee of his contract service'. A tribunal is likely to regard a reason 'relating to the conduct of the employee' as warranting dismissal with notice,

when it is somewhat less serious than that which warrants summary dismissal — but not much less. You must prepare your letter of dismissal accordingly.

96   Poor timekeeping

I have now warned you on at least . . . occasions that your failure to arrive at work on time was disrupting our production. I have also told you that if this continued, I would have to give you your notice. I must now do so. Your employment with the company will terminate on . . . .

I would only add that we do fully appreciate your difficulties, as you live so far from the plant. It is for this reason that we have been exceptionally patient in your case.

97   Alternative — extended lunches

Despite frequent warnings, you have seen fit to return late from lunch — culminating this week with your being over . . . late, on . . . days. In the circumstances, I enclose herewith your pay in lieu of notice. We shall no longer be requiring your services.

NOTE:

1   Warnings may not of themselves be enough to warrant dismissal. But if you have warned, say so.

2   Compensation for 'unfair dismissal' is only available to compensate ex-employees for financial loss suffered (including, now, loss of redundancy entitlement.) If your secretary finds other work during the period of notice represented by her pay in lieu — or, of course, by such period of notice as you see fit to give her — then she will no more get compensation than she would otherwise obtain damages for summary dismissal.

98   Denial that dismissal is because employee intends to join union

Thank you for your letter. It is not correct that you were

dismissed because of your intention to join the . . . Union. The reasons for your dismissal are set out in my letter to you of the . . . . Any employee of this company is fully entitled to join and take part in the activities of an independent union, as he sees fit. Your dismissal was completely irrespective of your intentions regarding union membership.

99   Pay in lieu – no reason stated

Your employment with the Company will terminate on the . . . , expiry of . . . days/weeks/months from your next pay day, the . . . . I enclose herewith your appropriate pay in lieu of notice; your accrued holiday entitlement; and your documents.

NOTE:
See Chapter 14 – written reasons must now often be given, at employee's request. But, in the absence of such a request, the law does not require employers to state reasons.

100   Take notice – with regrets

I must regretfully inform you that I am required (by the Board) to give you notice to terminate your employment by the above company. According to your contract, you are entitled only to statutory minimum periods of notice. As you have been with us over four weeks but less than two years, that entitlement is seven days' notice. But I am pleased to extend that period to . . . days.

NOTE:
1   This letter still gives no reason for the notice. It is best used in cases where there has been no misconduct, but where lack of 'capability' or 'qualification' is relied upon (see later in this chapter). Of course, if you do rely upon misconduct, it is not wise to send a letter which shows cordiality.

2   The fact that a contract of service provides for a period of notice never prevents you from giving more. A good employer often does so and nowadays, generosity of this sort is not entirely altruistic, especially where the dismissal may be 'unfair'. After all, he may have to pay compensation in the long run – and meanwhile he is not only giving both appearance and substance to his statement that he acted 'fairly in all the circumstances', but he is also giving his employee further paid time within which to find alternative employment. An employee remains (as before) under an obligation to mitigate his loss, as best he can.

101   Dismissal – no notice required

I am instructed to give you notice, terminating your employment as from the end of this week. You will appreciate that your contract of employment provided that you were entitled to minimum statutory periods of notice. As you have been with us less than 4 weeks, you are not, strictly speaking, entitled to any notice at all. However, we hope that by giving you . . . days' notice, this will help avoid unnecessary hardship.

102   Notice to terminate contract of employment – of executive

I must ask you to treat this letter as notice terminating your employment in accordance with your contract, at the end of the period of . . . weeks/months from . . . your next pay day.

NOTE:
1   A variety of letters of dismissal are offered in this book – please see Index. You must consider in each case whether or not to include details of the reasons for the dismissal.

2   The employee's rights accrue only if he is 'dismissed'. However harshly or kindly that dismissal is effected, if 'the contract under which he is employed by the employer is terminated by the employer, whether it is so terminated by notice or without notice . . . or if under his contract of employment he is employed for a fixed term and that term expires without being renewed under the same contract . . .' or if he leaves when he is entitled to do so because of his employer's conduct, he is dismissed.

3   You could probably give notice commencing from the date of the letter if you serve letter on the recipient that day. But it is preferable to do so from the next day.

103   With kindness

I am very sorry that it has become necessary for me to give you notice, in accordance with the terms of your contract. Your contract will therefore terminate on the . . . .

I do hope that you will be able to obtain alternative employment, at an early date – and if I can be of help to you in any way, please do not hesitate to let me know.

NOTE:
After a letter like this, it will be impossible to allege successfully that the employee was dismissed because of any misconduct.

104   Notice by employee to terminate contract earlier than expiry of notice

I hereby give notice to terminate my contract of employment on the . . . , which is a date earlier than the Company's notice to me . . . dated the . . . is due to expire.

With best wishes.

NOTE:
1   An employee may jump the gun by giving written notice to his employer, to terminate his contract. There is no rule (as in the case of redundancy payments – Chapter 12) under which the employer has power to serve a counter-notice, requiring the employee to stay on until his period of notice expires.

2   There is no specific 'prescribed form' for an employee's letter in the above circumstances – any words will do. In general, the briefer the letter, the better. But note: If the reason why the employee wishes to leave before his notice expires is that he proposes to take on another job, his loss as a result of the dismissal will be greatly reduced, and if he obtains other work at the same or at a higher rate of pay, it will disappear altogether. Anyway, he must 'mitigate his loss' – as in the case of any other contractual breach. Hence, if he is taking a job at a lower rate of pay, the following letter is suggested:

105   Employee jumps the gun — to obtain lower-paid job

I am happy to say that I have obtained another post, and I shall therefore be leaving prior to the expiry of the period of notice which has been given to me by the Company. My new employment starts on the . . . , and I shall therefore be leaving on the . . . .

Unfortunately, I shall not be earning the same salary/ receiving the same pay/remuneration/commission/terms, as I was receiving while working for your Company. The above notice is without prejudice to any claim which I may here-after find it necessary to bring for unfair dismissal.

NOTE:
The employee must still give the amount of notice required by his contract of service.

106   Allegation that employee has failed to 'mitigate his loss'

I was concerned to learn that you had rejected the offer of employment made to you by . . . . Where an employee is dis-missed, he is bound to mitigate his loss, if he reasonably can. You have been given the opportunity to keep that loss to the minimum — and if you see fit to carry out your threat and to institute proceedings for 'unfair dismissal' (as, of course, you are fully entitled to do), not only will the Company deny that your dismissal was 'unfair', but it will also contend that you have failed to mitigate your loss as you could have done.

107   Employee's reply — alternative job not reasonably comparable

I agree that I have been offered a job by . . . . But my status, responsibility and pay would not be comparable to those which I enjoyed while with the Company. I appreciate that it may be difficult for me to replace my former position with one which is as satisfactory, but I am certainly not pre-pared to down-grade myself, without at least a very firm effort to re-establish myself at a reasonably comparable level.

Incidentally, if I were to accept a lower paid job without

seeking a better one, I suspect that you would then criticise me for not having taken more energetic steps to mitigate my loss.

NOTE:
1 While an employee who seeks either damages for wrongful dismissal or compensation for unfair dismissal must do what he can to keep his loss to the minimum, this does not mean that he must take either the first job offered to him or one which would result in a vast change in his status. To take an obvious example, a Member of the Board need not accept work as a lift attendant.

2 Naturally, the question as to whether a dismissed employee has acted reasonably is one of fact, depending on all the circumstances of the case.

108 Allegation that dismissed employee has brought about his own downfall

I fully appreciate how you feel. But the circumstances of which you complain were, in our view, entirely brought about by your own actions. In particular, I would refer to the following:
* (a) . . .
* (b) . . .
* (c) . . .

I am sorry that the situation has reached this unhappy state. It is not of the Company's making.

109 Reply to allegation of 'contributory' actions

I vehemently deny that the alleged or any actions on my part have caused or contributed to the situation which led to my unfair dismissal by the Company. The facts are as follows:
* (a) . . .
* (b) . . .

110 Reply to unfair dismissal claim – dismissal agreed, not unfair

It is admitted that on the . . . , 19 . . , I dismissed Miss . . .

from her position as . . . with the above company. I attach hereto a series of memoranda/ letters of warning/written reasons for the dismissal. It is denied that the dismissal was unfair. We followed the procedure agreed with the . . . Union/ a fair procedure; gave her every opportunity to cease behaving in the manner complained of in the memoranda/warning letters; but as she continued to behave in the same way, we considered that we had no alternative other than to dismiss her.

NOTES:

1 If the employer's letter gives details of the allegations, then the employee's reply should do the same. Conversely, if the employer's letter is brief and unparticularised, a simple denial will do. This would be the same as the above draft, without the second (or the numbered) paragraphs.

2 It must be re-emphasised that when the executive – or any other employee – is attempting to protect his position, the basic rule remains the same: He is not bound to put anything into writing, but if he does so, he will find that a Tribunal is more likely to accept his case. On the other hand, anything he does commit to paper must be thoroughly accurate and carefully thought out.

3 It follows that if a letter is likely to find its way to Court, it is often wise to have it drafted by a solicitor – even if it is signed by the actual or potential litigant. There is no law which says that lawyers' letters must be signed by them. In practice, there are many occasions when they simply advise on the letter which the client should write – or draft that letter for his signature. So if you receive a well-drafted letter – either from the Company or from an employee – you may well suspect (correctly) the hidden hand of the lawyer.

Chapter 12

Redundancy

When the job goes along with the employee, then he is 'redundant'. If he is dismissed as redundant, he is entitled to such redundancy pay as is agreed between his employer and himself and if he is represented by a union, he will get much more than the statutory minimum which the law ensures for some redundant people.

To qualify for redundancy pay, the dismissed person must have worked for the same or for an associated employer for at least two years after the age of 18. His entitlement then increases up to a maximum (from 1 February 1981) of £3,900 after 20 years' service.

Selection for redundancy is a difficult misery. There are only three possibilities:

1 *Voluntary redundancy* – inviting people to apply to be sacrificed on the alter of worklessness. The best people still apply because *they* can get jobs elsewhere.

2 *Last in, first out* - a vile system which ensures that the new and energetic youngsters go first and the long-term employees, worthy or otherwise, remain. This removes the element of choice from the employer but at least ensures the absence of victimisation of any particular individual – hence is likely to avoid union disputes and will normally keep the employer away from industrial tribunals.

3 *Selection by demerit* – in other words: culling the workforce by sacking those who are considered least necessary, if the remaining workforce is to be kept viable. The trouble here, of course, is that few of those selected for redundancy will share their employer's view of their own lack of merit or poor service. And while 'redundancy' is a statutory reason for dismissal, selection for redundancy may be 'unfair'. So an employee who is genuinely redundant may have a claim stretching up to £10,000 or even beyond, based on his allegedly unfair selection for the sack.

The Redundancy Fund then pays out 41 per cent of any statutory redundancy payment. If an employer pays more than this required minimum, then he does so 100 per cent out of his own resources.

The following letters may be used or adapted by employers who have to make redundancies.

111   General announcement

I am very sorry to have to inform you that due to the recession in our industry and to the resulting shortage of orders, we shall shortly be forced to create a number of redundancies. We are doing everything in our power to keep this number to the minimum; we are engaged in urgent discussions with all unions concerned; and we urge all employees to help us to maintain the maximum level of productivity, so that we can keep the remaining business viable. The purpose of this letter is to dispel rumours and to assure all our workforce that there is no question of this company being put into liquidation. We are determined to ensure that this fine company shall continue in operation.

NOTE:
A letter of this sort will inevitably leave the reader worrying: 'Will I be among the survivors?'. But with rumours rife, it may be a necessity. Its terms need anguished care – and, where possible, should be agreed with any union involved.

112   Voluntary redundancy – applications invited

As you know, a drop in orders has made a cutback in staff absolutely unavoidable. In an effort to cause the least possible hardship, we are now inviting employees to apply for voluntary redundancies, if they wish. If you do wish to apply, then please inform your personnel manager *(or as the case may be)* within a week.

If your application is accepted, then you will receive your full period of notice *(or: . . . weeks/months' notice)*, together with your statutory redundancy entitlement.

If we receive too many applications or if for some other reason it is not possible to grant your application, you will be informed as soon as possible.

We are all very sorry that this situation has arisen — but we hope that the upturn in trade will not be far away and

when it is, we are determined that the company will be
ready to respond.

NOTE:

*1   Remember that a redundant employee is entitled to his proper
notice or pay in lieu. Indeed, only during the first 12 months of his
service (when he is not qualified for unfair dismissal protection) is
the employee's period of notice as important to him as when he is
made redundant.*

*2   Few redundancies are 'unfair'. And for most redundant employees
– at any level, including executive and managerial – the notice period
is the employee's only real cushion against disaster. So are you certain
that your own period of notice is the maximum you can negotiate
for yourself?*

113   Last in, first out

I regret to inform you of the serious drop in our orders
due to the present recession in our trade/industry. It means
that we are forced to make . . . redundancies in our . . .
department/factory *(or as the case may be)*. In accordance
with our agreement with the . . . Union, selection for
redundancy will be made strictly on the 'last in, first out'
basis. You will be informed of details within the next few
days.
   If you are one of those whom we shall have to lose,
may I thank you for your service to the company and tell
you how sad we all are that this situation has arisen. We
hope that business will expand again before too long and
that we shall then have the opportunity to offer you another
job with our organisation.
   If you are among those who will remain with us, may I
urge you, please, to help us in every possible way to ensure
that the company's business remains strong and viable.

114   Last in – employee redundant

We are all very sad that redundancies have become
inevitable. We have decided that the only way to avoid
individual ill-will is to stick to the principle of 'last in, first

out' as the basis of our selection for redundancy. So those employees who joined us most recently must be the first to be made redundant.

Unfortunately, you are among those whom we shall have to dismiss as redundant and in the circumstances, please treat this letter as giving you notice in accordance with your terms of service, terminating on the . . . As you will not have been with us for two years by that date, you will not be qualified for redundancy pay. *(Or:* at the date of your dismissal you will have been with the company/group for . . . years and . . . days and will therefore qualify for . . . redundancy pay. *Or:* The personnel department/accounts department/your departmental head will inform you of your/any redundancy pay entitlement as soon as possible.)

We are all very sad that this situation has arisen and we hope that trade will soon improve so that we may be able to offer you, if you wish, further work with the company. Meanwhile, we thank you for your service and wish you good luck in the future.

115   Selection by demerit

As you will certainly have heard, trade has slumped and the company is therefore forced to rationalise its work-force and in the process to create a number of redundancies. Obviously, this must be done on the basis that the remaining workforce will be as strong and viable as possible.

In the circumstances, it has been regretfully decided that we shall no longer be able to employ you as from the . . . . You will, of course, receive your full period of notice *(or:* your pay in lieu of notice) and any statutory redundancy entitlement. We are giving you this information as early as possible in the hope that you may find alternative employment.

By all means discuss this decision with your personnel manager/head of department *(or as the case may be).* May I emphasise once again how sad we are that this inevitable situation has arisen. We also regret that our efforts to find reasonably suitable alternative employment for you with the company/group have not been successful.

NOTE:

1 It is usually best to keep this sort of letter as general as possible. But if the employee asks for 'written reasons' for his dismissal, then you will have to give them – adequately and within fourteen days, or the employee will become entitled to an additional two weeks' pay, provided that he has been with you for at least six months when his employment terminates.

2 Where you select a person for dismissal on merit, then you may have two reasons for dismissal:

(a) Redundancy – because there is no longer the need to employ the same number of people to do the job at that place or time or at all.

(b) Capability – because the employee's performance was less satisfactory than that of others whom you are retaining. This is a subjective test (as opposed to the objective 'last in, first out' basis). It may therefore be challenged by the employee, if he does not share your assessment of his ability – or, indeed, even if he does. Then you must brace yourself for potential Industrial Tribunal battle – or for a claim which it may be wise or economical to settle.

116 Employee's response

Thank you for your letter of . . . which I was sad to receive. My reply is as follows:

1   I do not accept that it would be fair to make me redundant and I ask you to reconsider this decision. I shall be pleased to discuss the situation and its implications with you at your earliest convenience;

2   I do not accept your assessment of redundancy pay because (a) my employment did not begin on the date stated, but on the . . . ; (b) the calculation is incorrect because . . . ; (c) I believe that it would be possible to avoid these redundancies if . . . .
I would be grateful if we could meet at your earliest convenience because I have some further suggestions to put to you which I believe would be of great benefit to the business.

3   No period of notice is specified in my letter of appointment (*or*: while the period of notice which you mention is

stated in my original letter of appointment, I have since then been promoted several times and clearly I am entitled to such period as is reasonable in the circumstances which would be very much longer than that stated by you/ the accounts department.)

NOTE:

1   The fact that a decree of redundancy has descended from on high does not force the employee to accept it – on the terms stated or even at all.

2   If you *are made redundant, you may fight for the preservation of your job – and/or at the very least to ensure that you are getting your full legal entitlement – and hopefully more.*

3   If you are a member of a union or of a staff association, then put it to work. It may succeed in obtaining far more for you than the law guarantees. But if you are on your own, then you must do your best for yourself. Like your employers, you are entitled to consult ACAS – to ask the Conciliation Officer to advise you on your rights. Alternatively, your solicitor, whose initial advice you can get at little or no cost – or a Citizen's Advice Bureau. Do not take it for granted that your employers' calculations are correct, whether they are made by computer or not. 'Unfair selection for redundancy' is your claim.

117   Reasonably suitable alternative employment

I refer you to my letter of . . . when I gave you notice to terminate your employment on . . . . I am happy to inform you that it is now possible to offer you what we regard as reasonably suitable alternative employment from that date, working as a . . . in our . . . department/factory at . . . ; and otherwise on the same terms including remuneration as at present. I do hope that you will find this offer acceptable.

118   Trial period in alternative employment

Thank you for your letter. We were sorry to note that you do not regard the alternative employment which we have offered as suitable or satisfactory. But we were wondering whether you would not be prepared to give it

a try? The law provides that a person who is redundant
in your sort of case may take on alternative employment
offered for a trial period of up to four weeks, without losing
his redundancy rights. Both for your sake and for that of our
business — we would be very pleased to retain your services —
I do urge you to accept this suggestion.

119   No other employment available

We thank you for your letter and confirm that we have
made efforts to find reasonably suitable alternative employment for you. Unfortunately, there is none.

NOTE:

1   The Employment Appeal Tribunal said (in the leading case of British
United Shoe Machinery Ltd. *v.* Clark) *that when dismissing an employee
for redundancy, employers 'ought to make reasonable efforts to find
him other employment'. The standard to be applied is that of 'the
reasonable employer'. If there has been such a failure to make reasonable efforts to find the employee other work, it is still necessary for
the tribunal 'to consider what would have been the likely result had
that been done which ought to have been done . . . '.*

2   In Vokes Ltd *v.* Bear *no effort was made to find alternative work
for a 'middle-aged family man', employed as works manager of a
company in the Tilling Group. He was given no real warning that he
might be dismissed before the blow fell and no assistance whatever
in finding alternative employment. 'There was a redundancy situation
but no compelling reason . . . why the axe should have fallen before
the employer had done his best to help the employee. The dismissal
for redundancy was therefore unfair.'*

*3   It follows that you should always look for alternative employment.
And you may if you wish add to all redundancy letters (where appropriate) the following sentence. 'We regret that our efforts to find
reasonably suitable alternative work for you within the company/
group have not been successful.'*

120   Department closed

As we indicated to you some time ago, it has become

inevitable that your department must be closed. You will therefore be dismissed as redundant as from . . . . I enclose a calculation of the redundancy pay to which you will become entitled; you will also be entitled to . . . weeks' notice, in accordance with your terms of service; and if you have any queries regarding your redundancy, please do not hesitate to let me know.

We are sorry that there is no alternative employment which we can offer to you within the company/group – and hope that you will be successful in finding other work as soon as possible. If we can be of help to you in this regard, please do not hesitate to let me know. We all greatly regret this end to our long and happy association – and I wish you good luck in the future.

121   Redundancy – other employees retained

I was sorry to learn from your letter that you regard your dismissal as redundancy as being 'unfair' on the grounds that other employees who could have been dismissed have in fact been kept on. Unfortunately, in coping with the substantial decrease in trade, we have had to select people for redundancies on the basis of retaining the most viable possible workforce. Unhappily, it must be for us to judge the exigencies of the business – not least for the sake of the employees who will be remaining with us.

NOTE:

1   If it is shown that 'the circumstances which constituted the re-dandancy applied equally to one or more employees in the same undertaking who held a position similar to that held by the dismissed employee, and who has not been dismissed by the employer', then the dismissal may be 'unfair' – even if the dismissed employee was indeed redundant. The Tribunal would look, if necessary, at all the circumstances of the case to see whether or not the employer was using redundancy as an excuse to get rid of a particular employee unfairly.

2   The shorter the time that the employee has been with the company, the more important his unfair dismissal remedy becomes – as opposed to his redundancy pay. The moment he has served for 52 weeks (as defined – which may be a little less), he is entitled to his unfair dismissal remedies – which do not thereafter increase in amount. But his statutory minimum redundancy pay only starts accruing after he has served for at least two years after reaching the age of 18 and it takes 20 years before it reaches its maximum.

122   Employee rejects alternative

Thank you for offering me the alternative post of . . . . This is not a reasonably suitable alternative to my present job for the following reasons:

1   It would involve me in about an additional . . . minutes of travel, each working day.
2   My status would be considerably reduced.
3   . . . .
4   . . . .

I am anxious to continue my loyal and devoted work for the company/group/you − and I would therefore be very grateful if you would be able to make an alternative offer with you. I will most gladly call upon you at any mutually convenient time to discuss possibilities and I thank you for your consideration.

123   Procedure followed

Thank you for your letter. I am sorry that you consider that the arrangements are unfair. We have followed to the letter the procedure agreement made with your union and we suggest that you discuss the matter with your steward/ convenor/the father of your chapel/union representative. We recognise the inevitable hardship and unhappiness caused by our decision and its consequences − but unfortunately we have no alternative in the current wretched recession in our trade.

124   No 'dismissal'

I am sorry to have to inform you that the Department of Employment shares our view that you were not 'dismissed' − as redundant or at all. Having been warned that dismissals were imminent in your department, you in fact left before the date for the termination of your employment had been fixed. The departure was therefore voluntary — and I regret that you therefore forfeited any redundancy entitlement.

By all means take advice on this matter from your union or solicitor or Citizen's Advice Bureau. We are sorry that we cannot be of help to you.

NOTES:

1   The employee has ignored Janner's Law No. 1: 'Never resign — at least unless you have a better job to go to'. Those who resign are, by definition, 'not dismissed' — so they cannot successfully claim damages for wrongful dismissal, compensation for unfair dismissal for those remedies normally open to people who are dismissed as redundant.

2   An exception to this rule now follows·

125   Employee anticipates expiry of employer's notice

You served notice on me to terminate my contract of employment, on grounds of my redundancy. I hereby give you written notice to terminate my contract on the . . . , as I have found alternative employment commencing on that date.

NOTE:

If an employer gives notice to an employee to terminate his employment, the employee may himself give written notice that he wishes to leave before that period expires. He must do so within the 'obligatory period of notice' — if in doubt, take advice because the 1978 Act includes a very complicated definition of this term. Anyway, the employee may normally serve a counter-notice on you, saying that he wishes to leave early. You may then serve a further notice on the employee requiring him to withdraw his notice and saying that unless he does so you will contest any liability to pay redundancy money. An appropriate letter follows — but in this situation, please consult an expert.

126   Employer's counter-notice — stay on

Thank you for your letter of . . . , the notice that you wish to leave before your period of notice expires. I hereby require you to withdraw that notice and continue in the company's employment until the date when your notice expires. Unless you do so, the company will contest any liability to pay to you a redundancy payment in respect of the termination of your contract of employment.

We regret the necessity to serve this notice but we cannot do without your services during this period.

NOTES:

1 Think very carefully before you operate this procedure. The employee whom you force to stay on is unlikely to express his profound gratitude by excellent service. You will no longer have to pay the employee during the remaining period of notice – and you will generally be well advised to lead him happily on his way.

2 This is, of course, an extension of the good rule that where an employee gives notice, it is often better to give him his pay in lieu – despite a curious, recent decision which suggests that to do so may be a breach of contract by the employer.

Chapter 13

Exclusion from unfair dismissal protection

Certain categories of employee are excluded from protection under the unfair dismissal provisions. These include wives employed by husbands, or husbands by wives; people based outside the UK; people above retiring age and part-timers.

The current minimum normal working hours of part-timers necessary to qualify for protection under the unfair dismissal provisions is 16 hours, or 8 hours after 5 years' service.

For special rules for small businesses, please see Appendix 2.

127   Part-time employees

As you work for us under a contract which 'normally involves employment for less than 16 hours weekly', you could not under any circumstances qualify for compensation for unfair dismissal. By all means consult your solicitors, as you suggest. To assist them, I enclose herewith a list of the actual hours which you have worked during the past 52 weeks.

NOTE:
1   Here is yet another incentive to employ part-timers – for less than a normal 16 hour week.

2   If a part-timer is employed occasionally – or seasonally – for more than 16 hours a week, provided that his 'normal' working hours are less than this maximum, he will not get compensation for 'unfair dismissal', under any circumstances.

3   After five years' continuous employment, the part-timer is covered if he works 8 hours a week.

128   Part-time – over 16 hours at Christmas

I agree that during the Christmas season you worked well over 16 hours – but this was an abnormal situation. Your

work normally involves employment for less than 16 hours
a week. In the circumstances, quite apart from our vehement
denial that you were unfairly dismissed, it is our view that
you could not conceivably obtain compensation for unfair
dismissal against the company.

129 Part-time – special pressures

Although you were good enough to put in a full working
day during the recent rush job, you were normally employed
for less than 16 hours a week. In the circumstances, your
claim for compensation for alleged 'unfair dismissal' cannot
possibly be accepted.

I would add that in any event your dismissal was because
of the manner in which you carried out your job, and was not
'unfair', in any sense of that word.

130 Five years' continuous employment – 8 hour's work

Having now worked with the company for over five years,
I am covered by unfair dismissal protection because I normally work over 8 hours a week. In the circumstances, I
would invite you to reconsider your decision not to pay me
compensation for unfair dismissal; I am putting in a written
application for compensation and a basic award, so as to
protect my position; I shall be pleased to discuss the matter
with you – or, in due course, with the conciliation officer;
and I look forward to hearing from you as soon as possible.

131 Wives – and husbands

I agree that as a result of our unhappy matrimonial disputes it became impossible to employ you any longer in my
business, and you were dismissed accordingly. But I am told
that where the employer is the husband or wife of the employee, no remedy for 'unfair dismissal' could be obtained,
even if the dismissal were (as I deny) unfair.

NOTE:
The above exception applies where you employ your wife – but not

where your company does so. It protects the individual and not the corporate employer.

132   Employees outside UK

I appreciate your feelings about your dismissal – although I cannot agree that you have been unfairly treated in any way. In any event, under your contract of employment you were based and 'ordinarily worked' outside the UK and in the circumstances there can be no question of a successful claim by you for unfair dismissal. I am sorry that our relationship should have to end on this note.

NOTE:
The 'unfair dismissal' provisions do not apply 'to any employment where, under his contract of employment, the employee ordinarily works outside Great Britain'. This does not include people who 'ordinarily work' in Great Britain but are required to do jobs abroad – even if they are overseas for some considerable time. There will, of course, be many borderline cases.

133   On board ship

I appreciate that you were employed to work on board a ship registered in the UK. But where the employment is wholly outside Great Britain or the claimant is not ordinarily resident in Great Britain, he is to be registered as a person who under his contract of employment 'ordinarily works' outside Great Britain. You have not only been employed wholly outside Great Britain but are ordinarily resident, I understand, in . . . . In the circumstances, even if (which is denied) you would otherwise be entitled to compensation for unfair dismissal, you come within one of the exclusions provided by the Act.

134   Above retiring age – man

You were dismissed after reaching the age of 65 and in the circumstances there is no possible question of compensation for 'unfair dismissal'. We would like to point out, in any event, that we kept you on beyond retiring age because of our high regard for you — and we feel that we have acted more than fairly in your case. And we hope that on reflection you may agree.

135   Above retiring age — woman

Once a woman attains the age of 60, she is no longer protected against 'unfair dismissal'. So as you were beyond retirement age when you were dismissed, the unfair dismissal rule cannot help you.

In any event, I cannot agree that you were dealt with unfairly. We in fact kept you on as long as we possibly could. And you were given more than the required period of notice when we decided that you would have to leave us.

I am sorry that I cannot be of help to you.

136   Application out of time

We note your application to the Industrial Tribunal for compensation for alleged unfair dismissal. Without prejudice to our contention that this application is unfounded and your dismissal was entirely fair, we must point out that your employment terminated on . . . , but your claim was only dated . . . — more than three months later. In the circumstances, your claim is out of time and the company will if necessary contend that the tribunal has no jurisdiction to hear your claim. You may know that a claim can be brought out of time if it was not 'reasonably practicable' to do so within the three-month period. But as you knew from discussions with your personnel manager/as a result of your talk with your union representative/shop steward, that you did have potential unfair dismissal claims, there can be no lawful excuse for your delay.

NOTE:
It has been held to be 'reasonably practicable' to bring a claim within the three-month period if the claimant knew he had any rights at all. Even if he was misled by the wrong advice from a solicitor or from a Citizen's Advice Bureau — or even if the employer agreed that the dismissal was unfair and negotiations for an agreed settlement were

still going on — failure to lodge the claim within three months from the date of the termination of the employment would destroy the claim.

137   Negotiations admitted — but claim late

We have been informed of your unfair dismissal claim. But it is dated more than three months from the termination of your employment and we shall therefore, if necessary, submit that the tribunal has no jurisdiction to hear that claim. We have been advised that the without prejudice negotiations which have been going on since your dismissal in way affect the matter — save that they do indicate quite clearly that you knew that you had potential access to unfair dismissal remedies. Therefore it must have been 'reasonably practicable' for you to bring your claim within the statutory time limit.

NOTE:

1   The upper ages are the normal retiring ages applicable in the business, or 65 for men, 60 for women. There is no lower age limit (for redundancy pay, you have to be at least 20 — having continuously served for two years after reaching your eighteenth birthday). The absence of a lower age limit is particularly relevant when considering the rights of apprentices.

2   If the normal retirement age in your business is above the national retirement age, e.g. if you normally keep women as well as men on until reaching 65, your retirement age will apply. So, in effect, an employee will only lose his rights if he is above his employer's as well as the national retirement age, whichever comes later.

Chapter 14

Written statements of reasons for dismissal

When you dismiss an employee, you are not normally bound to give any reason for your decision. It may be wise, sensible and in accordance with good management and/or good industrial relations practice to do so. But the law leaves you to decide whether or not to keep silent.

However: if an employee who has been continuously employed by you or by any associated employer for six months or more * is entitled to a written statement of reasons for his dismissal, 'on request' that written statement 'shall be admissible in evidence in any proceedings'.

If an employer unreasonably refuses to provide a written statement within the two-week period or the particulars given are 'inadequate or untrue', the employee may complain to an Industrial Tribunal. If that complaint is upheld, then the tribunal 'shall make an award that the employer pay to the employee a sum equal to the amount of two week's pay' — with no upper limit.

If an employee requests written reasons, you may be fairly sure that he has been advised to do so by his union, or by a lawyer or other expert as a preliminary to an unfair dismissal claim. So be very careful how you phrase your reasons. Remember:

1 You are only entitled to dismiss for a reason known to you at the date when you dismissed. After the employee has left, you may find out other reasons which are even more serious than those which you knew at the time. These will be relevant, if and when the tribunal comes to assess compensation. They may show that the employee's 'contributory conduct' should greatly reduce — or even remove altogether — any payment which the employee would otherwise receive. But they do not go into the statement of written reasons.

2 Once you have put your reasons into writing, it will be very difficult for you to rely afterwards upon any other reason. For instance, if you do not replace the employee in his job, he is dismissed as 'redundant'; but if you have selected him for redundancy, instead of other employees who were kept on, then the basis for selection for redundancy was his 'lack of capability' or his 'conduct'. Both reasons should be given.

Note that this 26-week period remains unchanged, even though unfair dismissal protection now only begins after 52 weeks.

3   If the reason for the dismissal was that the employee failed to heed warnings previously given to him, preferably in writing, then you should repeat the warnings, stating the dates and manner in which they were given. It is not enough merely to refer to the written warnings, without repetition.

4   Unless you can refer to and repeat warnings and state that you were dismissed because the employee failed to heed those warnings, it is normally wise to get help in the drafting of the written reasons.

5   If the request for reasons comes in a badly drafted or even illiterate letter, do not presume that it was the handiwork of the dismissed employee. Lawyers frequently draft letters and other documents in a way that will not indicate the professional hand on the pen.

*   *   *

138 'Incapability'

You have asked me to put in writing the reason for your dismissal.

As you know, you have not been coping with your job as you used to. We accept that this was due to advancing years/ your ill health — but making all possible allowances and putting up with the situation for as long as we could, we eventually came to the reluctant decision that we could not retain your services.

Our specific complaints are as follows:
(1) . . . .
(2) . . . .
(3) . . . .

139 Ill health or old age — brief

The reason (as requested by you) for your dismissal was (as you know) that your capability for carrying out your work had been severely affected by age and ill health. This was evidenced by the following:
(1) . . . .
(2) . . . .
(3) . . . .

140   Technical qualification

When we modernised our administration, we tried to train our existing employees to do the work in the new way — and most of them managed to adapt themselves. Unfortunately, you did not. As you neither had nor are able to acquire the necessary technical qualifications for coping with the work, we felt that we had no alternative but to give you your notice.

141   Conduct

The reason for your dismissal was your conduct. Briefly, the company's main complaints were:
(a). . .
(b). . .
(c). . .

142   Illegal to employ

You have been given your notice because it is illegal for us to employ you. Your work permit has expired and in the circumstances it is not possible for us to keep you on without breaking the law.

143   Redundancy

The reason for your dismissal was that you were redundant. The reason why you have not received redundancy pay is that you had not been employed for the minimum two years. The minimum six-month period of continuous employment to which you refer applies only to the protection provided by *The Employment Protection (Consolidation) Act, 1978,* for people who are unfairly dismissed. It does not apply to a right to redundancy pay.

144   Denial of entitlement to written statement

Under the Employment Protection (Consolidation) Act,

you are only entitled to a written statement for the reasons for your dismissal if you have been continuously employed for at least 26 weeks ending with the last complete week before the effective date of the termination of your employment. You were only with us for . . . weeks — and therefore you are not entitled to a written statement (Nor, of course, are you protected by the unfair dismissal rules as such, because you have been employed by the company for less than 52 weeks.)

I would only add that it is denied that you were in fact dismissed unfairly, as alleged or at all.

145   Reasonable to refuse — breach of confidence

We are not willing to provide a written statement of the reasons for the termination of your employment because to do so would involve us in a breach of confidence.

146   Reasonable refusal — medical

Save that the dismissal was on medical grounds, we are not prepared to provide the written statement that you request. If, as you threaten, you present a complaint to an Industrial Tribunal — as you are fully entitled to do — we shall maintain that our refusal to give further details was in the circumstances wholly reasonable.

NOTE:
If a Tribunal finds that a written statement was unreasonably refused, then the employee will be entitled to the equivalent of two weeks' pay by way of compensation. But if you can satisfy the Tribunal that your refusal was 'reasonable', you will be in the clear. Reasonableness (as usual) is a question of fact.

147   Reference to written warning

You were given written warnings of intended dismissal on the following dates:
    (1) . . .
    (2) . . .
    (3) . . .

In those letters, I clearly stated the conduct complained
of and that if this continued, the company would have no
alternative other than to dismiss you. The complaints were
as follows:

(1) . . . .
(2) . . . .
(3) . . . .

The conduct did continue and you were accordingly
dismissed. In particular you were guilty of the following:

(1) . . . .
(2) . . . .
(3) . . . .

148   Alternative — reference to written warning

In reply to your letter of the . . . , requesting written
reasons for your dismissal, I must refer you to my letter
dated . . . . In that letter, I warned you that if the conduct
therein complained of persisted, you would be dismissed.
The complaints were as follows:

(1) . . . .
(2) . . . .
(3) . . . .

You did not mend your ways in the following respects:

(1) . . . .
(2) . . . .
(3) . . . .

The company therefore carried out its stated intention.

149   As warned — but additional reasons

Thank you for your letter requesting written reasons for
your dismissal. You were dismissed because in spite of my
letters to you dated . . . and . . . , you persisted in the conduct
therein complained of, and in particular:

(1) On . . . you . . . .
(2) On . . . you . . . .
(3) . . . .

In addition, the situation was made worse by the following
matters:

1   You were late at work on the following occasions . . . .
2   You failed to attend work on the following occasions, and did not produce a medical certificate. . . .
3   . . . .

Chapter 15

Demotion — and dismissal

An employee who is prepared to accept demotion is agreeing to a variation of his contract of service. He will not then be able to claim that he has been 'dismissed' — so he will have no claim to compensation for 'unfair dismissal'. Conversely: Demote with care. To reduce a man's status . . . his money . . . his future employability . . . could prove most expensive. So all letters of demotion are potentially perilous.

Remember that if you promote someone in the belief that he will cope with added responsibility but that hope proves unfounded, the fault is at least partially your own. Here was an employee obviously doing well in his job; you decide to put him up the ladder; and now you want to push him off? If he agrees to return to a lower level, then you will be lucky. If not, you must decide — to dismiss or not to dismiss?

If you do sack the employee who failed to perform well at a higher level, then he will probably regard the dismissal as unfair. And so it may be. Certainly a proportion of the responsibility for his failure to cope must rest upon you. So where you promote, you should provide for a trial period (see Chapter 3).

150   Demotion — after unsuccessful trial

After the most careful consideration, I have decided that it will not be possible to keep you on in the supervisory/managerial role to which you were promoted as from . . . . As you know, the burden of responsibility has proved too heavy for you. And I am sure that it will be best for both the company and for you if you were to revert to your former job, as provided for in the arrangement under which you were promoted.

For the avoidance of hardship, we will continue to pay you your present salary until . . . , whereafter it will revert to the normal pay for your previous and renewed grade.

Thank you for your effort in trying out the new role.

151 Concerning agreed demotion

I confirm our conversation — in which we agreed that you were not coping successfully with your job as . . . and that it would be better for all concerned — and in the interests of both yourself and the company — if we were to lift the burden of responsibility which has now rested on you for so long.

In the circumstances, it was agreed by us both that as from the . . . , you will serve as . . . at a salary/wage of £ . . . — and I feel sure that you will be much happier with this new arrangement. If you wish to see me in connection with the move or with your new job at any time, please do not hesitate to contact me.

With my best personal regards to you.

152 Demotion offered — no alternative

For reasons which I discussed with you, we are no longer prepared to keep you on in your present position of . . . . I fully appreciate the difficulties which you have had and am very sorry that this decision has become inevitable.

However, I am happy to confirm that we are prepared to move you across to the post of . . . — although necessarily not on quite the same terms. If you accept this change, your pay would be £ . . . per week/month — your period of notice will be . . . weeks/months; but in all other respects, your terms will be the same as previously.

I do hope that you will accept the alternative position. If not, then I am afraid that you must treat this letter as notice to terminate your employment on . . . . You will appreciate that you are, strictly speaking, entitled to only . . . weeks/ months notice — and the notice which I am now giving you is much longer. But I would like to emphasise once again that the company will be happy to retain you in its service, in a job which would impose less heavy burdens on you.

Please would you let me know your decision as soon as possible.

153 A move – which equals demotion

I am writing to confirm our conversation about the opening of the company's new office/plant/premises/department. The company is anxious to make use of your considerable experience and knowledge and to put you in charge of the new enterprise. It is true, as you pointed out, that you would be supervising/managing less people than at present – but there would be no change in your remuneration or other terms of service. In the circumstances, I earnestly hope that you will agree to this move.

We have carefully considered your suggestion that the move be for a trial period, and are agreeable to this if necessary. But we would point out to you the disadvantages from your point of view. The element of permanence provides stability for all concerned.

I look forward to hearing from you,
With best wishes.

NOTE:
However you may dress it up, the 'move' changes the employee's job – and is a dismissal in law. If you cannot obtain his agreement, then you either leave him where he is or, if you insist upon shifting him, then he will be entitled to regard that insistence as the destruction of his present contract of service. If he decides to claim compensation for unfair dismissal, then the burden of proving fairness will rest upon you.

154 Refusal of demotion

I have carefully considered your suggestion that I should accept less responsibility – but after anxious thought, I must reject it. I have served the company loyally and well for . . . years; I have received no complaints – oral or written – concerning my work; and while I appreciate that it might suit the company's short-term interests that I be moved across into the position suggested, I respectfully disagree that the company would benefit in the long run, and in any event I am not prepared to accept what amounts to a demotion/serious loss of status.

I am sure that on reconsideration you will understand my decision – and I assure you that I will continue in the future, as in the past, to devote my energies to the company's service. With best wishes.

155   Confirming agreed demotion — elderly manager

I was very pleased to have been able to tell you that the company has found a niche for you as its . . . . You have served the company loyally and well for many years and I believe that this new post will bring you not only security but also satisfaction. I confirm that your revised terms of service are as follows:-

1   Remuneration: £ . . . per week/month/year.
2   Holidays increased to . . . weeks per year — and holiday pay pro rata, when your employment terminates for whatever reason.
3   Otherwise, on the same terms as previously.
  With my best wishes to you.

Chapter 16

Admonition, warning, reproof and rebuke

One of the less happy jobs of every executive with subordinates working under him is the meting out of reproofs — which may be done orally on the traditional carpet, or in writing — probably so as to have the copy available as evidence. And the more elevated the subordinate, the greater the remedy he is entitled to win, if he is eventually dismissed 'unfairly'.

The letters that follow are designed as honest expressions of opinion, intended to produce results from the recipient or, at worst, a good impression on a tribunal or Court. They are written with one eye on the business and the other on the law. Some are alternatives to letters in Chapters 10 and 11.

*   *   *

156   Mild reminder

May I remind you of our conversation? You did promise to ensure that . . . . I do hope that you will not forget.
With best wishes.

157   Mild rebuke

You did assure me that you would . . . . But this has not been done. Please would you have it put in hand without further delay?

158   Explanation, please

The Chairman asked you some weeks ago to . . . . But despite your assurance that the job would be carried out without further delay, it does not appear to have been done. What is your explanation, please?

159   Appeal for mending of ways

As you know, I am concerned for your position in the company – and have been doing all that I can to turn away the wrath of the . . . . But I am no longer having much success in this. Please would you now ensure that . . . .

160   Excuses unacceptable

I have noted the excuses which you have presented to the Board, for your failure to do . . . . In view of . . . , these are totally unacceptable. In the circumstances, please would you now . . . .

161   Time limit

The promised reorganisation of your department has now taken . . . weeks/months, and is still not complete. I am asked by the Board to inform you that they insist upon the completion of the job within the next . . . days/weeks/by the of this/next month.

162   Tearing off strips

The patience of the Board is now exhausted. The following matters require your immediate attention:
   (a) . . .
   (b) . . .
   (c) . . .

NOTE:
Once you write details, these must be both accurate and provably so. It may be that you will receive a letter in reply – but the chances are that you will either get action or an oral retort. Your rule should be: Either keep your rebukes to general terms or ensure that they are fair, warranted, provable – and in moderate terms. An undignified loss of control resulting in the vocal harangue will happily go unrecorded. Its written equivalent can kill a case.

163   Warning

The Board has noted with dismay the failure of your department to balance its accounts/complete its stock check/ meet its norm. I am instructed to warn you that if there is any recurrence, the most serious consequences will inevitably result.

NOTE:
When employers can prove that they have given adequate warnings to dismissed employees, they seldom obtain compensation for unfair dismissal. And even if they do win their cases, the amount of compensation is generally reduced – the tribunal holds that the sacked man has 'contributed' to his own state of unemployment. So letters of warning are exceedingly important.

164   Second warning

May I refer you to my letter of the . . . , in which I warned you of the inevitable consequences of your failure to . . . . Please may I have an immediate explanation – together with an assurance that there will be no further delay in . . . .

165   Final warning

I am instructed by the Board to give you one final opportunity to carry out . . . in accordance with . . . .

Unless you comply with these requirements by . . . at the latest, the company will replace you with a . . . who is both willing and able to carry out the duties which have been entrusted to you.

166   Dismissal – with reminder of warnings

I must now refer you to my letters of the . . . , the . . . , . . . and . . . , and to the warnings therein contained. The work/stock taking/job evaluation/. . . has not been completed, satisfactorily or at all. In the circumstances, your employment is hereby terminated with effect from . . . . You will shortly receive the company's cheque in respect of all money due to you as at the date hereof, including salary and accrued holiday pay.

We trust that you will find some other post which suits you better, and are indeed sorry that our association must end in this manner.

NOTE:

1   The employment has been terminated without notice – but it may well be that the company would prefer to give notice or pay in lieu.

2   Even when dismissing summarily and after many warnings, it does no harm to attempt to end the association on good terms. Hence the final sentence.

Chapter 17

An executive's letters

Inevitably, a book of this sort is designed for executives in their business capacities. If, for instance, a man has to hire and fire, he must do his job as well and as fairly as he can — even if sometimes he finds it distasteful. But the executive must cope with these problems not only from his viewpoint as an employer's representative, but also from his own, as an employee — however mighty.

Here, as an antidote to some of the miseries doled out to others, are some letters (additional to those scattered through this book) which the executive may like to use and to adapt for his own purposes, if he is dismissed. Naturally, the object of the exercise is to ensure that his dismissal is 'unfair' — and that he receives a handsome, tax-free sum if he cannot get other work. Remember — applications must still be made, wherever practicable, within three months from the date when the employment terminates. Delay too long and you may lose your rights.

167   Executive's retort to dismissal

I acknowledge receipt of your letter of . . . , from which I was shocked to learn that I am to be dismissed by the company. I have devoted . . . years to the company's service; I have throughout been proud to carry out my duties with energy and skill; I have received no prior warning of intended dismissal; no fair procedures have been followed so as to enable me to represent my case, either to my immediate superior nor, still less, to a higher level of authority; and the pay in lieu of notice which I have received is no adequate remedy for the loss of my position.

In the circumstances, I ask you to reconsider your decision; and if it holds, then to supply written reasons for your taking this action.

I repeat once again that I have no wish whatever to cease working for the company — and so far as I am concerned I am ready, willing and able to return to my position.

NOTE:

1   Do you wish to return to your position? If so, then make your willingness plain – and stress your past service and loyalty to the company.

2   This letter does not specifically contain a threat to go to an Industrial Tribunal. Any executive or manager who does in fact make such a claim makes himself virtually unemployable. This threat should be held as a last resort – and anyway, the indications in this letter suggest to any well informed personnel chief or to a lawyer that you know your rights – which include the right to claim an order for reinstatement or re-engagement.

3   Assuming that you have been with the company for at least 12 months (as defined) you are entitled to unfair dismissal protection – but you remain entitled to written reasons within two weeks of your request, provided that your service has lasted at least six months.

168   Threat to instruct solicitors

I have no wish to prolong either the dispute or the ill-will that my dismissal has caused. But unless I receive an adequate offer of compensation from you within seven days, you will leave me with no alternative other than to place this matter in the hands of solicitors. I understand that my claim for additional pay in lieu of notice would go to the High Court and for unfair dismissal remedies to an Industrial Tribunal – but if you share my wish to avoid litigation, then may I now hear from you without further delay?

NOTE:

Unfair dismissal claims still go to tribunals and claims for damages for wrongful dismissal to the County Court (usually when the claim does not exceed £2,000) or otherwise to the High Court. Efforts to move all claims arising from alleged breaches of contracts of employment (wrongful dismissal, holiday pay, sick pay, etc.) from the courts to the tribunals have failed – mainly due to trade union opposition.

169   Denial of allegations made by employers

I am in receipt of your letter in which you see fit to allege

that I have been dismissed for misconduct/lack of qualifica-
tion/lack of aptitude. This allegation I strenuously deny. By
any standard, my dismissal was as unfair as it was unexpected.
Unless I hear from you with an offer of a very substantial
payment, I shall bring a claim for unfair dismissal before the
Industrial Tribunal.

NOTE:
*Just as it is important for employers to put their case on to paper as
soon as possible, so it is vital for the employee to do the same. If you
are dismissed in writing, then answer the letter – and keep a copy of
the answer. Deal with any allegations made, as briefly and lucidly as you
can.*

170   Executive unfairly dismissed

My dismissal has been unfair, in every sense of that word.
I have been unable to find alternative employment. In the
circumstances, I shall apply to the Industrial Tribunal for
my full remedies.
It would, of course, enable me to mitigate my loss considerably if I were to obtain other work. Perhaps you would
bear this in mind, when you are next asked for a reference
for me. Meanwhile, I am informing prospective employers
that my . . . years of service with the Company are likely to
provide the best reference that I can get in the circumstances.

NOTE:
*For rules on references see Chapter 19. Your employees are not bound
to provide you with a reference and if they do give a bad one, then
your chances of having any remady against them are highly remote.
So play it canny – as above.*

171   Passing the buck

Before I dismissed James Brown, I discussed the matter
with the Company solicitors/the Personnel Director/Mr . . . .
We both appreciate that there were risks involved in taking
this course, and that we might end up having to pay compensation for unfair dismissal. However, it was felt that this was

a risk worth taking in the circumstances.
  With best wishes.

NOTE:
*In all borderline cases involving 'unfair dismissal', management should
confer – and, in general, advice should be taken either from a superior,
or from the Company's solicitor and/or from Personnel. This is, of
course, a form of buck passing – but it is entirely legitimate. When
you deal with unfair dismissal, there is (potentially at least) over
£10,000 at stake and/or if you are are trying to cope with an actual
or potential industrial dispute, even an hour's break in production
may cost the company a small fortune.*

  *Still, it is as well to do any buck passing with appropriate dignity –
and to attempt, where possible, to take your fair share of responsibility
and more. The above letter is intended to strike a sensible balance.*

172   Refusal to resign

  I know that I have been overruled. I appreciate that I am
in a minority of one on the Board, but I adhere to my view
that the step which it is proposed to take is not in the interests
of the Company.
  I shall not resign.

NOTE:
*Never resign unless you have got a better job to go to or unless you
could prove that you were forced out, and hence dismissed 'constructively' (see Chapter 9). Only if you are dismissed can you hope to get
a remedy for unfair or wrongful dismissal – or for redundancy pay.*

173   Refusal to contract out of right to claim compensation
for unfair dismissal on expiry of fixed term

  Thank you for your letter, suggesting that – in return for
my long expected increase in salary – I should contract out
of my possible right to claim compensation for unfair dismissal, if the company decides not to renew my employment
when the present term comes to an end.
  I am sure that if you look at this matter from my point of
view, you will appreciate that this is not something that I

could possibly do. I appreciate that the company is not bound to increase my salary, as I am on a fixed-term arrangement. However, the Managing Director has made it quite plain to me on numerous occasions that – having regard to the completely unexpected and enormous increase in the cost of living and the fall in the value of money – it is unreasonable to expect me to continue to work as I am, on the basis of the agreed salary. Equally, it is not reasonable to expect me to give up my potential statutory rights against the company.

In the circumstances, could you kindly arrange for me to see the M.D. personally?

Meanwhile, you may be sure that I shall continue to use my best endeavours on the company's behalf.

NOTE:

1   Meet the Managing Director face to face, and you will probably get better results than you could do through any correspondence.

2   When you turn down a suggestion, it is important to do so in an amicable and dignified manner. After all, you will be continuing to work for the company, at least until your term does expire. You do not want to give anyone any chance of showing that you have given grounds for 'fair dismissal'. Hence,

3   Always state that the company has the assurance of your loyalty, support, conscientious work, etc., etc.

4   You can only contract out of your right to unfair dismissal remedies if you have a fixed-term contract of one year or more or if you come to a compromise arrangement that is recorded by a conciliation officer (Chapter 25).

174   Denial that executive 'ordinarily works outside Great Britain'

It is true that I have been employed by the company outside Great Britain for the past six months. It is not correct that I 'ordinarily work' outside Great Britain. According to the proper interpretation of my contract of employment, I was at all times based in Great Britain. In the

circumstances, I am advised that I am entitled to rely upon
my statutory protection against 'unfair dismissal'. From
my point of view, that is just as well – since you have seen
fit to dismiss me, I have not been able to obtain alternative
work. My loss is therefore enormous.

I hope that you will now deal with this matter speedily.

NOTE:

*Even if you are working overseas, provided that you remain based in
the UK, you retain your rights here – wherever you may be when you
are sacked. If, on the other hand, you are based outside the jurisdiction
of our courts, they cannot protect you – even if you are dismissed
here. If in doubt, look at your contract. And if you are offered work
abroad, by all means accept, if you wish – but get confirmation in
advance that you will remain based in the UK.*

175   Claim for compensation – not redundancy pay

I note that you say that I am being 'made redundant'. If I
am dismissed as redundant, then that would be thoroughly
unfair – and I shall take such steps as I may be advised in
order to protect my position generally, and in particular in
order to claim compensation for unfair dismissal in addition
to my redundancy rights.

Perhaps you will now reconsider the matter.

176   Denial that lack of qualifications a 'reasonable' ground for dismissal

I am astonished that you should have seen fit to dismiss
me for alleged lack of qualification, without at least giving
me the opportunity to acquire such qualification. I appreciate
that the new computer which you have introduced into the
office has affected my work, but I was and remain fully prepared to take such courses as may be necessary in order to
acquire the technical qualifications which I shall now need.
You gave me no such opportunity, but instead have given me
my notice.

In the circumstances, it is quite clear that I have been dismissed – and in my view, completely unfairly. I would ask

you to be good enough to reconsider this matter – and in particular my wish to undergo training, in order to cope with the new machinery and methods.

I look forward to hearing from you at your earliest convenience.

NOTE:
It is not enough to show a reason relating to 'capability' or 'qualifications' or 'conduct'. The law also requires the employer to act 'reasonably'. You allege that the employer was 'unreasonable' in the action he took. Put your case on record. This is as important when you are acting for yourself as when you are doing your duty for your company.

177 Employer's denial that employee has mitigated loss

I note your claim – which is disputed, in its entirety. In any event, I have seen no evidence that you have made any or any sufficient efforts to obtain alternative employment, and hence to mitigate your loss.

In my view, any loss which you may have suffered has been due not only to your own conduct while you were in the company's employment, but to your own inactivity thereafter. In the circumstances, any claim for compensation or damages will be contested.

178 Reply to allegation of 'contributory' actions

I vehemently deny that the alleged or any actions on my part have caused or contributed to the situation which led to my unfair dismissal by the Company. The facts are as follows:
    (a) . . .
    (b) . . .

NOTE:
1 If the employer's letter gives details of the allegations. then the employee's reply should answer each in turn. Conversely, if the employer's letter is brief and unparticularised, a simple denial will do. This would be the same as the above draft, without the second (or the numbered) paragraphs.

2   It must be re-emphasised that when the executive – or any other employee – is attempting to protect his position, the basic rule remains the same: He is not bound to put anything into writing, but if he does so, he will find that a Tribunal is more likely to accept his case. On the other hand, anything he does commit to paper must be thoroughly accurate and carefully thought out.

3   It follows that if a letter is likely to find its way to Court, it is often wise to have it drafted by a solicitor – even if it is signed by the actual or potential litigant.

179   Claim for compensation – with details of loss

Thank you for your letter, specifying alleged grounds for my dismissal. These I do not accept. I was unfairly dismissed. Even if (which I deny) I was guilty of the alleged failure to obey instructions, it was certainly not reasonable to treat such failure (which, I repeat, I deny) as sufficient grounds for terminating my employment. You appear to forget that I have been with the company for . . . years.

In the circumstances, unless I receive a substantial offer from you, I shall bring an unfair dismissal claim to compensate me for the very considerable loss I have suffered. This comes within the following categories:

1   Loss of salary/wage – at £ . . . per week, and continuing.
2   Loss of the following fringe benefits:
    a   subsidised meals;
    b   use of company car;
    c   sickness insurance;
    d   share option scheme;
    e   pension rights;
    f   . . .

In addition, I have had to move to London. The costs incurred have been as follows:
    1 . . .
    2 . . .

I have thought it best to place these facts on record, at the earliest possible opportunity. I shall be pleased to hear from you within the next seven days, failing which I shall place the matter in the hands of my solicitors.

This is indeed a very unhappy ending to a long and loyal period of service to the company.

180 Refusal to leave prior to 'dismissal'

I appreciate the warning which you have been good enough to give me, concerning forthcoming redundancies. However, I am not prepared to resign under any circumstances.

NOTE:
1 'Never resign'... well, hardly ever.... And at least not unless you have a better job to go to and/or you can prove that you were forced into resigning and hence that you were 'constructively dismissed'.

2 However, once you have been dismissed, i.e. given your notice, telling you that you will have to go very shortly, you may be able to jump the gun. If you do it properly.

181 Offer of re-engagement

In accordance with the order made by the Industrial Tribunal, I am pleased to offer you re-engagement by the company, in the capacity of . . . at a salary of £ . . . , i.e. on the terms specified by the Tribunal.

Kindly let me know at your earliest convenience whether this offer is acceptable to you.

182 Acceptance of re-engagement

Thank you for your letter offering me re-engagement on the terms set out therein. Your offer is accepted and I shall be pleased to attend for work on . . . .

183 Refusal of re-engagement

Thank you for your letter offering me re-engagement by the company. First, the terms set out are not those recommended by the Tribunal. They differ in the following respects:

(a) . . .
(b) . . .
(c) . . .

(In any event, having regard to the thoroughly unpleasant manner in which I have been treated by . . . , I do not feel

that it would be possible for me to return to working in the
same department/under the supervision of Mr . . . . If you are
able to offer some alternative arrangement, then I will of
course be only too pleased to consider it. Meanwhile, you may
be sure that I am continuing my efforts to obtain alternative
employment and hence to mitigate the loss caused to me by
your unfair dismissal.)

NOTE:
*It is vital in a letter of this sort to say why you are not prepared to
accept the offer of re-engagement – particularly if you can show that
the offer does not accord with the terms recommended by the Tribunal.
It is also important to show that you are attempting to keep your loss
to the minimum.*

184   Complaint of harassment

I wish formally to record my regret at the treatment which
I have been receiving during recent months. In particular:
(Insert details of treatment complained of)
In the circumstances, I am finding it increasingly difficult
to achieve the results which I seek, for the benefit of our
company. I would be grateful if I could discuss this matter
with you at your early convenience.

NOTE:
*It is not good enough simply to have a discussion with the Chairman.
It is vital to be able to prove your complaint, if necessary. If your
discussion takes place first – whether by accident or design – the
following letter may help:*

185   Confirmation of complaints made orally

It was good of you to spare me so much of your time, in
order to discuss my part in the company's business. It may
be helpful if I confirm the precise matters which have been
causing me so much concern. They are as follows:
(Insert details of complaints)
I would be grateful for anything that you can do in order
to put matters right. At the moment, and until we can get
our organisation back on to a level keel, the company's

business and its future prosperity are equally imperilled.
With best wishes.

NOTE:
It is always as well to emphasise your own good intentions. This is doubly so when you have been receiving letters of complaint. Some sample replies to such letters now follow:

186   Denial of complaint

Thank you for your letter. I completely deny the allegations which have been made against me by . . . . After my . . . years of hard work on the Board, it is most unjust that anyone should have made such allegations against me. I can only think that an effort is being made to oust me from the Board. This effort will be fiercely resisted. I have no intention whatsoever of resigning and I can only emphasise that I have been, remain and will continue utterly devoted to the interests of our Company.

187   Retort to letter of complaint

I was most distressed to receive your letter of the . . . . I do not know who has seen fit to give you the information which forms the basis of your allegations. It is completely untrue. I utterly refute in particular the following:
    1 . . .
    2 . . .
    3 . . .
The situation is in fact as follows:
    1 . . .
    2 . . .
I regard the attempt to oust me from the Board as absolutely shocking — and totally unfair.
If you think that any useful purpose would be served, I shall be pleased to discuss these matters with you. As you know, I have the greatest of respect for you personally and am only sorry that you have been dragged into this sordid controversy. Meanwhile, I shall continue to perform my duties and I trust that my efforts will not be frustrated by any further interference.

NOTE:

It is important, where possible, to separate off the Chairman from the Board – and to give him the chance to move in your direction, without losing personal prestige or face. Another alternative:

188   Stress on personal friendship with chairman

I have enjoyed and appreciated working with you over the past . . . years. Your letter therefore came as a particular shock to me. I have, if I may say so, the greatest possible respect for you – and I deeply regret that you have been drawn into the current personal controversy.

I absolutely deny the allegations that have been made – in particular:

    1 . . .

    2 . . .

May I suggest that we now meet to see whether we cannot get matters sorted out, before the Company – whose interests we both hold so dear – is torn apart?

NOTE:

The emphasis in all these letters rests upon your devotion to the Company's interest – and your determination not to be ousted.

189   Brief denial – and request for meeting

Your letter came as a deep shock to me. The allegations made against me are utterly without foundation. I would welcome the opportunity to discuss them with you. Could you spare me, perhaps, an hour before the meeting on . . . ?

190   Even briefer retort

No. These unfounded allegations just won't do. The attempt to oust me from the Board will fail. I will not willingly resign – and any dismissal would be grossly unfair.

NOTE:

1   A really brief bullet of this kind sometimes has killing effects. But it must be absolutely on target.

2   If you are forced *to resign you will be 'constructively' dismissed.*

191   To managing director — response to complaints

You are right — it has not been possible for me to
carry out my work with as much dispatch as I would have
wished. But the fault in this is not mine. I am desperately
under-staffed/the equipment ordered has not been supplied/
I have been refused the necessary equipment required . . . *(or
as the case may be).*

I would add that I bitterly resent the attempt to place the
blame for the current difficulties at my door. In the present
difficult circumstances, we are producing results which are a
good deal better than the Company is entitled to expect.

However, I am very anxious indeed to satisfy you — and,
above all, to produce thoroughly efficient results. Would you
therefore be kind enough to arrange for me to have the
necessary additional staff/to be supplied with the following
equipment, as previously requested . . . *(or as the case may be).*

I shall be pleased to discuss these matters with you at your
convenience.

NOTES:
*1   By all means offer to discuss the matter orally — but first get your
allegations into writing. Apart from impressing (if necessary) a Tribunal,
this approach often has a thoroughly salutory effect on the Board.*

*2   Remember to keep a copy — at home? A handwritten memo or note
should be photocopied.*

192   Complaint unfair — shortage of staff acknowledged

I was very upset to receive your memorandum dated . . . ,
in which you complain of deficiencies in the working of my
department/factory/office. As I have frequently discussed
with you, it is not possible for me to achieve better results
without additional staff. This I was promised. I understand
that current financial difficulties may have made it impossible
for you to provide the help that I need — but in the circumstances it is doubly unfair to blame me for defects which are

as inevitable as they are admitted and which are entirely due
to the burden of work shouldered by my present staff.

193   To managing director — asking that the matter be raised at board meeting

As you know, I do my best to shield the Board from
ordinary matters of day-to-day administration. But the
criticisms that are now being made both of me and of my
department have gone beyond the stage at which I can deal
with them on my own. They are creating an atmosphere of
tension and are interfering with my attempts to reorganise
. . . .

In the circumstances, I would be pleased if you would
agree to my placing this matter on the Agenda of the next
Board Meeting. I look forward to hearing from you.

With my thanks in anticipation.

NOTE:

*The fact that you are fighting back — or even the suggestion that the
matter may be raised at a Board Meeting — often has a lively effect. The
MD is quite likely to call your persecutor in to see him. You may even
find that there is a genuine and successful attempt to solve the difficulty,
behind the scenes. Hence the following drafts:*

194   Agreement to meeting

Yes, I fully agree that it would be better to sort this matter
out behind the scenes. But I must put firmly on record my
disquiet at the unwarranted allegations which Mr . . . has seen
fit to make against me.

Anyway, I shall be pleased to meet you on . . . at . . . .

195   Agreement to see chairman

I am always sorry to burden the Chairman with personal
problems, but if you think that his intervention would help
in the present case, I shall be very pleased to see him. However, I trust that the correspondence will be placed before
him and that he will know that the allegations made against

me are firmly rejected.

Perhaps you might also indicate to him that there appears to be an unhappy combination of executives seeking to drive me into the wilderness. As I consider that they are not acting in the best interests of the Company, I have no intention of leaving my post under fire.

196   Confirming satisfactory discussions

You were right − talks were indeed called for. I hope that now that we have had our frank discussion, we can once again work together as a team. I am particularly pleased to confirm agreement on the following specific points:

1 . . .
2 . . .
3 . . .

Without wishing in any way to labour the point, or to prolong the previous misunderstanding, I would like formally to record the fact that Mr . . . withdrew unreservedly the allegations made against me in his letter/notes of . . . .

197   Apology accepted

I happily confirm that I was only too pleased to accept the apology which you were good enough to give me at our meeting. I now look forward to working together with you, in harmony, as we did before the recent contretemps.

With best wishes.

NOTE:

1   An apology (like a contract) may be made orally or in writing. The oral variety is far more common and avoids loss of face. But (again like contracts) the oral word is far easier to contradict than the written statement. As you are unlikely to get a written apology, you can yourself confirm the nature of your conversation.

2   The above letter is one of thanks and is one which removes the knife from between the commercial shoulder blades. The recipient is unlikely to object to it.

3   As in the case of so many of these personal letters, it is generally

*better to have them handwritten. But make a photocopy for your own
records.*

198   Meeting unsuccessful

It was indeed good of you to spare so much time to meet
the Managing Director and myself last . . . . I am only sorry
that this meeting failed to resolve the unhappy situation.

Having given the matter further reflection, I can still find
no justification whatsoever for the allegations which have
been made against me. The threats of dismissal were particularly unfair, as the defects in the accounts/administration/
my office are in no way of my making. They are, as we discussed, entirely caused by . . . .

In the circumstances, I shall continue to do my best to
serve both the Company and yourself with all my energy. I
only hope that, despite the attitude taken up by Mr . . . at
our meeting and previously, he will not make my work impossible.

Once again, my thanks to you for your courtesy and
patience.

NOTE:

*1   Presumably, this letter will be shown to the Managing Director. It is
hardly likely to improve the situation – and may even precipitate your
dismissal. But you may regard your departure as inevitable – in which
case it is vital to have your case on paper, before the documents are
placed before the Court.*

*2   This letter (as opposed to the last one) should be typed. It should be
made formally clear that you intend to do battle. This may drive away
the wolves. As Stalin once remarked to that remarkable Indian leader,
Krishna Menon: 'The Russian peasant may be illiterate, but he is also
wise. He does not argue or moralise with the wolves who approach
his village. He shoots them. Knowing this, they keep away.' You might
even try the following:*

199   Any dismissal would be unfair

It is quite clear that efforts are being made to oust me from
my position – and hence, of course, from my livelihood. The

allegations that are being made against me are unfair and untrue. They are being made in order to protect others.

During our conversation, you asked me whether I proposed to substantiate my allegations concerning improprieties of which I informed you. I am perfectly capable of doing so; the documentary evidence is available; but I have no wish either to exacerbate matters or to create any further ill feeling. However, I am sure that you will appreciate that I have every intention of fighting back, if I am forced to do so.

Finally, I would like to emphasise once again my untiring loyalty to the Company. My work will continue to be devoted to the Company's interests.

NOTE:

1   This sort of letter is dynamite. Use it sparingly and adapt it carefully to suit your purposes.

2   Note in particular that the swipe from the rear is generally more effective than the assault from the front. The above letter suggests that the writer does not wish to use the ammunition available to him . . . that he has no desire for ill-will . . . that he does not wish to be forced to substantiate allegations made orally. This is a mature and sensible approach – particularly when combined with the renewed assurance of loyalty to the Company's best interests.

3   If you ever do put allegations into writing, they will almost certainly be libellous. Even though the occasion will undoubtedly be privileged, you may well be accused of 'malice'. So you are generally better off not to make allegations against other executives or employees. Indeed, if you emphasise your wish to avoid recriminations, it goes a long way to rebut any suggestion of malice.

200   Refusal to resign

I was shocked to receive your letter, suggesting that I should resign. This I will not do. I have no reason to do so. I have served the company well in the past and will bend every effort to continue so to do in the future,

201   Are you intending to dismiss?

I have found the treatment you have accorded to me of

late quite inexplicable. If it is your intention to dismiss me from the company's service, then I will be pleased if you would so inform me. Otherwise I shall continue to service the company in future, as I have in the past.

Chapter 18

Boardroom warnings

Personnel managers must treat their superiors with tact and with care, for fear of losing their own jobs. Among their greatest miseries are remarks like these:

'Get rid of him! I don't care how – that's your business. You are the personnel manager and it's up to you to find a way of sacking the man. So please get on with it . . . . '

'Sorry – but there's no money for more staff. How you get better results is a matter for you – but there is no question of expanding our workforce at the moment . . . . '

'There's no money for greater safety precautions, I'm afraid. You get together with the safety officer and use your safety committee and between you find ways to avoid these risks . . . without loss of productivity, of course . . . . '

Worst of all, the following two statements, often used together in glorious inconsistency:

'I'll deal with this industrial relations problem myself . . . . ' and

'It's up to the personnel function to keep the trade unions sweet . . . . '

Personnel chiefs often call in outside experts to address their Boards and other executives, to convey unpalatable advice and information. Otherwise, letters are sometimes useful. Try using or adapting the following.

202   Refusal to dismiss unfairly

I fully appreciate the reasons why you wish to dismiss Mr Green. But as he has been with us for more than 12 months and is in all other respects qualified for protection against unfair dismissal, I must respectfully point out that if he is dismissed as you wish, he will not only have a good claim for his pay in lieu of notice but he may also apply to an Industrial Tribunal for unfair dismissal remedies. These would include claims for compensatory and basic award which could stretch up to about £10,000, but also the possibility of a claim for reinstatement or re-engagement. If an Order is made that the company take him back into its service and we unreasonably refuse to obey that Order, then he could get an 'additional award' of several thousand pounds.

In the circumstances, may I suggest that you write to Mr Green, setting out your complaints and warning him that any repetition will lead to his dismissal. I will gladly help you to draft that letter. But if you dismiss without warning of following the procedures required by law, trouble is almost inevitable.

May I further respectfully point out that if Mr Green is dealt with in the way you have in mind, this could also create uncertainty and anxiety among other senior members of staff – which would be unlikely to help build the sort of teamwork which is being established under your leadership.

The decision, of course, is entirely yours   but I do hope that you will take these matters carefully into consideration. I will most gladly discuss them with you at any time you wish.

203   Please keep away

Thank you for your memo regarding our problems with the . . . Union. I greatly appreciate the interest which you and your Board colleagues are taking in our efforts to achieve the best possible industrial relations.

In the present case, I would be very grateful if we could discuss tactics together – and then my colleagues in the industrial relations/personnel department and I can continue to negotiate with the union – leaving you to step in if our efforts fail. In this way, we can alternate tactics, as and when required and not fire off all our ammunition at once.

NOTE:
Traditionally, top management was uninterested in industrial relations or personnel matters. Today, directors often step in far too early. Plan tactics with them – but usually keep their intervention as a last resort.

204   Forced resignation equals constructive dismissal

I note that you have informed Mr White that either he
resigns on the terms you have offered or he will be dismissed.
I do appreciate why you have taken this step. But I wonder
if you realise that if he is sufficiently well advised as to
accept your offer, he may still regard himself as 'dismissed'.
His resignation was forced upon him and we would therefore
have 'repudiated' the contract of service. He could therefore
take the company's money and bring an unfair dismissal
claim as well. The only way to prevent this happening would
be to get the agreement recorded by an ACAS Conciliation
Officer.

In the circumstances, as 'constructive dismissals' are
difficult to recognise and aggravating to contend with, could
I please call on you so that we could discuss tactics?

205   Firm fairness

I fully appreciate that the decision as to whether or not
Mr Green is dismissed is one for you and for your Board.
I know, though, that you have always respected frankness
and I have regarded it as part of my job to express my
views on personal matters completely openly. So I must tell
you that your decision is very worrying.

Mr Green has been with us for . . . years. He has always
served the company with single-minded loyalty. His mistakes
have been motivated by over-enthusiasm. He is well liked by
the workforce – and I fear that if he is dismissed, this could
lead to industrial relations difficulties. In addition, Mr Green
is, of course, protected by law against unfair as well as against
wrongful dismissal.

In the circumstances, would you like me to call on you to
discuss this matter? Of course I am in your hands – the
decision is one ultimately for you. But I am deeply
concerned to ensure the best possible industrial relations in
our organisation, particularly in the present hard times. So
I would be grateful if we could at least discuss your proposals
before they become irrevocable decisions.

Chapter 19

References

You are not bound to provide references. If you do so and you know the basic rules, though, you have nothing to fear — even if the reference is unsatisfactory or incorrect.

Speak ill of the person referred to and you defame him. If the defamatory statement is made orally, it is slanderous; if it is in writing or some other permanent form, then it is a libel.

In practice, there are three reasons why you need have no worries about a defamation action arising out of a defamatory reference:

1 The person defamed is unlikely to obtain evidence of the defamation — after all, why should the recipient of the references pass on the evil tidings?

2 The person defamed would have to spend his own money on the litigation — there is no legal aid for defamation actions. And any lawyer would tell him not to bother, not merely because of the risks involved (which Oscar Wilde discovered) but because of the defences open to the giver.

3 There are two main defences to this sort of action:

   a Justification — that the statement was substantially true. You cannot complain if someone takes from you a good character which you have not earned. On the other hand, a justification plea which fails leads almost always to increased damages — after all, the unkind statement has been repeated to a wider audience.

   b Qualified privilege. Unlike the MP speaking in Parliament or the Judge, Counsel, witness or litigant in Court, the privilege of the reference giver is not 'absolute'. It is 'qualified' — by the rule that if it can be shown that the reference was given out of malice — from a desire to harm the person defamed, rather than a wish to assist the recipient — then the defence will be defeated.

Still, defamation actions arising out of uncomplimentary references are almost unheard of. You may give them with impunity. If you are afraid that you may be charged with malice, though — then defame by telephone. Slander is even harder to prove than libel.

The real danger lies in statements which are incorrect — particularly trade references. You 'owe a duty of care' to the recipient. He is entitled to rely upon your reference, even if he made no payment for it. Therefore you must not be negligent.

If, then, you give a good reference to a man who deserved a bad one – perhaps because you got the name wrong; or (more likely) if you mislead the recipient of the trade or professional reference by saying that he is worthy of credit when you knew or ought to have known of his sad financial state of lack of credit-worthiness – you could be in trouble.

Here, though, a 'disclaimer' provides a watertight defence. You should take a leaf out of the bank manager's book and never give (nor permit your subordinates to provide) a reference without a disclaimer – saying that the reference is given 'without legal responsibility'. This phrase frees you from liability for negligence, but not, of course, for defamation.

206   Trade reference – with disclaimer

We are pleased to confirm that we have been suppliers of Messrs Smith Ltd for . . . years. They have paid their accounts promptly and we have no reason to suppose that they would not be worthy of the credit which you are proposing to give them.

This reference is given without legal responsibility.

207   Company sound – but disclaimer

We thank you for your letter of . . . concerning Messrs Smith Ltd. We believe that company to be well managed and financially sound.

While we are pleased to oblige with trade references, all references are given on the basis that no legal responsibility can be accepted.

208   Trade reference – unsatisfactory – with disclaimer

We thank you for your request for a reference for Messrs Smith Ltd. We trade with that company on a cash basis only.

This reference is given without legal responsibility.

NOTE:
A disclaimer of responsibility will free you from liability in respect of negligent misstatements, but not (I repeat) from potential libel actions. The disclaimer is addressed to the recipient – the libel action would be brought by the person defamed.

209   Unsatisfactory reference for ex-employee

We confirm that Mr Black worked for this company from ... to .... He was dismissed for misconduct/as unsuitable/ because ....

While we are pleased to provide references for former employees, all references are given without legal responsibility.

210   Least said

I confirm that Mr Black was employed by my company from ... to ....

NOTE:
Silence speaks. If you do not wish to say too much, then say little. And if you receive a reference of this kind and want further and better particulars, telephone the sender.

211   Request for written references

John Brown

The above named has applied to us for the position of .... We understand that he was employed by you, and in the circumstances, would be extremely grateful if you would kindly give us any information which may affect our decision as to his employment. In order to simplify matters, we are appending hereto a brief questionnaire. If you would be good enough to complete the same we would be most appreciative. Naturally, we shall be very pleased to return the courtesy, if at any further date we can be of assistance to you.

With our thanks in anticipation of an early reply,

Sample questionnaire
Name of Applicant: John Brown
Position applied for: . . .
1   What was the date of the commencement of the applicant's employment by you?
2   In what position was he originally employed?
3   Kindly detail any promotions or demotions
4   Upon what date did the applicant leave your service?
5   Kindly indicate circumstances in which employment terminated.
6   Did you find the applicant:
    a   In every respect, honest and reliable?
    b   Satisfactory in his relationships with members of the Board?
    c   Satisfactory with his relationships with subordinates?
    d   Well informed concerning:
        (i)   . . .
        (ii)   . . .
        (iii)   . . .
7   Would you consider him suitable for the position applied for, as indicated above?
8   Have you any further comments which would be of help to us, in deciding whether or not the applicant's request for the above employment should be accepted?

NOTE:
1   Under Paragraph 6(d), you should insert any particular qualities required for the particular post.

2   You may find from experience that there are certain employers who like to fill in a questionnaire of this sort – and others who do not. If in doubt, a telephone call to the employer or personnel manager concerned may be worthwhile.

3   It is usually wise and thoughtful to enclose a stamped, self-addressed envelope. And you may wish to send a copy of the questionnaire, for retention by the referee.

212   Asking for telephone reference for company secretary

We understand that Mr David Evans was employed by you

until recently as your Assistant Company Secretary. He has now applied to the above company for a similar position, and we would be extremely grateful if you could give us some guidance as to his reliability, honesty, efficiency, and as to his relationship with other employees, both those whom he supervises and those under whose supervision he comes.

If I do not hear from you within two or three days, then I shall telephone. It may be that it would prove more convenient to discuss this matter orally — and if so, then please do not trouble to reply to this letter, I shall be in touch with you shortly.

With my thanks in anticipation of your kind co-operation.

NOTE:
When asking for a reference, you should give the ex-employer the benefit of the doubt — and presuppose that they will know their law and be careful in the information they give to you. So oral references are often worth obtaining. But in case you wish to receive a written reply, the previous draft incorporates most of the questions which you may want to ask. Naturally, you will strike out those that do not apply and adapt the remainder, as necessary.

213   Please telephone

Thank you for your letter concerning John Jones. If you would care to give me a ring, either at the office or at my home (telephone . . . . .) I shall be pleased to discuss this man with you.

Trusting that you are keeping well and with kind regards.

NOTE:
Although a statement is just as defamatory if made orally as in writing — and where a person is defamed concerning his occupation, no actual financial loss need be proved by him, if he is to recover damages — the proof of slander is infinitely more difficult than that of libel (which, by definition, is in a permanent form). Consequently, it is often preferable to give a reference orally — and, conversely, often easier to obtain an accurate and helpful reference if you speak to the ex-employer in question, rather than writing to him. Alternatively, you could write the previous letter.

214   Reference for former company secretary

Thank you for your letter concerning Mr Talbot. He was employed by the company from . . . to . . . . I regret to inform you that he left after a dispute with the Board.

This reference is given in strict confidence and without legal responsibility on the part of the writer or of the company.

"THIS LETTER SETS OUT OUR FIRM'S POLICY ON
DISCRIMINATION IN BLACK AND WHITE ... "

Part Three

DISCRIMINATION, WOMEN'S AND MOTHERS' RIGHTS — AND RACE DISCRIMINATION

Chapter 20

Equal pay and discrimination

The Sex Discrimination Act amended the Equal Pay Act. A term is now implied into the contract of every woman employee that she will be treated on an equal basis to men − in particular, that she will receive equal pay for equal work or for work rated on an equivalent basis.

* * *

A person discriminates against a woman . . . if

'*(a)* on the ground of her sex he treats her less favourably than he treats or would treat a man or,

(b) he applies to her requirements or conditions which he applies or would apply equally to a man but −

(i) which is such that the proportion of women who can comply with it is considerably smaller than the proportion of men who can comply with it and

(ii) which he cannot show to be justifiable irrespective of the sex of the person to whom it is applied, and

(iii) which is to her detriment because she cannot comply with it'.

Equally, a man's 'marital status' must not affect his treatment. Nor must there be discrimination against a man or against married people in the field of employment. Nor must you victimise a person who seeks to exercise his rights under the Sex Discrimination Act.

After this opening salvo, the Act turns to discrimination in the employment field. Bearing in mind the increased temptation to discriminate against women in appointment to executive or managerial posts (see Chapter 21) and the rules on the reinstatement of mothers after child-birth, Section 6 of the Sex Discrimination Act, is important:

'It is unlawful for a person, in relation to employment by him at an establishment in Great Britain, to discriminate against a woman −

(a) in the arrangements he makes for the purpose of determining who should be offered that employment, or

(b) in the terms on which he offers her that employment, or

(c) by refusing or deliberately omitting to offer her that employment.'

Again, he must not discriminate in connection with promotion, transfer, training or any other benefits, facilities or services − or 'by dismissing her, or subjecting her to any other detriment'.

Exceptions: Women employed 'for the purposes of a private household' or where neither the employer nor any associated employer has a payroll not exceeding five people (leaving his home employees out of account). And you may also discriminate in connection with terms of employment relating to 'death or retirement' — actuarily, women live longer and are not necessarily entitled to the same pension opportunities.

With deadpan (or unconscious) humour, the Act makes one remarkable exception. You are entitled to discriminate in connection with the employment 'where sex is a genuine occupational qualification for the job' (*sic*). Your secretary, for instance?

There are other exceptions in Section 7. For instance:

1   Where the 'essential nature of the job calls for a man for reasons of physiology (excluding physical strength or stamina) . . . or for reasons of authenticity . . .'. Curiously, being a man is not a genuine occupational qualification for the job for reasons of physical strength. You must treat each 'person' who applies on his or her merits. Stakhanovite ladies may enter traditionally male areas — as they have done in other (often less advanced) countries.

2   You may employ a man where it is necessary so to do 'to preserve decency or privacy'.

3   Where 'the nature or location of the establishment makes it impracticable for the holder of the job to live elsewhere than in premises provided by the employer', then you may employ men if you wish.

4   Hospitals, prisons and other 'establishments for persons requiring special care and supervision' and where the inmates are male are normally excluded.

5   Providers of welfare, educational 'or other similar personal services' which are 'most effectively provided' by men are excepted.

6   So are jobs held by men because of legal restrictions.

7   Where a job is one of two held by a married couple.

8   Finally: where the job is 'likely to involve the performance of duties outside the United Kingdom in a country whose laws or customs are such that the duties could not — or could not effectively — be performed by a woman'. Your sales representative in Saudi Arabia, for instance.

Part 2 of the Sex Discrimination Act covers discrimination in the employment field.

Now follow sex discrimination precedent letters.

*   *   *

215   Denial that pay 'unequal'

My colleagues and I have given careful consideration to your allegation that you and other women employees in our office/accounts department are not being paid on the same basis as men.

We do not employ men in those departments, doing the categories of work which are the subject of your complaint. However, this is the result of chance, not design; when recruiting for posts in these departments, we select people irrespective of whether they are men or women (or, for that matter, without regard to their marital status); and we are satisfied that the rate which we are paying you and your colleagues is the same as that which we would pay men, if and when male applicants for these jobs are successful in obtaining them in the future. In other words we are paying the rate for the job, irrespective of sex and in the circumstances, while we have given full and careful consideration to your claim, we find no merit in it.

216   Work rated on equivalent basis

The work that you are doing is rated on an equivalent basis to similar work performed by men in our . . . department. There is therefore no justification whatever for your allegation that you are being paid at a lower rate because you are a woman. For many years, this company has prided itself on treating people fairly and on an equal basis, totally irrespective of their sex. We were therefore all the more disturbed at receiving your complaint; we have examined it with care; and we were pleased to find that it is unjustified.

217 Other companies' rates irrelevant

It is, we understand, correct that certain women are paid more by other companies in the district – but the circumstances are not the same. Other terms of work are less satisfactory/they do not have the same canteen facilities and other fringe benefits/their working conditions are far less pleasant/ they have not been hit by the current recession in the trade in the same way as ourselves/they are in a different sector of the industry/their pay structure is very different to ours (or as the case may be).

We pay women in our business the rate for the job – which is not assessed on the basis of their sex, but with regard to other terms of service and to what the company can afford.

218 Equal Opportunities Commission – consultant

We have taken your allegation of unequal treatment very seriously, although we regard it as unwarranted. We have therefore sought the advice of the Equal Opportunities Commission and as soon as we have any news for you, we will immediately be in touch again.

With best wishes.

219 Application to Equal Opportunities Commission for advice

Further to our telephone conversation, I am enclosing herewith correspondence which passed between the union and our company, concerning alleged failure to grant equal pay/ failure on the part of this company to comply to its obligations under the Equal Pay Act/Sex Discrimination Act.

After the most anxious consideration, we consider that we have complied with our obligations, in the spirit as well as to the letter. However, we shall be pleased if a representative of your commission would call upon us so as to discuss the matter and so as to attempt to resolve the current dispute in an amicable and fair fashion.

220 The Advisory, Conciliation and Arbitration Service – discrimination in appointment?

I was pleased to speak to you by telephone and am sending you herewith as promised, the correspondence in the matter of the alleged discriminatory practices by this company in connection with the non-employment of men/women in our . . . section/operation/plant/shop (*or as the case may be*).

As I told you, there is no discrimination in the above regard. (*Alternatively:* the company does employ only men/ women in the above job because . . .). In any event, we will be grateful if you or one of your colleagues will call upon us as soon as possible, in order that we may receive your advice in what may otherwise turn into a complicated dispute.

NOTE:
1   Whether to call in ACAS or the Equal Opportunities Commission is a matter of judgement – and often of personal contact.

2   It is almost always preferable to speak to ACAS or the Commission by telephone in order to set up the help you want. Equally it will save time and problems if those who are to assist you are given the necessary documents in advance.

3   For further details and precedents concerning ACAS, see Chapter 25.

221 Sex – essential qualification for job

We have carefully considered the representations made to the company by your union, alleging that we ought to open up the . . . job function to women. Having regard, however to the essential nature of the work/to the need to employ men in that job for reasons of authenticity/to . . ., we consider that the carrying out of the work by men is an essential qualification for the job. We have also written to your union to explain our view.

NOTE:
The Courts decide whether in a particular case sex is 'an essential qualification for the job', to use the Act's remarkable phrase. Meanwhile, the only certainty is that to be a female is to have an essential qualification for Bunny Girls.

Chapter 21

Women and married executives—complaints

Women executives and managers who are already in their jobs may be grateful for the protection legislation. They are entitled to equal pay; non-discrimination; maternity pay; and to reinstatement in their jobs after childbirth – in exactly the same way as any other woman employee. They are, though, far more vulnerable than shop floor employees, whose reinstatement rights will cause far less trouble to management, if only because (if you will pardon the expression) women 'turn over' so much faster than men. At higher levels, there is lower turn-over and those who decide on employment policies may discover that the problems of dismissing replacements are such that they prefer, where possible, to employ men – even where they cannot successfully maintain that 'sex is an essential qualification for the job'.

Anyway, there is no point in women executives having rights unless they know how, where and when to exercise them.

222   Equal Opportunities Commission – help required

I would be obliged for your advice, followed, if necessary, by your active help – in connection with my complaint against my employing company/firm, details of which are attached hereto. Please would you write to me at my home address. I would be pleased to call upon your appropriate officer, if this would be the best way to deal with the matter. For obvious reasons, I do not want my employers to know of this approach, at the present stage.

NOTE:
1   The address of the Equal Opportunities Commission is: Overseas House, Quay Street, Manchester M3 3HN (Tel: 061-833 9244).

2   The Commission will, of course, deal with any enquiries on a confidential basis. You can then discuss with the appropriate official the action which the Commission may be prepared to take in your case – which may be advisory; conciliatory; or even the appropriate assistance

with necessary litigation required to enforce your rights, by going to an
industrial tribunal.

223   Complaint – equal pay

I am sorry to have to trouble you about this matter, as it
only affects myself/a few of your staff/one category of em-
ployees/it really should have been sorted out without the
need to come to you. However, as I am anxious to have the
dispute dealt with speedily and without causing further ill
will, I know that you will not mind my approaching you/
putting details of our conversation into writing.

In my view, I/women employed as . . . in the office/
accounts department (*or as the case may be*) are not receiving
equal pay for the work that they are doing. They are being
paid less than men doing equivalent work/work graded on an
equivalent basis.

I trust that this matter can be rectified at an early date
and send you my thanks in anticipation.

224   Own pay unequal – protest

After all these years of loyal service to the company, I am
sure that you know that I make no unnecessary complaints
or protests – and that I am totally devoted to the success of
the business. It is therefore with regret that I find myself
impelled to write to you concerning my own pay/terms of
service. In particular, it seems clear that I (and, incidentally
, . . .)/other women employed in a similar capacity (*or as the
case may be*) find myself being treated less favourably in connection with terms of service/payment/promotion/transfer/
opportunities for advancement/training, than my men colleagues, working in a like capacity.

I have tried to raise this matter privately and informally
but without success. I would therefore be grateful if you
would be kind enough to arrange for this complaint to be
fully investigated – and I shall, of course, be only too pleased
to discuss it with you.

NOTE:
In practice, women executives and managers may be loath to risk their

positions in this way. But if a letter of this sort is followed (within at least any reasonable time) by dismissal, then the reason for that dismissal will be clear enough to enable the woman to obtain her remedy; and if she finds herself forced out of her job − pushed into resigning − then the existence of this letter will be great help to her, if she seeks to show that she was constructively dismissed.

An alternative to this approach would be a quiet word with the Equal Opportunities Commission or with ACAS.

225   Married man − discrimination alleged

I am writing directly to you in the hope that you will be kind enough to intervene, to avoid any further ill will or the perpetuation of a problem which could lead to anxiety not merely for me but also for the company. This letter is a confidential one; if you would like me to discuss it with you, then I shall be pleased to do so; but I hope that in any event you will understand that my complaint is one which I only make to you or at all after prolonged and anxious consideration.

I was appointed as . . . on . . . . I have worked very hard for the company and the results of my efforts/department show, I think, the products of this work − and, of course, of the team-work which I have been able to engender from my colleagues and subordinates. If proof be required, then I enclose herewith letters of thanks/congratulation from . . . , . . . and . . . .

It was therefore with great surprise that I found that another person/other persons had been promoted over my head. Having regard to remarks made to me − and to the absence of any other reason − I can only think that I was held back because of my marital status/I am a bachelor. Not only does this situation cause ill will, but it is, of course, an apparent breach of the Sex Discrimination Act.

As I said, I would be very grateful if you could look into this complaint − and I send you my warm thanks in anticipation.

NOTE:
This letter, of course, could easily be adapted to the needs of a woman who considers that she has been held back on the ground of her sex. But the Act gives no protection to single people ('gay' or otherwise).

Chapter 22

Maternity procedures*

The new maternity rules introduced by *The Employment Act, 1980,* have now been in force long enough to assess their effect in practice. Clearly, every employer who has not altered his maternity procedures should now do so. When he discovers that an employee is pregnant, then a full interview should take place; the woman should be asked whether or not she intends to return and urged to give an honest answer – but well advised employees will continue to state an intention to return, even if they have none. Above all, new forms are required, for the employee as well as for the employer.

The employer is not bound to provide notice of intention for the mother to fill in – but it is kindly and sensible to do so. And certainly the employer must have available his 'seven-week notice', if he wishes to confirm an employee's intention to return.

226   Employee's notice of intended absence through pregnancy or confinement

I am pleased to inform you that I expect to be absent through pregnancy or confinement from . . . . I intend to return to my job after my pregnancy.

NOTE:

1   This notice must be given at least 21 days before leaving – in writing, if so requested by the employer – even to qualify for maternity pay. It must be given in writing, to qualify for maternity leave, whether the employer so requests or not.

2   The employee should keep a copy of the notice, so as to be able to prove that she given it.

3   Notice must be given 'where reasonably practicable' – which it always is, if the employee knows that she has rights to maternity pay and/or leave.

*For small firms, see Appendix 2.

4   *Wise women always give notice of intention to return, even if they have none. If they then do not return, they lose nothing. But if they do not give notice and find that they need their job back – perhaps because the baby is stillborn – they have lost their jobs in return for nothing.*

227   Employer's seven-week notice – does mother still intend to return?

We hope that you are in good health and would be glad to have your confirmation as to whether or not you intend to return after your pregnancy or confinement.

Please complete the enclosed form and return it to us without delay. Unless you return this form to us within two weeks, confirming that you still intend to return to your job , we are required to warn you that you will lose your statutory right to your job.

May we remind you that you are now required by law to let us know of your intended return date not less than 21 days in advance. If you know that date when you return the form to us, then it would help both you and us if you would state it. Otherwise, please do not forget to give us that 21 days' notice in due course.

May we also remind you that your right to return expires at the end of the period of 29 weeks, beginning with the week in which the date of your confinement falls – although if you can produce a doctor's certificate at the end of that period to show that you are not well enough to return on that date, it may be postponed for up to a further four weeks.

If you have any queries about your rights, please do not hestitate to let me know. I repeat – do please complete and return the enclosed form as soon as possible.

With best wishes,

228   Mother's notice of continued intention

I, Mrs/Ms . . . of . . . now inform you that I:

(a)   Do still intend to return to my job. My intended date of return is   /I cannot yet tell you the date of my

intended return but I know that I must inform you in writing at least 21 days in advance. *Or*

(b)   I no longer intend to return to my job.

Date: . . .   *Signed:* . . .

(A stamped addressed envelope is enclosed herewith for your use.)

NOTE:
1   Remember that if you send this notice less than 49 days after the beginning of the expected week of confinement (or the date of confinement) notified to you by your employee, it has no validity. So when you receive your employee's notification, enter the relevant dates carefully into your diary – including especially the date when your seven-week notice will be sent.

2   No form is prescribed by law – and you are not required to send a 's.a.e.' Still less are you obliged to inform your employee of her obligation under the 1980 Act to notify you at least 21 days in advance of her date of expected return. But it is good and kindly management to take all these steps. Anyway, you must warn your employee that she will lose her rights unless she gives written confirmation of her intention to return within 14 days of receiving your request. She may do so at a later date if it is 'not reasonably practicable' for her to comply with the time limit – but if you have properly phrased and despatched your notice, then it certainly should be 'reasonably practicable' for her to comply.

3   As always when you may have to prove receipt of a document, post it by recorded delivery.

229   Not reasonably practicable to take back

We thank you for your letter dated . . . saying that you intend to return to your job on the . . . . Unfortunately, it is not reasonably practicable for us to permit you to return to work because your replacement has been doing that job now for some . . . months and it would not be fair to move her *(or as the case may be).* However: we are pleased to offer you employment under a contract of employment for work which is both suitable to you and appropriate for you to do in the circumstances and on conditions which are not substantially less favourable to you than if you returned to your previous job. In particular, we are pleased to offer you the job of:

We look forward to hearing from you that you are prepared to accept this alternative employment – and to seeing you at . . . on your day of return.

Meanwhile, we send you our best wishes,

NOTE:

1 This new right to offer reasonably suitable alternative employment was given by the 1980 Act – but it does not *apply where it is not reasonably practicable to give the employee back her job because of redundancy. If, then, the job has gone, the employee will be redundant as at the date of her intended return – and entitled to her normal redundancy rights and remedies, as at that date.*

2 We do not yet know what circumstances would in the view of court make it 'not reasonably practicable' to allow the woman to return to her job. I presume that the normal reason will be: That the replacement is well settled into the job. But watch out for judicial interpretation.

3 The reasonably suitable alternative employment may be offered by an associated employer, as well as by the original one – but that means: by any employer in the same group or . . . . And 'associated employer' means (as usual) any employer in the same group or under the same control.

4 The effect of excluding employees who cannot be returned to their job because of a redundancy situation is not altogether clear. It seems that employers may now look for reasonably suitable alternative employment to returning mothers on the same terms as they were always entitled to do so in the case of redundant employees. But where a redundancy situation exists, then the mother is treated as redundant on the day of her intended return – and precisely the same rules apply as they would to an employee redundant in any other circumstances.

230   Interview requested

I understand that you are expecting a baby and I send you my warm congratulations. Please would you arrange to see

me at your early convenience, so that I can inform you fully
of your maternity rights, and so that we can know of your
future plans.

With best wishes,

231   Job open – but not part-time

Thank you for your letter informing me of your intention
to return to work on . . . . Your job is available – but I regret
that I cannot offer you the same work on a part-time basis.
Please let me know whether or not you intend to work full
time, as before.

Hoping that you and the baby are well and with kind
regards,

NOTE:
*You are only bound to take the mother back to 'her job' – which
means the same job on the same terms. She comes back on the basis
that in theory she has never been away, So she is not entitled to return
to a different job – and working part-time is not the same, even if the
work is identical.*

232   Rights lost

You telephoned my office this morning stating an
intention to return to your job, having had your baby. Our
records indicate that more than 29 weeks have passed since
your confinement; and in any event, you have not given at
least 21 days' notice of your intention to return. In the
circumstances, we regret that we are not able to make your
previous job available to you.

233   Intention not stated

I am sorry, but we do not have a vacancy at present. Nor
can we reinstate you in your old job because we have engaged
a replacement. I must remind you that you did not follow
the procedures required by law in order to retain your job,
so we can only offer to keep your name on our list for

possible future vacancies.

Wishing you well in the future and with our renewed regrets that we are unable to assist you at present.

234   Position redundant

Thank you for your letter stating that you wish to return to your job on . . . . Unfortunately, since you left to have your baby, we have had to close the department in which you formerly worked. We have searched for an alternative position which would suit you, but regret to tell you that there is none.

In the circumstances, as you have been employed continuously by the company for more than two years, you will be entitled to a redundancy payment on the basis that you became redundant on the day of your intended return. So please do come back on that day and contact our accounts departments, so that appropriate arrangements may be made for you.

Naturally, we are all very sad at this departmental closure, but the current recession/shortage of orders for our goods/ *(or as the case may be)* made this inevitable.

With best wishes,

235   Not qualified – insufficient service

Thank you for your letter. You are not entitled to maternity benefits – either maternity pay or reinstatement in your job – because by the beginning of the eleventh week before the expected date of your confinement, you will not have been with the company for the statutory minimum qualifying period of two years.

236   Not qualified – left too early

To qualify for reinstatement in her job, a mother must remain at her job until 11 weeks or less before the expected date of her confinement. The only exception is where she leaves earlier than that date because of her condition and is then dismissed.

You left voluntarily more than two months before that date. In the circumstances, you are not protected by law and I regret that we have no job to offer to you. I am sorry.

237   Not reasonably practicable to give notices

Thank you for your letter. It was not reasonably practicable for me to give the appropriate notices because I did not know of my rights under the Act. In any event, I was in hospital and in no fit state to look after my affairs. And I did not realise at the time the reason for my indisposition was pregnancy.

Chapter 23

Race relations

The Race Relations Act, 1976, made provisions in respect of racial
discrimination which almost match those set out in Chapter 20
designed to forbid sex discrimination. It is unlawful, for instance, to
discriminate in connection with appointment, dismissal, promotion
or training on racial grounds. You must not discriminate against
a person on the ground of his 'colour, race, nationality or ethnic or
national origin'. There is no reference to religion, although it appears
that discrimination against Jewish employees is probably covered.

As in the case of sex discrimination, the unlawful behaviour may be
'direct' – like advertising: 'English applicants only' or 'No Blacks'.
But indirect discrimination is also banned – like advertising in an
area with a substantial, recent, Asian immigrant population: 'All
applicants must have lived in this area for at least ten years'.

Once again, discrimination is permitted where 'race is an essential
qualification for the job' – like the Chinese waiter in the Chinese
restaurant (but not the Chinese cook – English people may be expert
at Chinese cooking). Discrimination by employment agencies, vocational
training bodies and the like are covered, as is discrimination against
contract workers.

Finally: the Commission for Racial Equality has similar duties in
the area of racial discrimination to those exercised by the Equal
Opportunities Commission in the field of sex discrimination. Its address:
Commission for Racial Equality, Elliot House, Allington Street,
London SW1 (Tel: 01-828 7022).

238   Race relations – denial of discrimination

We were extremely upset to receive a letter from your
Commission alleging discrimination by this company, which
has always prided itself on the entire lack of prejudice which
governs its policies.

It is denied that Mr Smith was 'discriminated against' on
the grounds of his 'colour, race or ethnic or national origin'.
We declined to employ him because we did not regard him
as suitably qualified for the work concerned.

We are passing your letter to our solicitors, Messrs . . . and
. . . . If there is any further correspondence in this matter,
kindly address it to them, for the attention of their Mr . . . .

239 Facilities not refused because of colour

Confidential

It is denied that we refused to supply the goods/facilities/
services concerned to Mr Jones by reason of his colour. At
the material time, he was drunk/atrociously rude to our
manager/abusive to me personally/asking for goods/facilities/
services to be provided to him outside hours/when the business
was shut/ which we did not have available.

We are passing your letter to our solicitors, Messrs . . . and
. . . . If there is any further correspondence in this matter,
kindly address it to them, for the attention of their Mr . . . .

240 Invitation to Commission to send in officer

There was no discrimination on our part. But there is
clearly a misunderstanding, which we would be happy to
clear up. Perhaps one of your officers would call and see our
managing director?

241 Complaint of discrimination

We are making this formal complaint to the Commission
for Racial Equality Board in accordance with the Race Relations Acts, because we are convinced that our employee,
James Jones, has been discriminated against on the ground of
his colour. This most excellent man sought housing accommodation from Messrs . . ., on the new estate at Redville. Having
been told by telephone that several houses were available,
immediately he appeared at the office of the estate agents, he
was assured that all accommodation had been sold. This was
patently untrue, as the various 'For Sale' boards bore witness.

Would you kindly look into the matter?

Mr Jones is a most excellent, reliable, diligent and kindly
person and we have every confidence that his complaint is

justified. We have asked him to countersign this letter by way of written authority from him to make the complaint concerned.

242 Written authority for complaint to Commission

I, James Jones, of . . . in . . . , hereby authorise my employers, Smith Ltd, of . . . in . . . , to make complaint on my behalf in connection with unlawful discrimination against me by . . . Ltd, estate agents, of . . . in . . . .

(Signed) . . . .

243 TUC Equal Opportunities Clause

'The parties to this agreement are committed to the development of positive policies to promote equal opportunity in employment regardless of workers' sex, marital status, creed, colour, race or ethnic origins. This principle will apply in respect of all conditions of work including pay, hours of work, holiday entitlement, overtime and shiftwork, work allocation, guaranteed earnings, sick pay, pensions, recruitment, training, promotion and redundancy (nothing in this clause is designed to undermine the protections for women workers in the Factories Act).

The management undertake to draw opportunities for training and promotion to the attention of all eligible employees, and to inform all employees of this agreement on equal opportunity.

The parties agree that they will review from time to time, through their joint machinery, the operation of this equal opportunity policy.

If any employee considers that he or she is suffering from unequal treatment on the grounds of sex, marital status, creed, colour, race ot ethnic origins, he or she may make a complaint which will be dealt with through the agreed procedures for dealing with grievances.'

" I FIND THE BOOK INVALUABLE IN DEALING WITH
TRADE UNIONISTS___ ! "

Part Four

TRADE UNIONS, COLLECTIVE BARGAINING AND INDUSTRIAL DISPUTES

Chapter 24

Introduction

Our structure of law for collective and trade union rights and responsibilities has essentially arisen out of and following *The Industrial
Relations Act, 1971.* In 1974, the Trade Union and Labour Relations
Act repealed the provisions of the 1971 Act but reenacted the unfair
dismissal rules in strength and form. *The Employment Protection Act,
1975,* gave additional rights to trade unions and employees, including:
disclosure of information for the purposes of collective bargaining;
consultation about proposed redundancies; time off work for trade
union and public duties; maternity pay and leave; guarantee pay; and
protection when employers become insolvent.

The Employment Act, 1980, sought to reverse the process by
reducing the rights of individual employees, e.g. through changes in
the burden of proof in unfair dismissal cases, and (more especially) by
reducing the strength and power of trade unions, through the new
rules and restrictions on closed shops ('union membership agreements')
and on picketing and secondary action.

This part of the book contains crucial draft letters in the area of
trade union and collective bargaining, rights and disputes — together
with summaries of essential current law.

Chapter 25

The Advisory, Conciliation and Arbitration Service

The Advisory, Conciliation and Arbitration Service has been established on a statutory basis since 1975. Every employer and manager who is liable to run into employment difficulty on any scale — whether large or small — should know of the powers and responsibilities of the Service, which can do so much to achieve that splendid object — the avoidance of disputes and litigation.

ACAS was born out of the Commission on Industrial Relations and fathered by the Department of Employment. But it has long been totally independent. One of its top officials recently stated that never at any time has the Service been leaned on by any Government Minister, at any level. It is respected by all sides of industry for its independence. This is the touchstone of its ability to assist. 'The Service shall, if it thinks fit, on request or otherwise, provide without charge, to employers, employers' associations, workers and trade unions such advice as it thinks appropriate on any matter concerned with industrial relations or with employment policies'.

The Service is not bound to advise; it may do so of its own volition or on the request of any party; it is not permitted to make any charge; and its field of operation is as wide as can be conceived. The individual matters include:

1   The organisation of workers or employers for the purpose of collective bargaining.
2   Recognition of trade unions by employers.
3   Machinery for the negotiation of terms and conditions of employment, and for joint consultation.
4   Procedures for avoiding and settling workers disputes and grievances.
5   Questions relating to communication between employers and workers.
6   Facilities for officials and trade unions.
7   Procedures relating to the termination of employment.
8   Disciplinary matters.
9   Manpower planning, labour turnover and absenteeism.

10 Promotional and vocational training, recruitment and retention of workers.

11 Payment systems, including equal pay and job evaluation.

If you require advice on any of these matters – from the dismissal of one employee to a massive worry about the recognition of a trade union – do not hesitate to contact ACAS.

The Conciliation officers who provide the advice are a highly trained body, ranging of course in experience from new appointments to industrial conciliators of long standing. Conversations with personnel chiefs and trade union officials throughout the country, suggest that very few people regret seeking the advice of ACAS. It has two special advantages: it is free and you do not have to follow it.

If the advice does not produce a settlement, ACAS may then conciliate.

'Where a trade dispute exists or is apprehended, the Service may, at the request of one or more parties to the dispute or otherwise, offer the parties to the dispute its assistance with a view to bring about a settlement.'

Naturally, conciliation depends upon consent. 'We spend much of our lives dragging channels of communication between people who do not know how to talk to each other', a conciliator told me. ACAS provide industrial catalysts of a high order. Their success rate with incipient disputes is in the region of 50 per cent – a massive saving in industrial chaos and a huge avoidance of loss to industry, employers, employees and the country alike.

Third, the Service may arbitrate. Like any other arbitration, it can exist only because the parties agree in advance to accept the decision of an independent arbitrator, who acts as a judge in their cause. His decision is enforceable in the same way as that of a judge.

Commercial arbitrations have considerable disadvantages. They are often as expensive as litigation – in building disputes, for instance, the evidence may be paraded with the same mass of documentation by the identical skilled and highly paid lawyers as if the matter were before an official referee. But arbitration is often an acceptable and thrifty way of dealing with industrial disputes and of avoiding industrial action.

'Where a trade dispute exists or is apprehended, the Service may request that one or more parties and with the consent of all the parties to the dispute, refer all or any of the matter to which the dispute relates for settlement', by arbitration. Unlike advice or conciliation which may be provided at the request of one party, arbitration can only proceed 'with the consent of all the parties to the dispute'.

ACAS may appoint one or more persons to deal with the arbitration, but it is not entitled to appoint one of its own conciliators. Alternatively, it may refer the dispute to the Central Arbitration Committee (which replaced the Industrial Arbitration Board).

Advice; conciliation; arbitration – and the catalyst Service also creates new Codes of Conduct. Like the Highway Code on the road, ACAS codes regulate good industrial relations practices. So far we have the Disciplinary Code, the Code on Time Off Work and the Disclosure Code, which guide employers as to the information which they must disclose to independent, recognised trade unions during the course of collective bargaining.

Whether dealing with actual or possible disputes over the recognition of trade unions. when working out new payment systems or manpower planning policies – whatever the problem, if it concerns good industrial relations, ACAS can help you.

Naturally, ACAS officers vary in their skills, ability and experience. By all means inform your local ACAS office of your requirements. And if you are not totally satisfied with the help that you are getting, tactfully ask for someone else. Letters follow.

244   Collective bargaining – advice sought

We wish to extend collective bargaining arrangements within our plant/company. Please would you arrange for one of your experienced officers to call upon me as soon as possible in order to advise as to how this object may be accomplished.

245   Industrial dispute – experienced officer needed

I regret to inform you that we have now reached a deadlock in a dispute which is likely to lead to industrial action. As this could cause a total halt in our production and the laying off of large numbers of people, please would you arrange for a most experienced officer to assist with advice and, if necessary, with conciliation, at the earliest possible opportunity. This letter is being delivered by hand.

NOTE:
If you need the help of a particularly experienced person, do not hesitate to say so. You may be fortunate already to have a contact with an individual Conciliation Officer, thus:

246   Industrial dispute – particular officer needed

Urgent

I regret that the issue that I discussed with you concerning ... has not been resolved and it is now likely that the industrial action will be made official. Your services are most urgently required and I would be most grateful if you would contact me personally forthwith. I shall send this letter by hand and await word in my office.

With many thanks for your assistance in the past and in anticipation of the earliest possible response to this request.

247   Negotiating machinery – overhaul needed

We are not satisfied with our negotiating machinery – and nor are the various trade unions concerned. However, we are having difficulty in reaching agreement and the assistance of your Service would be much appreciated by all concerned. Please would you contact me as soon as possible.

248   Trade union facilities

We cannot reach agreement with the ... Union concerning the various facilities sought by them for extending their membership/calling meetings in working hours (*or as the case may be*). We would appreciate your guidance and help in sorting out this problem.

249   Unfair dismissal – advice required

We are suffering greatly from absenteeism and our disciplinary procedures will have to be invoked. We know that allegations are bound to be made of unfair practices – however carefully and fairly we proceed. Perhaps you could spare a few minutes at your earliest convenience to help us to establish some sort of procedure that will be both manifestly fair and accepted as such by the trade union?

250   Redundancy planning – advice

I confirm our telephone conversation when I told you that we are going to have to create redundancies. Please would you call by as soon as possible to help us to establish a procedure which will both operate fairly and enable the company to make the best of a bad situation.

With many thanks.

NOTE:
By all means telephone the Service or an individual officer with whom you have the appropriate relationship. Confirmation in writing, though, is often advisable.

251   Job evaluation – advice

We are proposing to instruct work study engineers to consider our pay structure and to do full job evaluation studies. Before giving them instructions, however, we would greatly appreciate your advice as to the best way to proceed.

With our thanks and best wishes.

252   Equal pay dispute

The . . . Union is alleging that its women members employed as . . . in our . . . are not receiving equal pay for like work to that done by men in other businesses. This we deny. However, we will greatly appreciate your advice and guidance as to how this matter may be resolved on an amicable and fair basis.

253   Enquiry invited

A most serious industrial relations situation is arising in

our business. This may be summarised as follows:

    1 . . .
    2 . . .
    3 . . .

We would greatly appreciate your advice as to how this matter should now be dealt with and we also officially request an enquiry into the question in issue in accordance with the powers given to the Service by Section 5 of The Employment Protection Act.

We look forward to an early reply and with my thanks in anticipation.

NOTE:

The Service has power 'if it thinks fit' to enquire into 'any question relating to industrial relations generally or to industrial relations in any particular industry or in any particular undertaking or part of an undertaking'. The findings may or may not be published – but will certainly have great weight. Before you ask for an enquiry, make sure that you are prepared to accept its outcome. Otherwise, remember the famous advice given by a factory inspector, asked whether it was wise to consult his Service. He quoted an ancient proverb: 'Love work; hate tyranny; live righteously; and do not let your name get too well known to the authorities'. This proverb is more applicable to the factory inspector and the tax man than to ACAS – but is nevertheless worthy of thought.

254   Codes of Practice – request for copies

We understand that the Code of Practice on . . . is/is likely shortly to become available. Would you kindly arrange for a copy to be sent to me, with an invoice if necessary.

Would you also please arrange for the appropriate person to inform me as to the current arrangements for me to be put onto the mailing list in respect of publications which are of concern to my company and which may from time to time be produced by your Service.

My thanks in anticipation.

255   Conciliation request – victimisation

Unfortunately, we have reached deadlock in connection

with the dismissal of the convenor of the . . . Union. For reasons which we have explained to you, we are not prepared to take him back; and the union is determined not to permit its members to return to work unless we do reinstate him. They allege victimisation – which we deny.

Could you please see whether the time has now arrived when conciliation might be possible? Alternatively, we will be prepared to consider arbitration, if this would be acceptable to the union.

Your early attention to this request would be most appreciated.

NOTE:
Letters individually addressed presume a relationship with a particular conciliation officer. Otherwise, refer direct to the Service – preferably after preliminary enquiries made personally or by telephone.

256   Arbitrator required

I am pleased to inform you that the . . . union has agreed that we go to arbitration in connection with the dispute concerning . . . . The question now arises: Whom do we appoint as arbitrator?

I appreciate that your Service does not itself appoint arbitrators from its own ranks, but perhaps you would arrange for someone to contact us immediately, to assist both sides to agree on an appropriate and acceptable person to arbitrate upon a dispute which, I would remind you, is causing severe disruption in production and much hardship to individual employees.

257   Arbitration urgent – chaser

You kindly promised that you would contact . . . with a view to seeing whether he would be prepared to act as arbitrator in the current dispute between our company and the . . . Union. It is now . . . days/weeks since our meeting and we have heard nothing further from you. The situation is getting serious. Please would you contact me, at once?

With many thanks and best wishes.

258   Arbitration requires submission − to union

We note that you are prepared to submit to arbitration but that you are not prepared to agree in advance to accept the arbitrator's decisions.

We must respectfully point out the essence of an arbitration is the prior acceptance by all parties concerned of the decision of the arbitrator − and while we are prepared to proceed to arbitration, this can only be on the basis that you, like ourselves, must agree to accept the judgement of the independent arbitrator.

The alternative would be to set up some sort of court of enquiry − which we do not feel would meet the purpose − which is, of course, to achieve a resolution of the unhappy dispute which at present divides us.

I look forward to hearing from you.

NOTE:
In a dispute involving ASLEF (the footplatemen's union) and British Rail, the union agreed to arbitration on the strict understanding that it would not commit itself in advance to acceptance of the arbitrator's award. Sensibly, the arbitration proceeded − but in fact it was a Commission of Inquiry, whose decision was in fact accepted. It is sometimes a mistake to worry too much about formalities, when results are required. Flexibility is essential − and ACAS is a splendidly flexible body, with wide powers sensibly used.

259   Thanks − to ACAS

We are all very grateful to you for the help which you gave to us in resolving the dispute with the . . . Union. All sides are convinced that the settlement is fair and reasonable − and it is clear that had you not intervened so effectively and patiently, industrial action would have been inevitable and grave harm would have been caused to the company and to all who work for it.

I am sending a copy of this letter to the chairman of ACAS.

NOTE:
Do not forget to give thanks where it is due − and, where appropriate, to let that thanks be known to those upon whom the individual depends for his position − and his prospects of promotion. Thanks cost nothing

– but they help to cement a friendly relationship which has been useful to you in the past and which you may require again in the future.

260   Dissatisfied – please send alternative

We have been very grateful in the past for the help given to us by your Mr John Smith, who is an expert in matters of unfair dismissal. But unfortunately, we are not happy with the advice which he has found it possible to give to us in connection with the serious dispute at present disrupting our production, and connected with . . . . In the circumstances, would you kindly send in a senior officer, experienced in this particular field, at your earliest convenience.

Chapter 26

Recognition of trade unions

The Employment Act, 1980, swept away the old recognition procedures – and replaced them with none. Gone is the power of ACAS to set up balloting arrangements, whether or not the parties agreed. No longer can they recommend recognition – giving unions the right to take employers to the Central Arbitration Committee, if a recommendation for recognition is flouted.

Today, management or unions may call in ACAS for advice or conciliation, if recognition causes problems. But if the dispute persists, then its outcome depends on shop-floor bargaining and muscle.

'Recognition' for this purpose means: Recognition to any substantial extent for the purposes of collective bargaining. Only a 'recognised' trade union has the right to demand disclosure of information for the purposes of collective bargaining; notification and consultation about proposed redundancies; appointment of safety representatives; appointment of trustees to pension funds . . . and other rights, reserved for those who bargain for and on behalf of their members.

As always, negotiation for recognition may be oral or in writing or both. But a recognition agreement should always be written.

261   Agreement to recognise

I write to confirm that the company agrees to recognise your union for the purposes of collective bargaining on behalf of the following employees/grades/all engineers in our . . . works/company *(or as the case may be)*. Details of the agreement are in course of negotiation and will be confirmed in writing in due course.

My colleagues and I look forward to continued cooperation with you and yours, for the benefit of the company and all who work for and with it.

262   Alternative: details attached

I am pleased to confirm that as from . . . this company

recognises the . . . Union as representing . . . for the purposes
of collective bargaining. Details of the agreement are enclosed
herewith. Assuming that you accept that the terms are
correctly set out therein, kindly sign and return these to
me at your early convenience.

I hope that this agreement marks the start of a long and
happy association and cooperation between the company
and the union, for the benefit of all concerned.

263   Refusal to recognise – insufficient membership

We have given most careful consideration to your application for recognition on behalf of the . . . Union, in respect
of employees in our/of the . . . grade *(or as the case may be)*.
In principle, we would be pleased to negotiate with the
union on behalf of our employees. But it appears that you
have in fact very few members among the employees
concerned and in the circumstances we do not consider
that recognition would be appropriate.

NOTE:
*No Statute, Regulation or Code lays down any minimum number or
percentage of members required for recognition. Some unions believe
that if 20 per cent of people in a particular unit or grade belong, then
it is reasonable to ask for recognition in respect of that grade. But
where a majority belong, management will find it hard to refuse to
recognise.*

264   Refusal – other unions involved

Thank you for your letter concerning recognition of your
union for the purposes of collective bargaining, in respect of
supervisors/managers *(or as the case may be)* in our . . . plant/
unit/company. In view of the opposition to such recognition
from the . . . Union, we do not consider that recognition of
your union would be in accordance with good industrial
relations practice. In the circumstances, we are not able to
agree to your request.

NOTE:
1   While most independent trade unions are affiliated to the TUC, a

non-affiliate may be 'independent'. But if a non-TUC affiliate seeks recognition, TUC unions concerned will almost certainly object – and sometimes back their objections with threats of industrial action.

2   Other battles over recognition may – through inter-union rivalry – be dangerous not only to the unions but to the management. Unions attempt to avoid demarcation disputes, in reliance upon the Bridlington Agreement, which bans 'poaching' of members by TUC affiliates.

3   If you run into difficulty over inter-union battles and ACAS cannot help you to sort out the trouble, try an approach to the TUC itself.

265   To TUC – help!

Personal and Confidential

We would be very grateful for your help in sorting out a dispute between two of your affiliated unions. The circumstances are as follows:

    (1) . . . .
    (2) . . . .
    (3) . . . .

Either I or my personnel manager would most gladly call on you or your appropriate officer at any mutually convenient time, in order that we may get your advice. We fear that if this dispute is not resolved, our production will be affected; the entire future of the company will be at risk; lay-offs and short-time working will become inevitable; and we may be faced with large-scale redundancies.

I look forward to hearing from you as soon as possible, please.

NOTE:

1   It is probably best for your managing or personnel director to address this letter personally to the General Secretary of the TUC – who will pass it to his appropriate colleague.

2   The TUC deeply dislikes battles between its affiliates. Ammunition should be fired at the enemy and not at your allies.

3   Unions in general and the TUC in particular are above all concerned – especially in times of recession – not to risk the loss of precious jobs.

266 Request to ACAS – recognition advice

I would be grateful if you would call upon me at your earliest convenience. A recognition issue has arisen which is likely to give rise to a dispute and your help with advice and, if necessary, with conciliation would be most appreciated.

267 Consultation arrangements

I note that you wish to consult with the company in connection with the recognition issue referred to you by the . . . Union. I am instructed by the Board to assure you of the full co-operation of the company. Please contact me at your early convenience to make the appropriate arrangements. And if and in so far as you feel that an enquiry is necessary, we shall be pleased to assist in any way.

The above is without prejudice to the view which we have expressed to the union, namely that recognition would not be justified on the basis of its present membership within the plant/office (as the case may be) within which recognition is sought.

268 To ACAS – for promotion of agreement

The company would be very pleased to settle the matter by agreement. In so far as you or any of your colleagues are able to assist in the promotion of such an agreement, we shall be obliged to you. We are prepared to accept conciliation and would be grateful if one of your experienced officers would call on us at the earliest possible date.

269 Recognition agreement after dispute

I am happy to confirm the agreement arrived at between your trade union and my company, which has happily put an end to the recognition dispute. The terms of the agreement are as follows:

1   The company agrees to recognise your union for bargaining purposes in respect of . . . employees working

in our office/workshop *(or as the case may be)*.
2   Your union forthwith to call off its work to rule, so that full production may be resumed immediately.
With best wishes.

270   Denial of failure to comply

I understand that the . . . Union has complained to your Service that the company has allegedly failed to comply with the current recognition agreement. This allegation is wholly denied. We were, are and will remain willing to continue to recognise the . . . Union for the purposes of collective bargaining. We are not prepared to accept a closed shop.

By all means visit us at an early opportunity. We shall be pleased to discuss the matter — but not to give greater rights than those contained in the agreement, a copy of which I enclose herewith.

Chapter 27

The right to belong—and Union Membership Agreements

An employee is entitled by law to belong to an independent trade union, i.e. one that is neither dominated nor controlled nor influenced by employers. The Certification Officer decides whether or not a trade union is 'independent' and if he certifies that a union is independent, that decision is final (see Chapter 28).

It is unlawful to discriminate against or to dismiss an employee for seeking to belong to or to take part in the activities of an independent trade union. Indeed, whereas normally an employee who seeks unfair dismissal protection must be continuously employed for six months, there is no such time limit where the dismissal is on grounds of trade union membership or activities.

Conversely, an employee is not entitled as of right to belong to or to take part in the activities of a non-independent trade union. Those staff associations which are 'tame' — or 'sweetheart' unions, as they are sometimes called — are not protected.

A closed shop is an agreement between union and management under which specified employees must belong to the union or one of the unions concerned. In a 'pre-entry closed shop' (usually: printers, actors or seamen) the employee must be a member before he is taken on. In a 'post-entry' closed shop, the employee must be a member, or become one within the time specified in the agreement.

Either way, the arrangement arises by agreement — and is properly (and in the 1980 Act, always) called: 'a Union Membership Agreement' (UMA).

Restrictions on UMAs were created by the 1980 Act — and explained by the Code. The Act created a new power for the Employment Secretary to make Codes which, unlike those of ACAS and the Health and Safety Commission, do not require the approval or agreement of TUC nominees. Breach of a Ministerial Code (Highway or ACAS or other approved Codes) does not render anyone liable to civil or to criminal proceedings. But evidence of the breach may be used in any proceedings, civil or criminal, to which it is relevant.

UMAs have not become unlawful. But an employee may opt out not merely (as previously) on religious grounds, but where he has a genuine *(i)* conscientious objection to belonging or *(ii)* deeply held personal conviction, which prevents him from doing so.

Otherwise, pre-existing UMAs remain unaffected. But for a new one to be enforceable, i.e. by dismissing a non-joiner, it must be 'approved' — in secret ballot by at least 80 per cent of those eligible to vote.

In addition, in a closed-shop situation, trade unions must not 'unreasonably exclude' or 'unreasonably expel' anyone from membership. Remedy: a claim to an industrial tribunal or (on occasion) to the Employment Appeal Tribunal (EAT).

In practice, these rules are having — and are expected to have — little effect, because:

1   No one wishes rows with trade unions.
2   Whatever their philosophical or political objections to closed shops, most managers prefer to deal with integrated, rather than with fragmented, workforces — and with one convener or other representative on behalf of the workforce (or the appropriate part of it).

The new law is not always clear. So look out for Court interpretations. Meanwhile, keep away from trouble as much as you can. And if in doubt, take advice.

Finally: if you do dismiss a non-joiner under union pressure (with threatened or actual industrial action) and if that person then brings an unfair dismissal claim against you, you may now 'join' the union as a party to the proceedings. You may claim from the union an indemnity or contribution, in respect of any payment which you may have to make to the unfairly dismissed employee.

Similar rules apply where you have a 'union labour only' sub-contract; where the sub-contractor then asks you to waive the 'union labour only' clause, so as to enable him to employ non-members on your job — but you decline; where the sub-contractor then dismisses a non-member, who claims that the dismissal was unfair; and where the sub-contractor then joins you in the proceedings, seeking contribution or indemnity from you. You may then join the union under whose pressure you declined to agree to the waiver.

In practice, if you do dismiss — or cause someone else to do so — in order not to fall out with the trade union, the idea of your then suing that union for pressurising you is so idiotic that one sample letter — hopefully, never to be used — will suffice.

271   Right to belong — alleged

I write to protest at the discrimination from which I am suffering, because I am seeking to belong/take part in the activities of an independent trade union, namely . . . . As I am exercising my proper, lawful entitlement, I trust that you will ensure that this discrimination ceases. The matters about which I complain are in particular:

1 . . .
2 . . .
3 . . .

272   Right to belong – conceded

Thank you for your letter dated . . . . You are indeed entitled to belong to the . . . Union. I have made enquiries regarding your allegation of discrimination, all of which are denied. However, I will be pleased to discuss these matters with you if you will call on me at my office at . . . a.m./p.m.

Dealing with the allegations of discrimination in turn, my investigations have revealed the following:-

1 . . .
2 . . .
3 . . .

I shall look forward to seeing you.

NOTE:
It is always useful to record in writing the answers to allegations which have themselves been made in writing.

273   Right to belong – denied

I am in receipt of your letter dated . . . , and clearly you are under a misapprehension. You have by law the right to belong to and/or to take part in the activities of any independent trade union. You are seeking to build up a staff association which has not been certified as independent. However, I will be glad if you will call on me to discuss the whole matter.

274   To union – threatening contribution or indemnity

I was most disturbed to learn that you have threatened industrial action if we do not dismiss Mr . . . who has refused to join your union on grounds which may be misguided, but are clearly (a) genuine; (b) conscientious; and (c) in any event, arising out of what the law calls a 'deeply held personal belief'.

We are giving urgent consideration to this matter, but must point out that if you do in fact force us to dismiss this man and if (as would appear very likely) he then claims that he was dismissed unfairly and seeks compensation from us, we shall be entitled to bring your union into the action and to seek a contribution or indemnity from you.

Perhaps in the circumstances we can discuss this whole unhappy affair together and see if we cannot find some other solution?

275   A closed-shop agreement

I write to confirm our agreement, which is now being drawn up in its final form. The company agrees that all future employees will either be members of your union when they are appointed or will agree to become members within . . . weeks of the commencement of their employment.

NOTE:
If you make a Union Membership Agreement, you should always attempt to ensure its application to future rather than existing employees. Nearly all serious and unhappy disputes over UMAs occur when employers try to force membership upon existing employees, who refuse to join.

276   Ballot for 'approval'

We are agreeable to the establishment of a post-entry union membership agreement, applying to future employees of our . . . factory/in the . . . department/employed as engineers *(or as the case may be)* in our works. You have told us that in your opinion over 90 per cent of employees who come into the category concerned are in favour of a closed shop and for our part, we are glad to accede to your request to set up arrangements for a secret ballot to establish their wishes. Hopefully, at least 80 per cent of those eligible to vote will in fact vote in favour, so that the agreement will be 'approved', in law as well as in fact.

277 Union's 'unreasonable expulsion'

I regret to inform you that Mr . . . has today told me
that he proposes to bring proceedings before an Industrial
Tribunal. alleging that in a closed-shop situation, your
union has unreasonably excluded him from membership,
thereby making it impossible for us to employ him. I have
told him that this is a matter between him and his union;
that in my view he should follow the union's own procedures
and if he is not satisfied with them, then he should use the
TUC appeal procedure; but of course the decision is his.

NOTE:
*1   If an employee does apply to a tribunal, then (says the law) the
fact that the unions' procedures have been followed will not
necessarily make the dismissal 'fair' – nor will a failure to follow
them make it 'unfair'.*

*2   Unions object fiercely to these provisions as an interference in
their own procedures. Management should (as the above letter indicates) keep its maximum distance from any resulting disputes.*

Secret ballots   The Employment Act, 1980, introduced a new procedure under which unions may apply to the Certification Officer for
payment out of public funds of all or part of the cost of operating
certain secret ballots. These include in particular ballots *(i)* for the
election or appointment of union officers; *(ii)* for calling or calling
off industrial action; or *(iii)* for the merger or amalgamation of unions.

There is no requirement that more secret ballots be held – and those
unions which have always used them (e.g. miners, engineers and
electricians) will continue to do so – and some may dip into public
funds for the cost. Meanwhile, union meetings in working hours (see
Chapter 34 on time off work) are having a much more profound
effect.

278 Secret ballot – agreed

I am pleased to confirm that we shall set up arrangements
for a secret ballot, as you have requested. Its purpose will be
to ascertain the view of employees in . . . /following cate-

gories *(or as the case may be)* concerning . . . . The ballot will be held on the . . . . Please would you see me as soon as possible, so that we can agree on all necessary arrangements.

Chapter 28

Independent trade unions

Nearly all important rights are given only to 'independent' trade unions. The right to be consulted about intended redundancies . . . to disclosure of information for the purposes of collective bargaining . . . to appoint safety representatives and trustees for pension funds . . . protection for actions civil and criminal, for unions that are 'independent' in law. The man who is in charge of the registration (or Certification) of independent trade unions is known as the 'Certification Officer'.

The Certification Officer maintains a list of trade unions, duly certified by him as 'independent'. His certificate is absolute evidence of that independence and is of immense value to unions, many of whose rights under the Act depend upon their being both independent and recognised. 'Sweetheart' and 'tame' staff associations are excluded from most of the new statutory benefits.

To be 'independent', a union must be free of control — direct or indirect — by or on behalf of the employer. Usually (but not always) the yardstick is finance. Who pays the piper?

A union which wishes to register may apply to the Certification Officer, sending a fee of £96 (or such other fee as may later be prescribed by regulations). Address: Certification Officer, Vincent House Annex, Hide Place, London SW1 (Tel: 01-821 6144).

Once an application is received, the Certification Officer must determine whether the trade union is independent — and if so, he will issue his certificate. If not, then he must give his reasons and the aggrieved trade union may appeal. The appropriate forms should be obtained from the Certification Officer, if and when the occasion arises.

When deciding whether or not a union is 'independent', the Certification Officer 'shall make such enquiries as he thinks fit and shall take into account any relevant information submitted to him by any person'. The employer is a 'person'. Most of the correspondence with the Certification Officer will inevitably be carried out by or on behalf of the trade unions concerned, to whom the above information should where necessary be provided. Employers may require these precedents:

1   Supporting application for certification.
2   Opposing it.
3   Sitting firmly (and with rugged and terrified independence) on the fence.

279   Certification application – supported

Re: Trade Union's Application for Certification

I am pleased to confirm that, to the best of my knowledge, information and belief, the above union is totally independent. Certainly in so far as its dealings with our company are concerned, it receives neither direction nor (still less) control from the company or any of its directors, managers or other officers; nor does it receive any financial support from the company, direct or indirect.

280   Application opposed

. . . Union's Application for Certification

I have been informed that the above union has applied for registration as an independent trade union. I feel bound to inform you of the following matters which may influence your decision and no doubt of which you will wish to take account:
1   The company has made the following payments to the union during the course of the past . . . months/years:-
2   The union's officers include . . . .
3   The company entered into an agreement with the union on the . . . , a copy of which is annexed hereto.
   In the above circumstances, this company does not regard the union as independent.

281   Non-committal evidence

Thank you for your letter dated . . . . The information you require is as follows:
   1 . . . .
   2 . . . .
   3 . . . .

282   Appeal against refusal to certify

We acknowledge receipt of your decision to refuse certification to the above named union and we wish to appeal against that decision. Kindly accept this letter as notice of that intention and supply us with any further forms and information.

NOTE:
1 *A trade union which is refused certification has a right of appeal to the Employment Appeal Tribunal. An objector to a successful certification (usually a TUC-affiliated union) has no such right.*
2 *Appeal forms (for this and all other purposes) available from the Employment Appeal Tribunal, 4 St James's Square, London SW1Y 4JB.*
3 *Time limit for appeal against certification — 42 days; other appeals — 42 days from date of entry in the register.*

Chapter 29

Disclosure of information

The rules allowing unions to claim disclosure of information for the purposes of collective bargaining were originally contained in the (Conservative) Industrial Relations Act – but they were not activated. Repeated in almost identical terms by *The Employment Protection Act, 1975,* they are now increasingly used. They are:

1 Only independent, recognised trade unions are entitled to disclosure.
2 The information sought and disclosed may be in the possession of the employer or of any associated employer, i.e. one in the same group or under the same control, at home or abroad.
3 Disclosure is only required at the union's request. Wise employers anticipate requests; do their best to keep their unions well informed; and make sure that all information given is properly explained – to them and to other levels of management. Great care must be taken not to mislead.
4 Information may be required for the purposes of collective bargaining – but not to individual negotiation.
5 Information need only be given if it is 'material' for the purposes of collective bargaining – information without which (as a union leader put it) union negotiators would be working 'blindfold'.

In this very wide duty of disclosure, there are many exceptions, including:

a Information that is confidential to other parties.
b Information the disclosure of which would cause serious harm to the company for reasons other than its affect on collective bargaining.
c When the cost of collating the information would be out of all proportion to its value when provided.
d Information collected for the purposes of litigation (and hence 'privileged').
e Information the disclosure of which would be contrary to the interests of national security.

283   Refusal to disclose — against interests of national security

I am in receipt of your request for information concerning . . . . I regret that it would not be proper for me to disclose this, having regard to the classified nature of the work in the department concerned. Such disclosure would be against the interests of national security. I am sure that on reconsideration you will agree with this.

Nevertheless, if you would care to meet me to discuss this matter, I think that I can provide you with sufficient information for your purposes, without going beyond the bounds of my proper authority — and I would be pleased to meet you at any mutually convenient time.

284   Information supplied in confidence

The information which you request was communicated to the management in confidence, and in the circumstances I regret that it cannot be disclosed.

We have already revealed to you a great deal of information — and it is hoped that you will now be able to proceed with the negotiations. If there are any further matters which can be disclosed without betrayal of a confidence, I shall, of course, be pleased to cooperate with you. We are only too anxious that our negotiations should be carried on in the most frank and friendly manner.

With best wishes.

285   Refusal of information relating to an individual

I am sorry. You ask for information relating to payments made to specific individuals. At your request, I consulted them to see whether they would be prepared to have their salaries or wages revealed — and they have declined. In the circumstances, I am not required or entitled to disclose this information to you.

In any event, the information which you have received should, I hope, be sufficient for the purposes of collective bargaining and the management is only too ready to co-operate with you in the hope of achieving a mutually satisfactory agreement.

I look forward to seeing you, as arranged, at tomorrow's meeting.

286   Refusal of information – serious harm

Confidential

The disclosure of [*e.g. the nature of the Company's over-drafts*] would cause serious harm to the Company's interests, for reasons other than its effect on collective bargaining. This information is highly confidential and if its disclosure were to lead to a leak, this would not only seriously affect the Company but also the jobs of the people whom we employ and whom you so ably represent.

I am sorry to have to convey this refusal to you, but I am sure that you will understand the position. If there is any other information which you require for the purposes of the current negotiations, please do not hesitate to inform me.

287   Refusal of information prepared for legal proceedings

The information you require was prepared by our accountants specifically for the purpose of defending a legal action brought against the Company by . . . . In the circumstances, the Company is not required to disclose that information. You will appreciate, I am sure, that the legal proceedings concerned are of great importance to the Company and the material to which you refer is privileged in law.

288   Refusal – information not necessary for carrying on collective bargaining

The information you request is not necessary for the purposes of collective bargaining. It concerns matters outside the scope of the current negotiations. In the circumstances, I would not feel justified in disclosing it to you.

However, I think that information which may concern you more and which we could probably disclose would be . . . .

May I suggest that we discuss the question of . . . ? I would
be pleased to look into the question of . . . with you.

NOTE:
*It is always good tactics – in negotiating with employees, in the same
way as in bargaining with potential suppliers or customers – not merely
to say no. Use the positive approach, wherever you can. This is both
helpful, fair and constructive. Suggest an alternative*

289   Employer's reply to criticisms of statement

Thank you for your letter. I have carefully considered the
points you make. My answers are as follows:

1   The information concerning . . . relates specifically to an
individual who has not consented to its being disclosed.
2   It would be seriously prejudicial to the Company's interests if the information concerning . . . were to be disclosed.
3   The information requested concerning . . . is highly
secret; its disclosure would be against the interests of
national security.

Now that you know the reasons for the non-disclosure, I
hope that you will appreciate our difficulties – and that you
will accept that we have in fact set out in the statement as
much as we properly can, in accordance with not only the
Regulations (and the Employment Protection Act), but also
in accordance with our firm wish that our employees – including, of course, members of your Union – should have the
fullest possible information, consistent with good industrial
relations practice.

290   No inspection of books

We have been pleased to disclose to you and through you
to your union full information concerning the following
matters:

1 . . . .
2 . . . .
3 . . . .

However, the law does not require the company to provide
you with a roving commission through the company's books.

nor are we prepared to do so.

We will be pleased, however, to provide you with copies of all information prepared for you for the purposes of collective bargaining and we trust that this will suffice for your purpose.

291 Cost of collating information too great

I have, as promised, asked the company secretary to set about collating the information which you required. He tells me, however, that the work involved would be enormous; that the cost of getting the information together would be vast; and that when all is done, the value of the information is unlikely to be very great.

In the circumstances, bearing in mind that the law provides that, where the cost of preparing information would be out of proportion to its value in collective bargaining, disclosure is not required, I would make the following compromise suggestions:

    1 . . . .
    2 . . . .
    3 . . . .

Chapter 30

Redundancy consultation and notification*

The early warning system operates in two directions — that of the trade union and its member; and that of the Employment Secretary.

Where you recognise a trade union for bargaining purposes, you must notify that union of any intended redundancy of any member or members — however few and however many — at the earliest practicable date. Notification (and hence consultation) is essential even if you do not reach the minimum of ten employees at any one establishment whom you intend to dismiss within a particular thirty day period — in which case the law requires at least 30 days' consultation with the trade union concerned. If you intend to make a 100 or more employees redundant at any one establishment within a period of 90 days, then you must give 90 days early warning to the union. Note:

1   You must consult even about the proposed redundancy of one union member or person on whose behalf the union negotiates.

2   When totting up the minimum statutory number for major redundancies, you include both union and non-union members.

3   Consultation is required in respect of non-union members, when a union is recognised as bargaining on their behalf as well as on behalf of its members.

Failure to consult will entitle the *trade union* to apply to an industrial tribunal for a 'protective award' on behalf of its member — that award being, in general, the employee's remuneration during the protective period, i.e. the period during which consultation should have taken place. The object of an award is to compensate the employee, not to penalise the employer.

The employer must also inform the Department of Employment where he intends to make ten or more people redundant at any one establishment within a 30-day period (30 days' notification) or where he intends to make 100 or more redundant at any one establishment within a 90-day period (90 days' warning). The sanctions for failure to comply: fines of up to £400 or a loss of up to 1/10th of the normal redundancy rebate (41 per cent of the statutory payment).

---

* See also Chapter 12 for main redundancy rules and letters.

The object of the exercise, of course, is two-fold:

1   To ensure that employees get the maximum warning of impending disaster, and so to help keep hardship to the minimum.
2   To enable trade unions and/or the Department of Employment to negotiate and/or to assist in efforts to avoid the loss of all or some of the jobs concerned.

292   Notification to union of intended redundancy – to members

As you know, we are in the throes of a rationalisation programme which will, we believe, enable us to keep the company on a firm and profitable basis for the foreseeable future. We are happy that we are able to keep redundancies to the absolute minimum. But it now appears certain that we shall have to make two of your members redundant in our . . . workshop. We shall be pleased to discuss these redundancies with you at your convenience.

With best wishes.

NOTE:
You do not have to select or to name the people whom you intend to make redundant. The choice of job losers may (and normally should) be discussed with the union.

293   Consultation invited – 10 to 99 redundancies

We greatly regret that due to . . . , we have no alternative other than to close the . . . department in our . . . works. We shall do our best to keep the department going for as long as possible and we hope not to have to start the run-down until *(state date – not less than 30 days from date when letter will be received)*.

We shall be pleased to consult with you over these proposed redundancies and I would be grateful if you would contact me at my office as soon as possible. The number of expected redundancies is . . . *(between 10 and 99)*.

NOTE:
1   In the absence of 'special circumstances', notification must be made

at least 30 days (or in the case of 100 or more expected redundancies 100 days) before the date of the first of the expected redundancies.

2 If you do not know the intended number, then say: about 10 (or as the case may be).

294   Major redundancies – 100 or more

It is with great regret that I must inform you that as a result of the collapse of our home/export market/absolute necessity of rationalising production to remain competitive/in business, that we shall be forced to close our . . . plant/department/warehouse/unit. Inevitably, this will cause large scale redundancies, probably in the region of . . . .

We have made every effort to avoid this unhappy situation, and we are still intending to explore every possible avenue of keeping the plant/department/warehouse/unit open. At present though, we see no alternative to closure. And we expect to have to start the run-down in . . . months time (*not less than 3*).

We are giving you this formal notification as required by law. But we have always valued the excellent industrial relations that have existed in the plant/the company – and we shall be pleased to consult with you at the first possible opportunity, to see whether any way can be found to avoid the redundancies or, if that proves as we fear, impossible, then at least to keep any resultant hardship to the absolute minimum.

Please would you contact me immediately at my office?

295   Special circumstances – customer insolvent

I am sure that you will have been as shocked and upset as was the Board of this company to learn of the insolvency of . . . Ltd. This collapse has meant that we have had to call a complete/partial halt to our production/production of . . . . Unfortunately, this will mean that we will be forced to give redundancy notices forthwith to not less than . . . employees, many of whom will be your members.

We are holding an immediate plant/department/works meeting/meeting with the company/area representatives of

the unions concerned at . . . in . . . . I do hope that you will
be able to attend or if that proves impossible, then to send
your most senior deputy.

I need hardly tell you how distressed we are at this turn
of events – particularly at a time when the company was
making such excellent progress. And we shall, of course, do
all in our power to keep the inevitable hardship that will
result from these unpalatable events to the absolute minimum.

With my warmest personal regards.

296   Seasonal work terminates unexpectedly

I regret to inform you that, due to the failure of the har-
vest *(or as the case may be)*, work which we had hoped
would keep our employees busy for another three months
has in fact collapsed. We shall therefore be forced to give
redundancy notices to . . . within the course of the next
seven days.

Please do contact us regarding any steps which might help
reduce any resultant hardship.

297   Expected order not obtained

I am afraid that our tender for . . . was not successful; the
work that we had been hoping for has not become available;
and when the present job at . . . is completed in about . . .
weeks time, we shall not be in a position to continue the
employment of . . . . We regret this very much – but the
matter was and is beyond our control.

We shall be pleased to consult with you regarding these
redundancies, at your earliest convenience.

298   Notification to the Department of Employment

I am instructed to inform you that the company intends
to make employees redundant as follows:
1   At our . . . plant, the first dismissals taking effect not
     earlier than . . . .
2   Through the closure of our . . . office/sales unit, approx-

imately . . . redundancies, taking effect not earlier than
. . . .

3   Through the transfer of our Accounts Department from
. . . to . . . , commencing on or about . . . .
Please send me your appropriate forms.

299   Explanation for delay in notification — unexpected events

I have to inform you that it is the Company's intention to
make . . . employees redundant at our . . . plant/office commencing . . . . Unfortunately, it was not possible to notify the
Employment Secretary through you at an earlier date because
of the following events which were both unexpected and
beyond the control of the company:

1 . . . .
2 . . . .
3 . . . .

300   Denial to union of undue delay

Thank you for your letter dated . . . . It is correct that we
were unable to consult with your union about the proposed
redundancies more than 30/90 days (*as the case may be*)
before the first of these redundancies were due to become
effective. The delay was caused entirely by special circumstances beyond our control, and in particular:

1 . . . .
2 . . . .
3 . . . .

That said, the company remains ready and willing to explore any possibility of avoiding all or any of the redundancies and/or of avoiding any hardship which may result to
any employee as a result. It would be wrong to hold out any
real hope — but we would welcome consultations with you
at the earliest opportunity. So do please contact me/the
personnel director/. . . as soon as you can.

301 Denial of right to protective award

Your member was one of four people whom we unfortunately found it necessary to make redundant. We did consult
with you at the earliest practicable opportunity. In the circumstances, if you see fit to apply for a protective award on
behalf of your member, the proceedings will be vigorously
defended.

We have always done everything within our power to be
fair and reasonable towards our employees and to encourage
good industrial relations. We are therefore particularly disturbed at this allegation which you have seen fit to make
against us.

302 Consultation adequate – major redundancy

The period of consultation required in the case of your
members was 30 days and not 90 days as stated by you – we
did not intend to make 100 people redundant, nor, happily,
were we forced to do so.

We consulted with you at the earliest possible opportunity
which was in fact more than 30 days before the date of the
first dismissal. There can therefore be no substance in your
claim for a protective award and any proceedings would be
most vigorously defended.

None of this removes our regret that these redundancies
became necessary. And in any event, we shall continue to
consult with you in the hope that the hardship caused by the
redundancies may be kept to an irreducible minimum.

NOTE:
*You will have to work with the union even after the dispute has been
settled. So preserve courtesy, dignity and goodwill – especially in letters
which are liable to end up before Tribunals.*

303 To Employment Secretary – notification adequate

We were disturbed to receive your letter alleging that you
did not receive sufficient notification of the redundancies at
our . . . plant/office. You were in fact notified at the first
reasonably practicable opportunity – which, as it happens,

was in excess of the statutory minimum period specified in the Act. The facts are as follows:

1   (*Date of notification*).
2   (*Number of employees to be made redundant*).
3   (*Date of first dismissal*).

304   Original intention, less than 10

I write to inform you that in about four weeks we shall have to make approximately 15 people redundant at our . . . plant/office/works. The reason why you did not receive the 30 days' notification was that we had originally intended to make only six redundancies. Unfortunately, the collapse of certain orders has forced us to cut our work force by more people than we had intended.

I should add that we shall do everything in our power to ensure that as many redundancies as possible are voluntary; and we would be pleased to see your conciliation officer at any mutually convenient time.

NOTE:
1   Do not hesitate to call in ACAS – particularly where a dispute is possible.

2   You are only obliged to give notice of 'intended' redundancies – and you would claim that in the above case that there were 'special circumstances' which made it impracticable to give the statutory notice even in respect of those whom you intended to make redundant, i.e. less than 10.

3   Remember: there is no minimum number of people who you are required to consult when trade unions are involved.

305   Intended redundancy – union notification

On . . . I told your representative in the factory of the problem foreseen for employment in the next few months, as a result of a shortage of orders, which could result in up to 70 employees being made redundant. I gave notice of a 30-day consultation period commencing . . . during which the fullest information would be supplied to you. This letter sets out the circumstances and we shall be pleased to commence consultations with you at your earliest convenience.

1   Reasons for redundancy

In spite of intense sales and tendering activity the Division has been unsuccessful in obtaining manufacturing orders to support the current programme. The effect of this is being felt progressively in the . . . Unit, where, when current orders are fulfilled from mid-May onwards, there are no contracts to follow on. Because of this the direct operators involved, as well as some of those on . . . and other support services throughout the factory will be affected.

The problem results from no intake of . . . orders for . . . assemblies usually covered by Stores Orders and obtained by competitive tendering. This complete absence of orders is significant at a time when the . . . has reduced its purchasing because of cuts in Government spending as part of the counter inflation policy.

2   Consequential action

As a direct result of the shortage of orders in the . . . Unit it has been necessary to revise the complete manufacturing organisation. The existence of two separate unit management structures can no longer be justified and a single production unit with responsibility for all shop production work now replaces the previous two-unit structure.

This major change means the loss of some indirect jobs in management and elsewhere because of duplication quite apart from the reduction in volume of work caused by the shortage of orders.

Although the effects are most strongly felt in Manufacturing there is a follow-through effect into Quality Assurance, Contracts, Sales and Accounting where diminished workload will also be felt.

Finally, the loss of direct effort means reduced recovery of overhead and all departments have been instructed to economise in manning and other expense areas to ensure the continued viability of the Division in these reduced circumstances. In some instances this means simply keeping within budgeted limits, but where reductions in actual workload are certain, reductions in manning are also inevitable.

3   *Numbers of employees involved*

As far as can be seen at this time the original overall estimate is still substantially correct although the make-up of the total now varies slightly from that originally tabled.

Unless circumstances alter, the number of employees affected in jobs and areas for which unions have rights of representation are:

Direct Employees

Job Category	Numbers Affected	Total No. Employed
(1)		
(2)		
(3)		

Indirect Employees

Job Category	Numbers Affected	Total No. Employed
(1)		
(2)		
(3)		

Total of Direct and Indirect

Until employees have been identified by name you should not assume that these numbers represent your members only, but it is possible that at least some of them are in membership with you in appropriate jobs. Similarly, until volunteers have been matched with job categories, it should not be assumed automatically that the numbers quoted will result in enforced redundancy.

In Manufacturing, where the problem is greatest, redundancy selection will, in general, be determined by the association of employees with the specific product lines affected by shortage of work. Within these areas it will be necessary to transfer some employees to other product lines where their skills and experience can be utilised. Where this is not possible it will be the Division's intention to release employees who have reached or passed retirement age and part-time employees in that order. If further action is needed to achieve the reduction required the service of employees will become a major factor in selection for redundancy.

Where contract labour can be suitably replaced by company employees this will be done.

It is appreciated that, for the union, membership is of course a key factor. Equally, the Company must necessarily have regard to the welfare of all employees and to the need for them in their particular jobs. In practice, because of the existence currently of 33 voluntary applications and the high level of union membership among direct employees, it may be possible to preserve both viewpoints without difficulty. Other departments involved will follow the same general rules varying them only when specific circumstances, peculiar to them, make it imperative.

Regarding volunteers, the Division will, where practicable, release them at a mutually agreed date, either during or after the end of the 30-day consultation period, but reserves the right to refuse an application if it is not in the future interest of the Division to approve it whatever the reason.

4   Redeployment

In addition to internal attempts to redeploy employees who have been warned of redundancy every attempt will be made to help them find alternative work externally. To do this close liaison on job opportunities has already been established with other local employers. The services of the Department of Employment will also be fully utilised and, for those employees who are willing to consider re-location, use will be made of the Company's jobs finding facility and redeployment agency.

A general willingness to consider opportunities by employees and your active support will help to achieve success in this respect.

5   Method of dismissal and timing

Apart from volunteers, no employees will be made redundant

until the expiry of the 30-day consultation period. From that date onwards groups of employees will become redundant as work runs out progressively in the period to the end of . . . . As soon as the employees involved have been determined, each will receive a letter giving them advanced warning of redundancy. Not less than 14 days prior to actual redundancy each will receive a final letter giving the actual date of redundancy.

On that day their employment with the Company will be terminated and each will receive redundancy payments due to them from State and Company schemes together with payments for unused holiday entitlement and money in lieu of notice. They will also be able to exercise any options open to them under the Company's Pension Plan where appropriate.

The foregoing provisions will apply if and when redundancy actually occurs. Unusual efforts are being made to try to get orders with sufficient work content to render redundancy unnecessary. If we are successful it will be my pleasure to inform you of any withdrawal of redundancy notices we are able to make.

In any event, you may be sure that in the present difficult and unhappy circumstances, the company will make every effort to keep hardship to a minimum — and production to a maximum. It will comply with the spirit as well as with the letter of the new legislation and will be pleased to consult with you at every stage.

I will be glad if you would contact me at your early convenience, so that we may discuss both how the redundancies and their effects may be kept to a minimum and how the maximum protection may be provided not only for those employees who have to leave but also for the remainder of the workforce. We greatly regret the necessity for redundancies today and look forward to your co-operation so that we can do whatever is possible to preserve jobs in the future.

NOTE:
With the exception of the final paragraph — which I regard as an essential addition — and with alterations made so as to disguise the circumstances, this is an excellent example of a letter which was carefully drafted and sent out by a personnel manager.

Chapter 31

Short time, lay-off and guarantee pay

When you 'lay-off' an employee or put him on short-time working, you fail to provide him with the remuneration to which he is lawfully entitled under his contract of service. You are therefore in breach of that contract.

If the employee accepts the new arrangement, then the contract of employment is varied. He no doubt prefers to work less days or hours or even to be laid off altogether until business picks up, rather than regarding himself as dismissed. However, if the employee does not accept the new situation, you will be left with the alternative – to dismiss or not to dismiss.

You may dismiss the employee actually by giving him his notice or pay in lieu. You may then, if you wish, take him back on revised terms – under which, for example, he may be offered specified pay for hours worked, but no guarantee of any minimum.

Alternatively, if you simply lay off the employee or put him onto short-time without his consent, he may regard himself as dismissed 'constructively'.

If the employee suffers from 'workless days' not caused by any industrial dispute in his own or any associated company or employer, then he will be entitled to 'guarantee pay' for a maximum of five days. As from 1 February 1981, the maximum guarantee pay is £8.75 per day – making a total of £43.75 for five days, after which he must wait a further period of three months before he can qualify for any further guarantee money *(The Employment Act, 1980).*

306   Notice of short-time working

As you will certainly know by now, the company is suffering greatly as a result of the current recession and I regret that it will no longer be possible to keep you on full-time working. In the circumstances, I regret that you/your department will go onto short-time working as from . . . . Initially, we hope to keep everyone employed for four/three/at least two days a week, but the situation will be kept under constant review. And of course the sooner we can go back to full-time working, the happier we shall all be.

I am sorry to have to give you this bad news, but you do know that the management is doing everything within its power to seek further orders — and we have put off making this decision until the last possible moment. We have, of course, consulted the . . . Union/all unions concerned before making this sadly inevitable decision.

307   Notice — before short-time working

We have done our utmost to ensure full time working for all the company's employees — but the state of the market is so bad and the recession so deep that we are now forced to put all the workforce/all employees in the . . . department *(or as the case may be)* on short time. I am therefore giving you notice in accordance with your contract of employment, to terminate your current service on the . . . . Thereafter, we shall be pleased to retain you in our employment. We cannot guarantee you any particular amount of employment in any week — but we will, of course, do our best to maximise the work for you.

We hope that you will be prepared to stay on with us on this basis, but if you are able to find alternative employment or decide to accept voluntary retirement or redundancy, then we shall quite understand. Please would you convey your decision to . . . /your personnel manager/your department head, as soon as possible and in any event not after . . . .

Once again, I must repeat our very great regret at having to take this decision — but the state of our order book has made it absolutely inevitable.

NOTE:
1   If you dismiss your employee in these circumstances, then that dismissal is 'attributable wholly or mainly to the fact that the requirements of your business for employees to carry out work of a particular kind . . . have diminished or are expected to . . . diminish . . . '.
2   An employee is 'laid off' if his pay depends upon the work — and you provide him with none for a particular week. Beware if his re-

muneration is 'less than half a week's pay'. Then he is 'taken to be on short time for that week'.

3   If the employee wants to be treated as dismissed as redundant by reason of being off or kept on short time, then he must give notice in writing of his intention to claim redundancy pay. Before the service of that notice, he must either have been laid off or kept on short time for four or more consecutive weeks leading up to the date of service of his notice or ending not more than four weeks before that date or he must have been laid off or kept on short time for six or more weeks (of which not more than three were consecutive) within a period of 13 weeks ending on the date of service of his notice or not more than four weeks previously.

308   Employee's notice of intention

I hereby give you notice that I intend to claim a redundancy payment by reason of being laid off/kept on short-time working, as I have been laid off/kept on short time during the following periods: . . . .

I hereby give you a week's notice/ . . . notice, in accordance with the terms of my contract of employment, to terminate my contract on . . . .

NOTE:
If it is 'reasonably to be expected' that the employee will – not later than four weeks after date of service of his notice as above – 'enter upon a period of employment of not less than 13 weeks during which he will not be laid off or kept on short time for any week', then he will not be entitled to redundancy pay. But in that case you must give him notice in writing within seven days after receiving his notice of intention to claim, as follows:

309   Employer's counter-notice – contesting liability for redundancy payment

Thank you for your notice dated . . . stating your intention to claim redundancy pay. We reasonably expect that within four weeks of the date of your notice we shall enter upon a period of employment of not less than 13 weeks during which you will not be laid off/kept on short time. In the circumstances, we will contest any liability to pay a redundancy payment in pursuance of your notice of intention to claim.

We are giving this notice on the advice of our solicitors, and in accordance with Section 88 of the 1978 Employment Protection (Consolidation) Act. But we would like you to know that we are anxious to retain your services, which we appreciate; and we greatly regret having to lay off employees/put you and other employees onto short time, due to the recession in the trade — but that we are very pleased that immediate prospects are improving and I hope to be in touch with you again in the course of the next few days/week or two, with further information.

Chapter 32

Insolvency

If you need to use this chapter, your company is unlikely to be able to afford the cost of the book. The insolvency rules are designed to provide a substantial cushion for employees when (in ordinary terms) their employer goes bust.

First, new items join the 'preferential payments', floating to the top when the assets have been accumulated and the creditors are to be paid off.

Priority debts now include guarantee payments; remuneration on suspension on medical grounds, i.e. in certain cases where the employee is laid off due to breach by employers of the Health and Safety at Work Act etc.; payment for time off; and remuneration under a protective award.

Much more important, though, are the new claims which may now be made from the Redundancy Fund. If the cupboard is bare and the employee does not receive the following amounts, he may claim them from the Fund (up to £130 a week in each case). The Fund itself, of course, receives extra money from all employers to cover its new obligations.

These rights apply to the following debts, owed by an insolvent employer to his unfortunate employee:

1 Arrears of pay for up to 8 weeks.
2 Pay in lieu of notice.
3 Holiday pay (up to 6 weeks).
4 Basic award of compensation for unfair dismissal.
5 Reasonable reimbursement of fee or premium paid by apprentice or articled clerk.

310 Claim for preferential debt

I am owed the following:
(a) . . . .
(b) . . . .
(c) . . . .

I claim the above as preferential debts.

If the company/firm does not have sufficient assets to cover the foregoing, then I claim the same and each of the same from the Redundancy Fund.

In addition, I claim the following items under Section 64, which do not rank for preferential treatment:

(1) . . . .
(2) . . . .
(3) . . . .

NOTE:

1   The above letter should be addressed to the officially appointed Receiver of the company, who will give the necessary forms to be completed and returned. If there is no Receiver appointed, or where no reply has been received within 6 months, applications should be made to the Secretary of State for Employment through the local office of the Department of Employment.

2   The employee who believes that he has rights which are not being accorded to him (or which are in doubt) under either of these sections should consult his association or trade union and/or its solicitor or his own.

Chapter 33

Itemised pay statements

An employee must be told in writing not merely how much he is entitled to receive but also its breakdown. This rule avoids disputes. It enables employees to study, to consider, and if necessary, to challenge the amounts paid — and to make these challenges either personally or through a trade union.

311 Itemised pay statement — Board to Company Secretary

I have received complaints from the . . . Union, that pay statements received by its members who are employed by our company, are not fully itemised. Please would you ensure that this situation is rectified as we do not want any difficulties with the law.

312 Individual request for itemised pay statement

I regret that the payments of salary and commission which I have been receiving are accompanied only by a slip setting out the net total. I would be very grateful if I could in future receive itemised pay statements, as required by law. I hope that this will not prove a nuisance for the accounts department, but will enable me to check in a proper manner as to the make-up of my earnings from the company.

My thanks in anticipation and kind regards.

313 Denial of failure to provide itemised statements

Thank you for your letter. I am sorry that your pay statement last week appears to have set out only the sum paid — But I am assured by the accounts department that this is a rare exception to the general rule. Our pay statements are itemised and we will do our best to ensure that your earnings are sufficiently detailed in future.

With best wishes.

Chapter 34

Time off work

When is an employee entitled as of right to time off work — with or without pay? How are the statutory rights, as explained by the Time Off Work Code, working in practice? And how are these affected by *The Employment Act, 1980?*

An employee remains entitled to such time off work as may be reasonable in all the circumstances of the case:

1   *For public duties* — such as those of a JP, school governor, local councillor or member of a Statutory Authority. An employer is not required by law to pay the employee when he is off work for this reason.

2   When an employee is made *redundant,* he is entitled to reasonable time off work at his normal pay in order to seek *(a)* alternative work and/or *(b)* training for such work.

3   *A trade union official* may claim paid time off work for trade union duties. These include not only duties in connection with collective bargaining but those 'concerned with industrial relations with his employer or any associated employer or employee' — plus training for such duties.

4   *An expectant mother* is now (thanks to the 1980 Act) entitled to reasonable time off work without loss of normal pay, to attend upon a doctor or midwife for *pre-natal advice* and care. If required by her employer, she must produce a certificate of pregnancy and (after the first occasion) evidence of her appointment.

5   *A safety representative* is entitled to reasonable time off work for the carrying out of his duties (as laid down by the Health and Satety Regulations, Code and Guidance on Safety Representatives and Committees).

The ACAS Time Off Work Code expands the rules as they apply to trade union officials and members. For instance, an official, i.e. one who holds office in the union, should be given reasonable paid time off work: *(a)* for necessary meetings; *(b)* to represent members before Industrial Tribunals; *(c)* to inform new employees of the union's activities; *(d)* to consult with colleague officials in the same or an associated company, i.e. one in the group — although there is no requirement that the employer should pay travel expenses (these are frequently the subject of negotiation).

The Code also suggests that it may be in the interests of management as well as of unions that election meetings and those concerned with possible industrial action should be well attended. In practice, management almost always recognises that it is in their interests to achieve a maximum attendance. Election meetings (and sometimes others) are now more often than not held in working hours and without loss of pay, by members as well as by officials. This remarkable evolution is having and will continue to have far more effect upon union meetings than the 1980 Act provisions entitling unions to claim the cost of secret ballots from public funds (see Chapter 27).

314   Tribunal threat

I write to confirm that I have been invited to accept an appointment as a Justice of the Peace for the County of . . . . Unfortunately, you have refused to give me sufficient time off to sit on the bench — and I am writing to ask that you be good enough to reconsider this decision.

As a loyal and enthusiastic member of your management team, I certainly have no wish to create any difficulties, but if you persist in your refusal I will be left with no alternative than to bring proceedings before an industrial tribunal on the ground that the time off is reasonable in the circumstances. I do hope that this step will not be necessary and look forward to hearing from you.

315   Threat rejected

Thank you for your letter. We are always prepared to give our employees reasonable time off in order to attend to public duties, and there is no need to invoke the law nor, still less, to threaten proceedings before an industrial tribunal in order to encourage us to comply with our moral and legal obligation. However, I must point out that we are only bound to grant such time off as is reasonable in the circumstances; in your case, it is wholly unreasonable that you should have a day a week/fortnight *(or as the case may be)* off from work because your absence would gravely affect the operation of our office/plant/works/of the team which you head/manage.

We have reconsidered the situation with care, as you requested. I regret that we cannot change our decision.

However, if you would like to discuss the matter further so that we may explain our reasoning in more detail than is possible in a letter, please do not hesitate to contact me.

316   Redundant employee – time off for interview

I confirm that you are attending interviews for alternative jobs as follows:

1 . . . .
2 . . . .
3 . . . .

Please let your immediate supervisor know how long you will need to be away in order to attend those interviews and time off will be given. We wish you the best of luck in your endeavours to find other work.

317   Redundant – training time off refused

I have carefully considered your application for seven days' time off in order to train for alternative work. As we are attempting to run down the department as slowly as possible and to keep our team together for the purpose, it would not be reasonable to give you the time off you seek. However, if you will ask your shop steward to see me I will be pleased to discuss with him the possibility of making some alternative arrangement.

318   Time off – trade union duties – agreed

Further to our conversation, I am happy to confirm that the company is agreeable to your having time off, as you request, during working hours for the following of your duties as an official of the . . . Union:

(a) . . . .
(b) . . . .
(c) . . . .

May I take this opportunity of saying how much the company appreciates the happy relationship which has so long existed between your union and its officials and the manage-

ment — to which I would add that I personally am delighted
in your appointment/renewed election as convener/works
chairman (or as the case may be).

NOTE:
*1 It will be a matter of judgement, in each case, whether it is better
to confirm arrangements in writing or to leave them with the flexibility
which an oral arrangement (like the unwritten British constitution) may
produce.*

*2   The final paragraph — with its emphasis on personal relationships —
is infinitely variable but extremely important in an area in which,
whatever the formal agreements, personal relationships will decide
whether or not industrial relations are satisfactory. It follows that you
should not hesitate to make equivalent additions to any of these
precedents, which will personalise a letter — in any event when there
are words of appreciation or goodwill to be set out. Bear in mind, too,
that letters of this sort are likely to be passed higher up the union line,
so the effect of your words not merely on the official concerned but
on his branch, area or national body should be borne in mind.*

319   Unreasonable time off — refused

We have given very careful consideration to your request
for time off during working hours in order to . . ./for the
purposes of . . . .
Having had careful regard to the terms of the Code of
Practice and especially to the problems which will be created
for your colleagues/in your operation (*or as the case may be*)
as a result of your absence, we cannot consider the request
to be reasonable.
However: As you know this company is always ready,
willing and anxious to assist, in so far as it can — and if you
would call on me, at my office, perhaps we could sort out
some mutually agreeable compromise.
With best wishes.

NOTE:
*Once again, remember that this letter may go forward — and if it is not
couched in a friendly and kindly terms, it could cause an unnecessary
row. Conversely, even a refusal may be laced with goodwill and
suggested possible compromise.*

320 Training time – agreed

Thank you for your letter concerning the proposal that
our Mr Brown should attend a training course organised by
. . . at . . . on the . . . (from the . . . to the . . .). As you have
specifically asked that he should attend; as we agreed that
the course is relevant to the carrying out of his industrial
relation duties; and as the course is approved by the TUC
(or: laid on by your union), we shall be happy to arrange for
Mr Brown to attend. I am further pleased to confirm that he
will receive his normal remuneration while attending the
course.

When you are next in this vicinity, do please call by for a
chat. There are a number of matters which I would like to
discuss with you.

NOTE:
*Where you are agreeing to a request or making a concession, by all
means use this as an opportunity to invite further discussion – perhaps
on thornier problems.*

321 Training time – unreasonable

Thank you for your letter concerning the 10-day course on
industrial safety, organised for officials of your union who are
also safety representatives under the Health and Safety at Work
Act.

While we congratulate you on the course and on the
obvious thoroughness with which this vital topic is to be
covered, we would like to draw your attention to the extensive safety training facilities which are already provided by
the company. These have included, during the past few
months, the following:
(a) . . . .
(b) . . . .
(c) . . . .
In the circumstances – and also bearing in mind the difficulties which the absence of Mr . . . would create in the office/
department/section, we do not feel that we can reasonably
agree to his being away for such an extended period.

However, we have discussed with him the possibility of his
going on a rather more intensive course, if you arrange one in

the future — so do please keep us in touch. We are sure that you, like Mr . . . , will understand that while we must decline your invitation to send him on this particular course, we in no way underestimate the importance of the training work which your union is arranging — nor our appreciation for your efforts in the field of industrial safety.

With best wishes.

NOTE:

Before replying to the letter, you will have discussed the matter with the individual official. Any indication that he has accepted the decision should be included in the letter. If he is dissatisfied, try the following:

322   Refusal — discussions continuing

We have had preliminary discussions with your Mr Jones, concerning the request that he should attend a 10-day industrial safety course provided by your union. Our initial view is that the course is too extensive for the particular requirements of our business — in which not only the accident record is excellent but the dangers are not great. And we also have a special regard to the instruction and training which is already provided and which already includes:

(a) . . . .
(b) . . . .
(c) . . . .

However, Mr Jones is not happy about our decision and as we regard safety training as being of paramount importance, we are having further discussions on the matter with Mr Jones/ with our Safety Committee and with Mr Jones. I shall be in touch with you again shortly.

323   Time off for trade union activity — agreed

Thank you for your letter concerning time off for your members, Mr . . . , Mr . . . and Mr . . . , in connection with activities for your trade union. We are agreeable to the arrangements you suggest; we regard these as in accordance with good industrial relations and with the Code of Practice; and we would only add the following cautions;

1   Time off must be confined to . . . .

2   We are sure that your members will bear in mind the following difficulties which may arise because of their specific work . . . .

3   . . . .

With kind regards.

324   Trade union activities – refusal

We have given most careful and anxious consideration to your request that Mr . . . , who is a member of your union, should have time off for . . . .

Unfortunately, we are unable to agree to this request for the following reasons:

1   The activities referred to themselves consist of industrial action (in contemplation of furtherance of a trade dispute).

2   Your trade union is not certified as 'independent'.

3   The time off is in excess of that which is 'reasonable', having regard to the relevant provisions of the Code of Practice.

4   To agree to your proposition would result in a wholly disproportionate disruption in the work of the firm/ department/section.

We are sorry that we cannot comply with your request on this occasion, but we would be happy to meet you, if you wish, to see whether some mutually acceptable compromise can be arrived at.

NOTE:
Have you discussed the position with ACAS, before sending the refusal?

325   Local councillor – refusal

We are indeed in favour of our employees taking an active part in public life. But we do not consider that – having regard to the nature of your job and the responsibilities you bear – it would be possible for you to find that compatible with the active work required of a local councillor. Naturally, it is entirely a matter for you whether or not you stand for office. But we cannot guarantee to give you time off in order

to attend committee meetings and the like. We shall be pleased
to help in any way we can — but we must emphasise that
yours is one of those positions in which availability is vital.

326   Threat of complaint

I was most concerned to receive your letter, refusing to
grant me time off from work in order that I may carry out
the duties of a local councillor. I fully appreciate the necessity
for my services to be available and of course the company's
needs would have priority. But I would most respectfully
ask that you reconsider your decision in this matter, not merely
because of the law and the rights given to employees to make
complaints to industrial tribunals in such cases, but in order
to preserve the excellent repute of the company and the good
industrial relations which have proved so important.

I shall be most pleased to come to discuss this matter with
you or any of your colleagues if necessary. But you will
appreciate the importance of this request to me.

NOTE:
*Letters of this sort have to be written with the greatest of tact — but if
the threat of industrial tribunal proceedings (however veiled, as in the
above precedent) leads to 'constructive' dismissal, appropriate letters
are provided in Chapter 9.*

327   Pre-natal care

Thank you for your note, informing me that you are
expecting a baby. My congratulations to you. I would be
grateful if you would call on me so that we can discuss
your maternity rights and proposed arrangements.

Meanwhile, I note that you wish time off work for
ante-natal care and we will, of course, be pleased to make
appropriate arrangements. Please let me/your immediate
superior have a copy of your Certificate of Pregnancy and
a note of confirmation of your proposed appointments and
I am sure that mutually convenient arrangements can be
made.

"IT WAS A VERY SAD CASE – HE WAS TRYING TO RETRIEVE A DRAFT LETTER AND FELL INTO HIS OWN SHREDDER — ! "

Part Five

HEALTH AND SAFETY
AT WORK

Chapter 35

Introduction

A cynical old MP once advised a new recruit to the Commons: 'Never do good by stealth!'

Under the Health and Safety at Work Act, it is not enough to be good. You must, if necessary, be in a position to prove your virtue. If you are prosecuted for an offence, your defence will almost certainly be: 'I took such steps as were reasonably practicable in the circumstances'. In that case, the Act says: 'Prove it'.

This Part contains samples of the letters which you are most likely to need, when coping with the Act and attempting to avoid trouble. Use and adapt the precedents to suit your circumstances and you will go a long way towards keeping out of trouble.

That is the negative side. The positive is more important. Suppose that your employee refuses to follow the safety rules which you have laid down for his protection. By all means speak to the offender and try to induce him to mend his ways. If that fails, after appropriate consultations with shop stewards or workers' representatives put your complaint into writing. In that way you will not merely protect yourself if you have to prove that you used 'all reasonable persuasion and propaganda' to induce the employee to comply with the rules. With luck, the fact that you have taken the trouble to make a written complaint may embed itself sufficiently into the mind of your employee to induce him to be more careful in future.

The Act repeatedly demands that employers take steps that are 'reasonably practicable'. Reasonableness is the key to avoiding trouble. Reasonable care is (once again) essential when using these drafts. They are provided in the knowledge that if properly used, they can avoid headaches, accidents — and, potentially, heavy penalties.

Finally, Section 2(3) of the Act requires you to prepare and whenever necessary to revise written statements of your Health and Safety policy, organisation and arrangements and to make these statements available for your employees.

Chapter 36

Health and safety statements

The Act requires that every employee be provided with a health and safety statement. This falls into three parts:

1 *Policy* No problem — the employer's policy is undoubtedly to give paramount importance to the health and safety of his employees at work.

2 *Organisation* You cannot set out your organisation unless you have one. Who is in charge of safety in your business? What part is each level of management expected to play? Have you set up any (and if so what) safety committees?

3 *Arrangements* Each employee is entitled to know what arrangements you have made to protect him. The statement should identify the main hazards faced by the particular employee at his work and state how to avoid them.

Usually, one statement of policy and organisation will cover most if not all employees, even in the largest concern. Statements of arrangements, though, often have to be individual. The Act requires (for the first time) that employers apply their minds to the dangers involved in each job.

The Health and Safety Commission's guidance document on safety statements is set out in full in Appendix 4.

Next time your factory inspector pays a visit, his first question may be: 'Where is your safety statement?' If you have no statement, you are breaking the law. If your statement is defective, you are asking for trouble. If your statement sets out satisfactory organisation and arrangements and you do not adhere to them, then what defence could you possibly have to a charge that you have failed to take 'such steps as were reasonably practicable' to protect your employees, in accordance with the procedures which you yourself have set out as necessary?

328   Request for statement

I do not appear to have received a written statement of the company's safety policy, organisation and arrangements. I would be very grateful if this could be made available to me at your early convenience.

329   To inspector – statement under preparation

I confirm that the safety statement for our new plant at . . . is under preparation. Thank you for agreeing that it is better for us to take a little more time in order to ensure that statement is first class, rather than rushing through a document which may be less effective.

NOTE:
Factory inspectors are very reasonable – and if a statement is genuinely under preparation, there will rarely be problems.

330   Denial that statement defective

The company's safety statement does indeed set out not only our policy and organisation, but also our safety arrangements. We have to strike a balance in connection with the arrangements. While we must identify the main hazards faced by each person in his job (and we have done so), we must not put in so much that the statement will not be read or understood.

Anyway, we shall be pleased to discuss your comments both with you and with the factory inspector, so that if we are wrong in our view, revised statements can be provided very swiftly.

Thank you for drawing this matter to our attention – and with our best wishes.

Chapter 37

Duties to employees

'It shall be the duty of every employer to ensure, so far as is reasonably practicable, the health, safety and welfare at work of all his employees.' Section 2 of the Health and Safety at Work Act codifies, strengthens extends — and moves further into the law of crime — the bulk of the civil law on health and safety at work. Into the bargain, it adds 'welfare' — a word which the Act does not define.

Therefore, it is now a criminal offence, punishable at worst by two years imprisonment and/or an unlimited fine — *not* to ensure, so far as is reasonably practicable, the health, safety and welfare at work of all your employees.

The Section breaks down the duties (again, in most cases) mirroring the civil law by saying that they include the following specific duties: That of:

> '*(a)* the provision and maintenance of *plant and systems of work* that are, so far as is reasonably practicable, safe and without risk to health;

> '*(b)* arrangements for ensuring, so far as is reasonably practicable, safety and absence of risk to health in connection with the *use, handling, storage and transport* of articles and substances;

> '*(c)* the provision of such *information, training, instruction and supervision* as is necessary to ensure, so far as is reasonably practicable, the health and safety at work of his employees;

> '*(d)* so far as is reasonably practicable as regards any *place of work* under the employer's control, the maintenance of it in a condition that is safe and without risk to health and the provision and maintenance of means of access to and egress from it that are safe and without such risks;

> '*(e)* the provision and maintenance of a *working environment* for his employees that is, so far as is reasonably practicable, safe, without risk to health, and adequate as regards facilities and arrangements for their *welfare* at work.'

The employer, then, is not his employees' insurer. The fact that someone is injured while at work — or suffers ill health as a result of his work — would not of itself make the employer criminally liable, any more than it can of itself make him (or his insurers) liable to pay compensation at civil law. The employer who has taken all such steps as are 'reasonably practicable' to protect his employees and to comply with the law will be in the clear. Unfortunately for the employer (or his manager or executive), though, Section 40 of the Act provides that it is 'for the accused to prove' that he took such steps as were 'reasonably practicable'.

If, for example, you wish to prove that you could not reasonably have been expected to do more than you did, for the protection of your employees, then the burden of proving that contention rests upon your bowed shoulders.

How can an employer discharge this unusual burden? He may be able to give oral evidence (personally or by calling on a colleague, a subordinate or even a superior). Yet the spoken word is always suspect — if only because the human memory is so fallible. The best evidence is always in writing.

Or take Section 3, which (again) codifies the law — this time on an employer's duty *not* to his own employees but to anyone else who may be affected by his work — a visitor, a neighbour, a member of the general public.

'It shall be the duty of every employer to conduct his undertaking in such a way as to ensure, so far as is reasonably practicable, that persons not in his employment who may be affected thereby are not thereby exposed to risks to their health or safety.'

Once again, the Act uses those crucial words: 'So far as is reasonably practicable'.

A visitor — perhaps the employee of a contractor or of a sub contractor . . . a child, brought in by a driver (your own or that of your supplier) . . . a representative or a buyer . . . is injured on your premises. The Inspector's attention is drawn to your activities and you are questioned about your safety organisation and the steps taken to protect that visitor. Could you prove that you had done that which a reasonably prudent occupier of premises would and could and should have done, in the circumstances, for the safety of visitors?

Or suppose that the employee or the visitor is injured through his own failure to comply with your safety rules or procedures. It will not be enough for you to tell the Court: 'I warned him. . . . The protective clothing or equipment was available. . . . The system was a good one. . .'. You would have to prove — positively — that you took all reasonably practicable steps to persuade and to propagandise the employee into making use of the procedures or systems, the equipment or clothing, provided by you.

Once again (as always) the finest formula for the avoidance of trouble with the law lies in the pen in your hands, the pencil poised by your secretary, the dictating machine – in the appropriate letters, duly recorded, copied and filed.

To preserve your own safety from the dire dangers of prosecution and punishment, you must now consider (if you have not already done so):

1   Does your organisation need reviewing or tightening up, to cope with the requirements of the Act?

2   Do your employees and colleagues know of your system – and are they instructed and trained in how to operate it? And

3   Have you the necessary precedents, to be used or adapted to suit those most worthy of twin purposes: The protection from harm of your employees and of others 'affected' by your 'undertaking' – and the protection of your company, firm and/or yourself from trouble under the Act?

*   *   *

331   Instructions to department to tighten up safety procedures

The Board has been disturbed to receive a number of complaints regarding the lack of adequate safety procedures in your plant/office/workshop. Bearing in mind the heavy burden of care placed on employers and their managers by the Health and Safety at Work Act – and the potentially stringent criminal penalties which may result from non-compliance – I must insist that you take immediate steps to ensure, so far as is reasonably practicable, that those of our employees who come under your management are not submitted to unnecessary risk to their health or safety.

In particular, but without prejudice to the generality of the foregoing, please take immediate steps to deal with the following:

1   The failure of employees in . . . to wear their safety helmets/spectacles/protective clothing.

2   The removal by employees of guards from lathes/ machinery.

3   The general untidy state of the . . . resulting in obstructions in the gangways.

4   . . . .

Please formally acknowledge receipt of this letter and let me have your assurance that these matters will be dealt with, without delay.

NOTE:

1   With full responsibility placed on those at fault, and with directors and managers at every level personally responsible in law, it is vital to be able to show, if necessary, that you were not at fault. The above letter makes an excellent start to that worthy end.

2   As usual, getting a signature from the recipient has two useful functions. It emphasises to him the importance placed by you on compliance with the rules in general and your requirements in particular; and it avoids any possibility of doubt as to whether or not your letter was both written and received.

332   Report from manager

Thank you for your letter concerning safety measures in my department/office/workshop. I fully recognise that the system is far from perfect. However, as I have explained to you, and through you, I hope, to the Board — on several occasions, it is not possible for me to make other than marginal improvements, for the following reasons:

1   In order to avoid the continued risk of backstrains, we must either be provided with more mechanical lifting equipment or with additional help.
2   In order to obviate the risk with the . . . machine, it would have to be replaced by a . . ./adapted by . . . .
3   To induce my workforce to make proper use of their safety helmets/equipment, I require the full time service of a safety officer/adequate resources made available for safety training.

I am as concerned as the Board with the safety of our employees, and would be very happy to discuss these matters with you. I fully appreciate the importance of the Health and Safety at Work Act and I am doing all that I can — but I do hope that the Board will now give consideration to the need for additional resources to be devoted to the health and safety aspects of our work — and I look forward to hearing from you.

NOTE:

1   As with master, so with man — writing counts.

2   Just as it is possible for the buck to be passed downward — so it may also go up the line. Further precedents in Chapter 53.

Chapter 38

When the employee causes the hazard

Sometimes death or injury at work is due to the fault of management; sometimes because employees will not co-operate — on some building sites, for instance, it is said that workers only don their safety helmets when it starts to rain.

How far, then, can you be held criminally liable under the new Act, if your employee fails or refuses to follow the safety rules? And can *they* be held personally to blame?

The Act not only requires employers to achieve high standards of health, safety and welfare for the benefit of employees, but it also demands that employees shall cooperate in the carrying out of the safety and health measures. Duties placed on them by existing legislation are extended.

Every employer must do what he can to ensure that his employees know of and follow the rules; that all reasonable 'persuasion and propaganda' is used to encourage and persuade them to take proper care of themselves and others; and only if the procedures are sufficiently clear and established is the employer himself likely to avoid prosecution and punishment if an accident occurs or even if the inspector considers that the Act is being flouted.

Here are some suggested procedures, designed to put the maximum fair pressure on employees to look after their own safety and so to avoid accidents to them and their colleagues, and (at the same time) to fend off either civil or criminal liability which may otherwise fall on you. Check this list; keep it by you; follow the suggestions — and you should keep out of trouble.

1   Check that your employee's *system* of working is safe. When have accidents occurred in the past and why and how can they be eliminated? Are you satisfied that all the equipment or machinery provided for the use of your employees is really adequate and satisfactory?

2   Is your system of training, instruction and supervision beyond reproach — both as regards new and existing employees? And can you, if necessary, prove that system? Is it sufficiently documented?

3 Have you won the approval and co-operation of your employees, individually and collectively, to your safety procedures? Is yours a large enterprise with trade union membership or a staff association? If so, have you consulted the organisation or committee concerned so as to ensure that your employees fully understand and approve of your safety, health and welfare set up — and have you sought their help in the enforcement of the rules? (*Note:* You must comply with the regulations requiring consultation with appointed representatives of recognised trade unions. These 'safety watchdogs' do not bear personal liability arising out of their duty in that capacity — but, if properly harnessed — can greatly help keep the business safe and hence keep management out of trouble with the law.)

4 You need a system separate from your normal disciplinary and dismissal arrangements to deal with employees who fail or refuse to follow safety rules or procedures. Suggestions:

(a) Speak personally to the employee who is not complying; emphasise the importance of his doing so; warn him of the consequences of failure.

(b) Refer the employee to Sections 7 and 8 of the Act, which require him to take proper care for his own safety and not to interfere with safety equipment and the like — and which render him liable to the same penalties for breach as the employing company or its managers.

(c) If the first effort fails, try again — this time in company with a fellow employee (if union representatives are involved, try to bring the shop steward with you); and this time or the next deliver a written warning; if possible, get a signed duplicate or receipt.

(d) If danger (actual or potential) is being caused not merely to the employee concerned but to others, then emphasise the unfairness of the conduct.

(e) If dangerous behaviour persists, consider dismissal. Factors to be taken into account include:
   (i) The nature and extent of the danger — to the employee himself and to others.
   (ii) The effect of dismissal on good industrial relations.
   (iii) The employee's length of service, degree of responsibility and general conduct. And
   (iv) All the circumstances of the case which might make the dismissal 'unfair', so as to give the employee a right to compensation.

(f) Deliver second written warning, preferably by hand — and once

again, if possible, accompanied by a workers' representative. This warning should state:

(i) If applicable, that further non-compliance will leave you with no alternative other than to dismiss; and in any event

(ii) Drawing attention to previous warnings; to the rules under the Act; and stating that no responsibility can in any event be accepted by the company in the event of the risk giving rise to injury, loss or damage to the employee. (Note: This disclaimer may be of help in a civil action, but it will not necessarily free the employers from criminal liability. But it does emphasise the seriousness with which the employee's misconduct is regarded).

(g) Consider whether your equipment or system of work requires redesign or change — perhaps to remove employees' objections or so as to make it impossible for the machine or equipment to be used in the dangerous manner complained of. *Typical example:* A noisy operation — and operatives who refuse to wear 'ear defenders'. Can the noise be reduced sufficiently to obviate the need for the ear muffs?

An employer will not necessarily wish to use the above steps in the suggested order. These should be adapted, as best suited to his business and circumstances. But if he follows the rules, it can hardly be said that he did not take 'reasonable steps' to influence his employee. In the event of an accident, he would probably avoid liability — the employee's contributory negligence would be 100 per cent. The employee knew of the dangers; and the employer (or his insurers) could prove their case — so that the responsibility would rest on the employee.

Equally: If the employer is prosecuted either under existing legislation or under the new Act, his defences would be well prepared.

Above all: The Act is not designed to produce actions or prosecutions but to avoid accidents. These procedures will help.

333   To trade union representative seeking cooperation

As you know, we are very concerned with the failure of some of your members to wear their safety helmets/use equipment provided for their safety. We appreciate that in the past, the rules have often been treated in a very relaxed way. But clearly this is no longer possible − both as a result of the Health and Safety at Work Act and also (and especially) because of the suffering caused through accidents, many of which could have been avoided, had the rules been complied with.

In the circumstances − and knowing how concerned you are with the health and safety of your members − I would be very happy if you would meet me [Mr . . . , our safety officer, and myself] so that we can discuss the best ways to persuade people to take proper care of themselves.

Looking forward to hearing from you and with all best wishes.

NOTE:
It is essential to obtain union co-operation − and this must be done on the basis of persuasion, in the interests of members. Any aggressive approach − such as the unexplained quoting of Section 7 − is likely to produce a hostile response.

334   To shop steward − for personal approach to member

I have/our safety officer has/spoken to John White on several occasions, because of his failure to wear his safety boots/his insistence upon removing the guard from his machine/the slipshod way in which he risks danger to himself and to others by removing the guard from his lathe. Obviously, it is essential for his safety/and for the safety of others that he comply with the rules − and I am sure that a word from you would be of enormous help. Please would you let me know whether you think it would be best for you to tackle Mr White personally or whether you would prefer to do so together with me; Perhaps you would drop by and see me in my office as soon as possible about this.

With best wishes.

335   To shop steward − please accompany me

Once again, I ask for your kind cooperation in connection with a serious infringement of the safety rules − this time by your member, Mr Jim Smith. I tackled him last week about his continued failure to wear his safety mask — he will be lucky if he is not blinded as a result and anyway there is now a serious breach of the Protection of Eyes Regulations and of the Health and Safety at Work Act.

In the circumstances, I would be grateful if you would come with me to see this man, so that between us we may persuade him to mend his ways — and to retain his eyesight!

I shall be along to see you about this, later in the day.

With very best wishes.

336 First written warning — by hand

In spite of our conversation last Tuesday in which you promised that you would never again leave the guard off your machine, I was most concerned to observe this morning that you have again infringed the same important safety rule. This rule is designed, of course, for your own protection. But the company is bound to enforce that rule, not only so as to keep you safe but also so as to protect both the company and indeed you from possible prosecution under the Factories Act and/or the Health and Safety at Work Act.

I am writing to you personally as an indication of the seriousness with which this matter is regarded — and to ask that you never again cause unnecessary danger to yourself by removing the guard from your machine.

I am delivering this letter to you by hand [in company with your shop steward] — please sign the duplicate/carbon/receipt, which will acknowledge that you have received, read and understood this letter.

337 Record of warnings — to manager

I must inform you that I have had to warn Roger Price for not wearing his safety spectacles (*or as the case may be*), on the following occasions, each of which is recorded in a note on his file:

    1 . . . .
    2 . . . .
    3 . . . .

May I suggest that you now consider what further action might be taken?

338   Request to employee to sign record

I have now had to warn you on four occasions (on the following dates: . . .), as a result of your failure or refusal to wear your safety spectacles. I have therefore reported the matter to the personnel officer. Please sign carbon copy of this letter to show that you have duly received it.

NOTE:

As usual, the law does not require the giving of a signature, but it has two effects: It proves beyond doubt that the document was received; and it emphasises to the recipient the importance that you place on the letter.

If the employee refuses to sign, a note should be made on the carbon accordingly – and the carbon should be placed on the file. (See also Chapter 41 – on receipts and acknowledgements.)

Chapter 39

An employee's duty to take care of himself

Section 7 of the Health and Safety at Work Act:
  'It shall be the duty of every employee while at work —
    (a) To take reasonable care for the health and safety of himself and of persons who may be affected by his acts or omissions at work; and
    (b) As regards any duty or requirement imposed on his employer or any other person by or under any of the relevant statutory provisions, to co-operate with him so far as is necessary to enable that duty or requirement to be performed or complied with.'

So an employee is criminally liable if he does not 'take reasonable care' for his own health and safety at work and that of his colleagues or workmates. And he must 'co-operate' with his employers, so as to enable or help them to comply with their statutory 'duties or requirements', under the Factories Act, the Offices, Shops and Railway Premises Act, the Health and Safety at Work Act, the Explosives Act, the Alkali and Works Regulations, the Nuclear Installations Act, the Mines and Quarries Acts . . . etc., etc., and all regulations made under them.

In addition, Section 8 reads: 'No person shall intentionally or recklessly interfere with or misuse anything provided in the interests of health, safety or welfare in pursuance of any of the relevant statutory provisions'. Luddites, beware! And note: The Act uses the words 'intentionally or recklessly', rather than the (more difficult to prove) 'wilfully', used in the Factories Act.

These duties are real — but, in practice, unlikely to be enforced through criminal prosecution, other than as a last resort or where there is full union backing. No one wants to turn this Act into a second Industrial Relations Act, regarded as a club to beat the workers. If the Act is to be used to best effect to reduce industrial accidents, then the co-operation of workers and their organisations is essential. Still, it is fair to draw the attention of employees and their representatives to Sections 7 and 8.

It is not wise, though, to threaten prosecutions which will not occur or to cry industrial wolf by warnings to workers of prosecutions which may produce precisely the opposite effect to that intended — to frighten them away from responsibility and to prevent the workforce from regarding health and safety as at least one matter on which they and management can unite their efforts.

The following brief letters are variations of letters in the previous Chapter. They may be used on their own, but they may also be included in warning letters (as in the preceding and next chapters).

* * *

339   Employee may be prosecuted

I was sorry to hear that your foreman, Mr Black, had to remind you once again that the law requires the wearing of protective goggles or spectacles, when working at an abrasive wheel/lathe. Please would you ensure that you never again fail to wear your protective gear.

Please bear in mind that the Health and Safety at Work Act places a positive duty on employees themselves to take reasonable care for their own safety. Failure to do so may lead to prosecution — and while we are primarily concerned with the protection of your eyes, we must point out that if the Inspector were to note your breach of the law, you could well be prosecuted.

340   Danger to mates

By failing to follow the safety rules — and in particular, by removing the guard from your machine and allowing swarf to accumulate in the gangway — you are causing a danger to your colleagues. You are also in breach of the Health and Safety at Work Act and if this breach is noticed by the Factory Inspector, you would be liable to prosecution.

To protect your colleagues as well as yourself, please do ensure that there is no future breach of the company's safety regulations.

341   Simple warning

By your dangerous behaviour in removing the guard from

your machine (*or as the case may be*), you have not only caused a hazard to yourself/and to your colleagues, but you have been in clear breach of Section 7 of the Health and Safety at Work Act. The Act, of course, is a criminal statute and offenders against its rules may be prosecuted.

Please do not give any further cause for complaint on this score.

Chapter 40

Further and final warnings*

The time must come when an employer must lay down the law —
especially the law on health and safety at work — and must do so in
writing. Oral requests and demands for co-operation in health and
safety measures have failed? The first written warning (as in the previous
Chapter) has been given? Then comes the great problem: What do we
do if the employee continues with his wrongful behaviour?

If the danger is sufficiently great — to the employee or to others —
then you may have to threaten dismissal. But this threat should never
be made idly or if you are not prepared if necessary to carry it out. So
before threatening the ultimate deterrent, consider:

1   Would it be 'fair' to dismiss in all the circumstances of the case?
2   Are you seeking to make an example out of one person when the
    practice is widespread?
3   Have you really tried all reasonable persuasion and propaganda to
    induce the employee to comply — so as to treat dismissal as the
    very last resort?
4   What would be the results of the dismissal on good industrial
    relations?

There are, then, two sorts of second or further written warnings.
Some contain a threat of dismissal — others do not. A variety of such
letters now follows.

*   *   *

342   Second warning — simple

I have been told that in spite of my letter to you dated . . .
you are still, on occasion, removing the guard from your
machine. I hope that this information is incorrect because —
as I both explained and wrote to you — any further infringement of the rules could lead to serious consequences.

*For general 'dismissal' letters, see Part 2.

343   Regrets at breach of undertaking

As a result of my letter to you dated . . . , you undertook
to comply in future with our safety rules and in particular
. . . . This you have failed to do and I must now warn you
that if you again cause danger to yourself/and to others in
this way, disciplinary action will have to be taken.

NOTE:
*You are, of course, not bound to state the nature of the disciplinary
action which you have in mind. A generalised warning not only gives
scope for the employee's imagination but leaves your options open.
However, if you propose taking a specific step, then it may be preferable to say so. Thus:*

344   Suspension

Once again and in spite of my letter to you dated . . . , you
have seen fit to smoke in close proximity to inflammable
materials. This behaviour cannot be tolerated and unless I
receive your immediate assurance that there will be no further
repetition, I shall have no alternative other than to suspend
you for a period of a fortnight without pay, in accordance
with the company's rules. This letter is being delivered by
hand and I shall be glad if you will immediately call on me
in my office.

NOTE:
*If your disciplinary rules do not provide for suspension, do they need
revision? Clearly, the threatened action must be in accordance with
your contract with the employee concerned.*

345   Dismissal warning – safety

After repeated oral requests that you wear your safety
helmet/ear defenders, and in spite of my warning letter to
you dated . . . , you are continuing to ignore the safety rules
– which are, of course, designed to protect you. Especially
as a result of the Health and Safety at Work Act, it is not
possible for the company to ignore these breaches of rules
any longer. I must warn you that if you again fail to wear

your safety helmet/ear defenders, I shall feel bound to give
you your notice/terminate your employment.

I trust that you will now treat this matter very seriously
and that you will not put me in the position of having to take
this very unpleasant step.

Please sign the duplicate of this letter, so as to acknowledge
not only that you have received it but that you have understood the seriousness of the position.

346 Dismissal – danger to others

You have chosen to ignore the repeated requests of your
shop steward and myself that you keep the guard in place on
your lathe, so as to avoid causing danger not only to yourself
but to your work mates. You have not taken heed of the
warning contained in my letter dated ... – nor have you
complied with your repeated promises to obey the safety
rules. In the circumstances, I must now warn you that any
further breach of this rule – which, I repeat, is necessary both
for your safety and for that of other employees – will result
in my having to dismiss you.

As you know, dismissal is regarded in this company as an
absolutely last resort. We have all tried our best to persuade
you to co-operate in taking reasonable care of your own
health and safety and that of your colleagues – but so far we
have failed. We cannot permit any continued failure.

347 Protective clothing must be worn – or else

If employees do not wear protective clothing, they are
liable to suffer dermatitis – and we cannot guarantee that
they will not suffer serious personal injury in the long run.
As I explained to you in my letter dated ... , it is vital that
all employees wear the protective clothing provided – and
breach of this rule cannot be permitted.

In spite of that warning – and despite also the entreaties
of your shop steward/foreman/departmental manager – you
are still not wearing your gloves/coat/apron.

As you have ignored so many polite and friendly requests,
I am now forced to warn you that any further failure will
inevitably lead to your dismissal. I would be very sorry to

have to take such serious action — please do not remove my alternatives.

348   Forklift truck — driver warned

I have now warned you — both orally and in writing — of the dangers involved both for you and for your colleagues in the way in which you are handling your forklift truck. In particular:

1   You are riding on the truck, when it should be controlled only on foot.
2   You are manoeuvring the truck far too close to the edge of the dock.
3   . . . .
4   . . . .

As this behaviour is risking injury to yourself and/or to others, I must now warn you that any further breach of the rules will force me to give you your notice.

I would be very sorry to have to dismiss you — and I hope that you will now appreciate the seriousness of the position and comply with the rules — not merely because the Health and Safety at Work Act so requires, but for the sake of your own safety and that of others who work with you.

349   Pallets not carefully stacked

If a stack of pallets were to fall, injury or even death could easily result. I have had to warn you — both by word of mouth and in writing — of the slovenly way in which you have sometimes been stacking.

As you know, I have now received a complaint about your stacking from Mr . . . . The Board have therefore instructed me to refer to my letter to you dated . . . , complaining about your carelessness; and to warn you that any further complaint will lead to your dismissal.

350   Further infringements at own risk

It is true that your continued failure to wear your safety mask endangers only your own safety. But you are in breach of Section 7 of the Health and Safety at Work Act and are liable to be prosecuted; you are taking risks which are wholly unnecessary and which could bring disaster to you and to your family; and because you are such a valued and long serving employee, your behaviour worries us very much.

Once again — and repeating what I wrote in my letter to you dated . . . I must ask you to comply with the safety rules. I must also warn you that the company can accept no responsibility whatsoever, if you continue to behave in such a reckless and dangerous manner.

Please sign the enclosed receipt to show that you understand the situation.

NOTE:
The fact that you said no responsibility is accepted will not, of course, free you from such responsibility. In civil law, there should be no problem — you have taken all reasonable steps to persuade and to propagandise your employee into complying with the law. But under the Health and Safety at Work Act, the question will still remain: Have you taken such steps as are 'reasonably practicable' to avoid danger — and if so, can you prove it? This letter should do the trick — provided, of course, that the practice complained of is not sufficiently dangerous. A balance must be struck between the degree of danger and the employer's wish not to dismiss the employee.

351 Too dangerous to tolerate

I am sorry — but we cannot permit you to continue . . . . This practice is far too dangerous, for your colleagues as well as for yourself. I repeat the warning given to you in my letter dated . . . . But this time I must add a further warning: If at any time your conduct is repeated, I shall have no alternative other than to terminate your employment.

352 To union — asking for support in dismissal

Whatever our differences on other matters — and I am happy to think that these are not great — we share the same concern for the health and safety of those of your members who work for our company. It is therefore with great regret that I must tell you that your efforts and ours to induce your members to use their protective clothing/not to remove guards from machines have failed. Because the practice is so dangerous – and especially in view of the Health and Safety at Work Act and the penalties contained in it – we shall have no alternative other than to dismiss those members who are risking their own lives and limbs – and those of their colleagues/ workmates if the practice continues. We have now sent out final warnings. This letter is to keep you in touch; to ask that you renew your efforts to persuade your members to take care; and to thank you for your support in our efforts to reduce to an absolute minimum the toll taken by accidents in our enterprise.

With best wishes.

353   Warning to all employees

I am writing to you – and to all other fitters/operatives/ shop floor workers/furnace men (or as the case may be), to remind you of the grave danger caused to you/and to your colleagues/workmates by the deplorable practice of . . ./by the continued failure of some employees to keep guards on their machines/stack pallets with sufficient care/operate fork-lift trucks with due regard for their own safety and that of others. I am instructed to warn all employees concerned that they are not only in breach of the company's rules but also the Health and Safety at Work Act. In the circumstances, any continuation of the practice by any individual may lead to the termination of his employment.

This letter is being sent on my responsibility, but with the knowledge of all relevant trade unions – who are as concerned as we are to avoid any unnecessary accidents, and who recognise the unnecessary risks at present caused.

I trust that you will take this warning very seriously.

NOTE:

1   It is always advisable to obtain the full co-operation of all relevant trade unions. This helps to exert pressure on their members, for their own sakes – and, of course, to avoid undesirable effects on industrial relations.

2   It is best to address serious warnings of this sort to individual employees – and, where possible, to obtain receipts for the letters (see

Chapter 41). Alternatively (but second best) they could be put in wage packets. Third (and worst) they could be exhibited on the appropriate notice boards.

354 Final warning – general

I am writing to you and to all other employees employed in . . ./on . . . to issue a final warning that anyone found smoking in our . . . shop/. . . area will be dismissed instantly and without notice. Leniency has been exercised in the past – but in view of the Health and Safety at Work Act – and of the considerable danger caused by this practice, not merely to the smoker but to anyone else affected – employment will be terminated forthwith in all future cases.

Please treat this warning seriously. It is given with the full knowledge and approval of all relevant trade unions – who are as anxious to preserve safety in our works as we are.

NOTE:
1 No threat should be made unless you are prepared, if necessary, to enforce it.

2 I repeat: Dismissal must be regarded as a last resort, when all else has failed. To be regarded as 'fair', it must not only be preceded, where possible, with warnings – it must not be used as an excuse for victimisation or 'picking on' individuals whom you would be happy to dismiss for other reasons.

3 The employee who does not follow safety rules might be held to have been dismissed 'unfairly', but his compensation is almost certain to be reduced, to take account of his own irresponsibility for his own downfall.

355 Denial that employer's general duty has been breached

I accept that it is the duty of every employer to ensure, so far as reasonably practical, the health, safety and welfare at work of his employees. But it is also the duty of employees.

I am passing your letter to the company's insurers for their attention, but I cannot hold out any hope of your obtaining the sort of compensation which you apparently have in mind.

NOTE:

If insurers are to be involved, either deny liability or say nothing. Admission may be a breach of the contract of insurance.

Acknowledgements, receipts and undertakings from erring employees

356   Receipt of warning – acknowledged

I agree that I have received, read and understood your letter dated . . . , in which you insist on my keeping the guard on my machine in position.

NOTE:
If the employee refuses to sign, then make a careful note of that refusal on the document – and file it.

357   Alternative receipt

Thank you for your letter concerning the wearing of safety helmets. This I have read and understood.

358   Undertaking for the future

I have read and understood your letter dated . . . , concerning the importance of my wearing my safety mask/using my ear defenders. I appreciate the importance of this rule and undertake that in future I will wear the mask, as required.

359   Agreement to guard lathes – danger to others appreciated

I have received your letter dated . . . concerning my failure to keep the guard on my lathe in position, and you have explained to me the danger which may result not only to myself but also to passersby, who may get grit/splinters in their eyes. I will keep the guard in position in future.

(Signed) . . . . . .

360   Simple acknowledgement

I have received, read and understood your letter of . . . ,
regarding . . . .

(Signed) . . . . . .

361   Acknowledged that letter handed over

You [and my shop steward] have handed to me the letter
dated . . . concerning my failure to . . . . You have explained
to me the seriousness of the matter — which I fully understand.

362   Acknowledgement to chairman of safety committee

You have explained to me the importance placed by the
Safety Committee of my not . . . . You have also handed to
me the letter from the Committee — which I have read and
understood.

Chapter 42

Contractors and sub-contractors on your premises

As we have seen (in Chapter 37), Section 2 of the Health and Safety at Work Act codifies the civil law on an employer's liability to his employees and transfers it to the law of crime. Section 3 has the same effect on an employer's duty towards visitors, neighbours and the general public.

Thanks to Section 2, you must take all such steps as are 'reasonably practicable' not to submit your employees to risk to their health and safety while they are at work. Thanks to Section 3, you must do all that is 'reasonably practicable' to see that people other than your employees do not suffer risk to their health or safety as a result of work activities under your control.

The Occupiers' Liability Act, 1957, imposes a 'common duty of care' on all occupiers towards their lawful visitors. That is a duty to take such care as is reasonable in all the circumstances, to keep those visitors safe while on the premises for the purposes for which they are permitted to be there.

As always, what is or is not 'reasonable' depends on all the circumstances of the particular case. A warning (says the Act), none too helpfully, 'may or may not be sufficient' – everything depends on the nature of the warning and of the person who receives it.

Again: Contractors, sub-contractors and others who visit your premises 'in the exercise of their calling' – that is, while doing the jobs for which they are employed by their employers and engaged by you – may be expected to take all necessary precautions to protect themselves against those risks which are 'ordinarily incidental to their calling'. You must protect them, in so far as you can, against unusual risks – or risks which result from their use of your premises or on equipment supplied by you. But they may be expected to know their job and to guard against the ordinary risks which they would expect to encounter while doing those jobs.

Conversely (says the Act), you must expect child visitors to take less care of themselves than would adults in similar circumstances. This rule has become particularly important since a series of High Court rulings which put most child trespassers in the same legal position as most lawful visitors.

You owe no duty to take care for the safety of trespassers. You must not set traps for them — do not dig a pit at the entrance to your works, nor set a spring gun by your stores. But the trespasser — the person who comes onto your premises without your consent, express or implied — visits you at his own risk, *unless* you should have reasonably expected him to be there. In that case, the Court of Appeal has held that you 'owe a legal as well as a humanitarian duty' to take reasonable care for his safety.

So, where you know that children are likely to come onto your land, precisely because they are children you must take as much care of them as you would if they were your own. And if there is any 'allurement' — in one important case, an open fire; but it might just as easily have been a trolley on rails, or even a pile of sand or bricks — then you must do what you reasonably can to guard the allurement.

How old is a child? (Or, as one wit put it: When does infancy become adultery?) Unlike the criminal law, which sets the limit at 10 — below which age every child is presumed absolutely to be incapable of crime — there is no such limit in civil law. Nor is there any specific mention of children in the Health and Safety at Work Act.

Naturally, at civil law the plaintiff only has to prove his case 'on the balance of probabilities', while those who prosecute under the Health and Safety at Work Act must satisfy the Court of the guilt of the accused 'beyond all reasonable doubt'. However: Once an unsafe practice is proved — whether affecting employees, visitors or strangers — the burden of proving that reasonable steps (or 'reasonably practicable' ones, as the case may be) were taken rests on the accused.

As with Section 2, so with Section 3 — to show that you were not guilty of unsafe or unhealthy practices — or that you took all those steps which would have been taken by a 'reasonable' employer in the circumstances — you will need letters.

Again: While you can pass the buck both upwards and downwards in the case of your own employees because if you can establish that the fault was that of 'some other person', you will be entitled to be acquitted — so, in the case of contractors or sub-contractors — you may well be able to prove that the fault lay with those who employed the people at risk.

The Inspector decides upon whom to serve the improvement or prohibition notice (Chapter 49). He will also decide whom to prosecute, — and when. If your documentation is in order and shows that you are not at fault, then you will have achieved one major victory. It is great to be acquitted if you are prosecuted — but far greater not to be prosecuted in the first place.

363 Warning to contractors – dangerous premises

I enclose herewith, as arranged . . . copies of our safety pamphlet, one copy of which must be given to each of your employees before he enters our premises. This important document summarises the main hazards which your employees may face when working in our factory/shop/works. I would, however, especially draw your attention to the following:

    1 . . . .
    2 . . . .
    3 . . . .

Kindly acknowledge receipt of this letter and of the pamphlet and confirm that copies will be given to your men.

With best wishes.

NOTE:

1 In due course, regulations may be made under the Act, requiring information to be given to specified classes of visitors. Meanwhile and in any event, the provision of a safety booklet for visitors is highly advisable – and really well-run businesses already provide this. If you do not, then why not?

2 An alternative to sending copies of the pamphlets is to hand one to each visitor, when he first enters your premises. Thus:

364 Contractors' employees handed safety pamphlet

Welcome to the premises of . . . .

In order that you avoid any unnecessary risk on our premises, you will be handed together with this letter a pamphlet, setting out the main hazards. Please read it with care and follow the rules laid down for your safety.

In addition, of course, you will be required to take proper care in connection with your own job – and not to cause danger either to yourself, to your work mates or to employees of our company, as a result of your work here.

You will be required to sign that you have received this letter and the enclosed pamphlet.

With best wishes.

NOTE:

1 As with your own employees, so with those of others – no signature is required by law, but once the visitor has signed that he has received a document, he will be unable successfully to deny receipt of that document. He will also be presumed to have read and understood its contents.

2 If your pamphlet is in any way obscure – or likely to be so to a visitor who does not know the premises and/or who is not particularly intelligent, then by all means add a paragraph to read: 'If you have any queries about the meaning of this pamphlet or regarding safety measures in our premises, please contact [our safety officer, Mr . . . , in room . . .].

365 One major hazard – be warned

This company takes pride in looking after the health and safety not only of its own employees but also of all visitors to its premises. Please adhere to all safety rules and in particular, note the following:

     1 . . . .
     2 . . . .
     3 . . . .

Because of the nature of our work/the siting of our premises/the nature of the work which you will be doing, the major accident risk is likely to arise from . . . .

In the circumstances, please take special care to . . . .

366 Warning to employers – major hazard

I am very pleased that you will be sending in your men on . . . to carry out . . . on/at our premises at . . . .

Please take careful note of one major hazard, caused by the nature/siting or our premises/the work which you will be doing. That is: *[Insert particulars of hazard – and of steps necessary to reduce it to a minimum]*.

367 Protest to contractors – danger to your employees

I am extremely concerned at the unsafe manner in which

your employees are carrying out their work on our premises. In particular, I have received serious complaints concerning the following:

1   The leaving of packing cases/wiring/obstructions in gangways.
2   Careless stacking of equipment/supplies.
3   Reckless operation of cranes/hoists/forklift trucks.
4   . . . .
5   . . . .

Please do ensure that immediate measures are taken to rectify these complaints. Apart from the danger caused to employees of this company – and, of course, to your own employees – the enforcement of the rules laid down by the Health and Safety at Work Act could be disastrous – and we would have to hold you fully responsible.

This letter is being delivered by hand. Please would you contact me personally, without delay.

368   Danger to own employees

I have noted with anxiety that the scaffolding erected by your employees in our premises is in a dangerous condition/ that your employees are not wearing the safety goggles which we have provided for their use while on our premises. I appreciate that the prime responsibility for any resultant accident would rest upon you – both in civil law and under the Health and Safety at Work Act. But for the sake of your employees and also because of the Act, I would be obliged if you would look into the above matters at your earliest possible convenience.

NOTE:

1   Whatever the weight of the burden placed on occupiers by Section 3, if you spot a dangerous practice which does not affect your employees but which could cause injury or even death to employees of your contractors, do you not have a moral duty to protest and to warn?

2   Because you do not 'employ' your contractor's workmen – you do not deduct PAYE from their pay nor hold their cards (a good rule of thumb, this, when trying to decide whether or not a person is your 'employee') – *you may still have a legal responsibility for their safety. You 'control' your premises? Then you are bound by the Act not to cause danger to others (do you provide them with defective equipment? Are your staircases or gangways defective?).*

3 Conversely: While your visitors must take care for the safety of those whom they employ – or, for that matter, for those they manage (see Chapter 37 for duties of directors and managers), they must also avoid causing unnecessary risks to your employees. The trouble is, though, that if you do not handle the matter tactfully, your visitors may down tools. Therefore an approach by one of your top men to one of theirs is normally best. If in doubt, try this one – brief but incredibly effective:

369   Warning – the inspector cometh

In view of the current state of your scaffolding/as your employees are not using guards on their machines/as a result of the way in which wiring and boxes are cluttering up the gangways, I thought you might like a tip off: We are expecting a visit from the Inspector any time/day now. And he is busy enforcing the Health and Safety at Work Act.

I have thought it best to contact you direct, rather than to speak to the people on site – which I am sure that you will wish to do yourself.

With best wishes.

370   Immediate danger – warning to foreman

I write to you as foreman in charge of the work being carried out by your company on our premises at . . . . We have been most disturbed to note the use of/failure to use . . . /your employees' unsafe practices in connection with . . . As a result, considerable danger is being caused not only to your own people but also to ours – and I must ask that you ensure that the practice concerned is discontinued/that safety rules are immediately complied with.

I am contacting your Head Office, but because we consider that there is an immediate danger here, this note is coming to you by hand.

371 Architect – to site occupier

When visiting the site at . . . this morning, I was concerned to note the following dangerous practices:

1 The scaffolding is unsafe.
2 Ladders are not properly footed/lashed.
3 . . . .
4 . . . .

The responsibility – both in civil law and under the Health and Safety at Work Act – rests upon the occupiers of the site and upon the employers of the people concerned. However, we are not only concerned with the safety of our clients and their employees but also with these liabilities – and I am sure that you would want to look into these matters without delay.

With my best wishes.

NOTE:

There is considerable dispute as to the extent (if any) that architects are liable under the Health and Safety at Work Act, in respect of dangerous practices at sites on which work is being carried on which they are supervising. In my opinion, Section 3 is quite wide enough to cover them. The architects 'undertaking' includes the supervision not only of the structures but of the way they are being erected. In any event: An architect who sees a dangerous practice which is liable to cause death or injury on a construction site should not close his eyes. Construction accidents cause far too high a percentage of industrial disasters.

372 Erectors and installers – take care

I write to you officially because your engineers are in the process of erecting vessels/machinery at our premises at . . . . I am sure that you would wish to know that their methods of work appear to be dangerous in the following respects:

1 . . . .
2 . . . .
3 . . . .

We appreciate that erectors and installers are made personally responsible under Section 6 of the Health and Safety at Work Act – in addition to their normal duties to their employees under Section 2. But as we are also concerned for the safety of our own employees – and as we know of the high repute of your company and your wish to carry out your work in a safe manner — we decided to have this letter delivered to you by hand/sent to you express.

I would respectfully suggest that you arrange to have matters put right without delay. You may also wish to know that we are due for a visit from the Factory Inspector at any time now.

Chapter 43

Contractors and sub-contractors— replies to warnings

If you believe that complaints made concerning your health or safety measures or those of your employees are unjustified, then say so – in writing. Just as site occupiers may seek to place the blame on you, so you are entitled to pass it back whence it came. Oral complaints should not be ignored – but written ones should most definitely be replied to – in kind. Thus:

373   Contractor denies danger

Thank you for your letter concerning . . . . I respectfully disagree that there has been any breach of building regulations/the Factories Act/the Health and Safety at Work Act – nor any avoidable danger . . . to my employees or yours.

Without prejudice to the foregoing, I am of course concerned to preserve the highest standards and I am immediately arranging for one of my senior managers to visit you, and to discuss the entire matter with you.

NOTE:
1   The magic words 'without prejudice' keep appearing in this book – and should be used whenever you are prepared to make a concession which you would not wish to have put before a Court.

2   Even if you do not agree with the allegations of a dangerous or unhealthy practice, you should still investigate – if only because failure to do so would inevitably be negligent and a subsequent accident may be as disastrous for you personally as it is for your company – and especially for the person injured or killed.

374   Defects remedied

Thank you for your letter dated . . . . I appreciated not only the concern which you have shown for the employees of this company, but especially the trouble you took in bringing to my personal notice the dangerous practice concerned. I took immediate steps to ensure that the defect was remedied/the scaffolding was strengthened/my employees wore their safety helmets/used their protective clothing.

I trust that similar circumstances will not arise in future – but if they do, perhaps you would care to telephone me? My company places paramount importance on health and safety at work and is always pleased to co-operate in the taking of safety precautions – for the benefit not only of its own employees but all others affected.

With kind regards.

375   From window cleaners to clients

As a result of the Health and Safety at Work Act, we are reconsidering all measures for the health and safety of our employees at work. Our employees are now required to wear safety harness when working at heights – and I would ask for your kind cooperation in ensuring that adequate hooks or other anchor points are made available to them, so that all unnecessary accidents may be avoided. I look forward to hearing from you.

376   Sub-contractor blames head contractor

Thank you for your letter drawing attention to . . . .

The fault (if fault there be) is not ours. The system of work is provided/equipment specified and provided by our head contractors, . . . Ltd of . . . – to whom I have sent a copy of your letter. I hope that you will be hearing from them very swiftly.

NOTE:
Buck passing is not a routine confined to employers – but it has its dangers. Having been put on notice of the risk concerned, the sub contractors are certainly justified in requesting action from their head contractors, if the fault lay with those head contractors. But equally, they should take immediate steps, in so far as they can, to avoid any further risk to their own employees.

377   Contractor blames site occupier

I acknowledge receipt of your letter dated . . . . I deny that there is any avoidable danger in the system as operated by us. Any danger is caused through defects in the structure of the premises in/upon which we are working. I would draw your attention especially to the following:

1 . . . .
2 . . . .
3 . . . .

No doubt you will arrange for these matters to be looked into without delay — and as our company is, of course, far more concerned with the existence of danger than with the element of blame, please do not hesitate to contact me.

Chapter 44

Child visitors—wanted and unwanted

The Health and Safety at Work Act makes no specific reference to children – but courts are likely to apply the same principles as those established under the Occupiers' Liability Act. You must take special care for child visitors because they are likely to take less care for themselves.

Recent Appeal Court decisions have established that if you know that children (or, indeed, adults) are likely to be on your premises, you may 'owe them a duty of care' – in civil and in criminal law. This is a 'humanitarian' as well as a 'legal' duty.

378   Children – banned

Our security men at the gate have instructions to hand a copy of this letter to every driver – our own and those of other companies.

CHILDREN ARE NOT PERMITTED
TO ENTER THESE PREMISES

If you have a child with you in your cab, then he must be left at the gate. These premises are dangerous for children – do not risk disaster for your own child – or anyone else's – by ignoring this warning.

Please sign the duplicate of this letter, to acknowledge that you have received, read and understood it.

NOTE:

1   There are many establishments which ban children. Leaving them in the gatehouse may cause aggravation, but drivers should soon get the message.

2   If you believe that drivers do not bring their own children into your premises you could be right! But in case you are wrong (as is, alas, probable), consider having this follow-up letter available:

379   No children – further warning

Once again I remind you that no children are allowed on
these premises. In future, please do not bring children with
you in your cab – or this could lead to serious consequences.
Please sign the receipt for this letter.

NOTE:
*For rules on acknowledgements, receipts and the signature of docu-
ments, see Chapter 41.*

380   Children – not to leave cab

These premises are dangerous for children. The child with
you must not be allowed to leave your cab under any circumstances, once you have passed the gatehouse. If he needs to
use the toilet, facilities are available at the gatehouse and you
must personally take the child with you and accept full
responsibility.

In future, we ask you not to bring children with you when
making deliveries to our works/factory/cold store/warehouse.

I hope that you will understand that we have made this
rule in order to protect the health and safety of children. We
ask for your co-operation, for their sake.

381   Children in grounds – parents beware

I was sorry to note that your child has been wandering
about our grounds. THIS IS DANGEROUS.

As I expect you know, a child tragically drowned in our
quarry last year – it is not possible for us to fence off the
entire area and we must ask you to ensure, as best you can,
that your child does not again come on to our land.

We would especially draw your attention to the following
dangers on our premises:
1   Piles of sand, which are attractive to children but may
     collapse upon them.
2   Trenches which may seem ideal to explore, but which
     are not shored up and cannot be made 'child proof'.
3   Trolleys on rails – which are fun to play on – but which
     may easily crush a child who gets in the way of one
     when on the move.

4   Roofs – particularly glass ones – which children like to
     climb on, but through which they may easily fall.

We do, of course, appreciate your difficulties in preventing
your child from coming on to our land – but we must warn
you that while we will continue to take every reasonably
practicable step to protect children who come on to our
premises, we regard them as trespassers; we do our best to
keep them off; but the ultimate responsibility must rest with
parents. So please take this matter very seriously – for the
sake of your child.

382   Older child trespasser – beware

As I am sure you know, you are not permitted to enter
these premises/this land. The reason is that there are dangerous places/processes/machinery which could easily cause you
to suffer injury or even death. That is why the rule forbidding
young people to come here is very strictly enforced.

You must leave these premises/this land at once – and not
return.

Our security guard will ask you for your name and address.
Please give them to him – and sign the enclosed sheet to say
that you have received this letter and that you have either
read it or had it read to you and that you understand it.

NOTE:

*1   Naturally, you have to catch the youngster before you can push a
letter in his hand – and he may refuse to give his name and address. If
you suspect that he may be coming to steal, then you would in any
event be entitled to call in the police and to hold him until they arrive –
private individuals may arrest when they reasonably suspect that a theft
(or other 'arrestable offence') has been committed and they reasonably
suspect the individual held to have been guilty of that offence. If you
do keep a youngster until the police arrive, where he is trespassing on
your land, the chances of your getting successfully sued for wrongful
arrest (or 'false imprisonment') by or on behalf of the individual arrested
are almost nil. The same principle, incidentally, applies to adults –
including your own employees – whom you wish to arrest – perhaps
because they refuse to submit to search.*

*2   As usual, requiring the individual to receive – and, if possible, to
sign – a letter will not only emphasise to him the seriousness with*

*which you treat the matter but will help you to prove that you have
taken 'reasonably practicable steps' to keep him safe in future.*

383   Lawful child visitor — take care

We are very pleased to welcome you to our factory/works/
premises, and hope that you will have an interesting time here.

Please remember, though, that this is a place of work which
could cause danger to you, if you are not careful. I remind
you especially of the following:

1   Take special care when . . . .
2   Keep away from . . . .
3   At all times wear the safety helmet with which you will
be provided . . . .
4   Do not remove the cap/hat with which you will be provided — this is required for reasons of hygiene and health.
5   Under no circumstances leave your guide. If you wish
to use the toilet, tell us and you will be taken there.
6   Co-operate with your guide's requests, at all times — for
your own safety. You will be safe, if you follow his
instructions — but the company can accept no responsibility for your health or safety if you wander off on
your own or otherwise fail to keep to the rules and to
obey your guide.

Please sign the tear off slip at the foot of this letter, to say
that you fully understand what I have written.

With all best wishes to you for a happy and safe visit.

NOTE:
*1   If the party is organised by a school then teachers will always be
pleased to co-operate in getting these letters handed out and signed.*

*2   You may like to sugar coat the pill by attaching the letter to your
handout or pamphlet or other literature — so that the youngsters
receive it as part of a major package. Alternatively, to emphasise the
importance of the letter, you may in any event like to deal with it
separately.*

384   Warning to child of particular danger

Please take special care when you are visiting these premises/on our land. Children/young people have in the past been injured by/when on/as a result of/. . . .

To emphasise the importance of your avoiding risks by . . . , this letter is being handed to you personally. Please sign to show that you have received and understood it.

With best wishes to you.

Chapter 45

Defences — health and safety

Companies, firms and 'authorities' all owe duties under *The Health and Safety at Work etc. Act, 1974*. So do 'directors, managers and company secretaries' – as well as individual employees. If, then, you are prosecuted under the Act – in your individual or in your corporate capacity – you need to know your defences and to be able to put them clearly into writing.

Essentially, there are only three possible defences, one of them most unlikely to succeed. They are:

1   That there was no hazard. Inspectors – who normally have the sole right to decide whether or not and whom to prosecute – very rarely take action without hazardous cause.

2   That you took all such steps as 'were reasonably practicable' to avoid the danger. Unfortunately the Act (most unusually for a criminal statute) says: If the accused relies upon this defence, then it shall be for him to prove his innocence. Or:

3   You may rely upon 'the act or default of some other person'. In that case, you may be let off the hook – or prosecuted together with or separately from the party blamed.

The Health and Safety at Work Act (like the Trade Descriptions Act before it) seeks to lay the blame on the guilty head – and on none other. Thus:

1   If the company is to blame, it may be fined (up to £1,000 by the Magistrates, or an unlimited sum by a Crown Court).

2   If the individual manager is guilty, then he may be fined (as above) and/or, in some cases, sent to prison for up to two years by a Crown Court.

3   If either the company or an individual is charged and alleges that the fault lay with some other person, that other person may be charged with the offence, whether or not the charge is dropped against the original defendant.

4   If the buck is passed to the true culprit and the company or the individual is free of guilt, then (unlike the civil law) the criminal law will free the employing company or the managerial superior from blame. Under this Act, you are only held responsible if you were guilty of a crime. The civil rule on 'vicarious liability' of an employer for the misdeeds of his employee does not apply.

It follows that:

1   As an individual, you may need to pass the blame to others. The fearsome penalties under the Act do not encourage a brave acceptance of fault.

2   Conversely, each must watch out for possible attempts to shift the blame for dangers onto him.

Documentation is essential.

Here, then, are some precedent letters, addressed to your Inspector and setting up these defences. The allegations may, of course, be used separately or together.

385   Hazard denied

We have noted carefully your allegation that the . . . machine/system/operation/workplace is hazardous. All examination and enquiry has not borne out this allegation — and in the circumstances, we would be glad if you would call upon us so that our safety officer/scientific experts *(or as the case may be)* may discuss the matter with you. We are, of course, very anxious to ensure the continued absence of hazard in our workplace and will be glad to cooperate with you in any way we can. We look forward to hearing from you.

386   Reasonably practicable steps

We have noted with concern the allegation you make in your letter dated . . . /to our safety officer when you visited our premises, namely that we are in breach of Section 2 of the Health and Safety at Work Act by reason of . . . .

In fact, we have taken all such steps as are reasonably practicable to avoid the hazard referred to. In particular, we have done the following:

    (1) . . . .
    (2) . . . .
    (3) . . . .

I also enclose the following documents which clearly show the instructions given and steps taken by us in this regard.

NOTE:

In this respect as in most others in law, documentation is the key not only to the winning of cases but (more important) to their avoidance. So send the Inspector photocopies of all relevant documents – including entries in record books, etc. Two such documents now follow.

387 Confirming instructions to subordinate

I was deeply concerned to discover that employees in your department are still removing guards from machinery/failing to wear their protective glasses/ear muffs/hard hats. This is in blatant disregard of instructions given to you and to them, copies of which I enclose herewith.

Please would you now ensure that these instructions are followed and that any violations are reported immediately to me/to the safety officer.

I am sending copies of this letter to . . . *(e.g., The Safety Officer, Works Manager, Personnel Manager, Works Director, Chairman of Safety Committee, etc.)*

388 Complaint to superior

I noted with concern the decision of the Board not to invest in . . . /carry out the remedial/maintenance work/ safety precautions recommended by the Safety Committee. I fully appreciate the difficult circumstances in which our business is carried on/current cash-flow problems. And of course the ultimate decision is that of your colleagues and yourself on the Board. But as we all have a direct and personal responsibility under the Health and Safety at Work Act, and as the Safety Committee is unanimous in its anxiety in this regard, I most respectfully ask that the Board should reconsider this decision.

NOTE:
The last two letters form the basis for the avoidance of personal liability in reliance upon 'the act or default of others'. Remember that the case of Tesco v. Nattrass *established that if the company has taken all reasonably practicable steps to ensure compliance with the rules, it is the individual who may be held responsible. Thus:*

389   Company denies liability

It was denied that the company had failed to take such steps as are reasonably practicable to avoid the hazard complained of. In particular, we have done the following:

(1) . . . .
(2) . . . .
(3) . . . .

I enclose copies of relevant documents.

NOTE:

The company, of course, remains 'vicariously liable' to compensate anyone who suffers as a result of the negligence of any employee, 'in the course of his employment'. But criminal liability depends upon fault – and a company is not liable in criminal law unless it has itself failed to comply with its obligation or has been itself guilty of a criminal offence. In the Tesco case, the House of Lords held that the manager (if anyone) should be prosecuted, not the company – which had given full and proper instructions and had exercised that degree of care and supervision as was required (in that case, to avoid breach of the Trade Descriptions Act).

390   Blaming others

It is denied that the company is at fault in the matters stated or at all. If (which is not admitted) any fault lay on anyone, then it must rest on . . . . The basis for this allegation is . . . .

I enclose copies of correspondence/notices/instructions which clearly establish that the company was not to blame, as alleged or at all.

NOTE:

While Inspectors are serving about 15,000 prohibition and improvement notices a year under powers given by The Health and Safety at Work etc. Act, 1974, *there are still some 1,500 prosecutions. Usually, the company, firm or corporation is put in the dock – but individuals are also held personally responsible.*

Chapter 46

Neighbours and nuisances – and pollution of the air

At 'common law' – as a result of the decisions of judges over the centuries – no one may use his land in such a way as unreasonably to interfere with his neighbour's enjoyment of his (the neighbour's) property. We may all have to put up with a certain amount of noise, smoke, fumes, vibration or dust as 'part of the give and take of neighbourly life'. But when the degree of disturbance goes beyond that which a normal, reasonable, healthy person would expect to have to put up with, then it becomes a 'nuisance' in law, as well as in fact. Nor is it any excuse to say that the nuisance has existed for some time and that the complainant 'came to it'.

Still, the neighbourhood is taken into account. Anyone who lives in a factory district cannot expect the same degree of peace as someone else who dwells in a smart residential neighbourhood.

The neighbour disturbed may apply to a Civil Court for an injunction, restraining the continuation of the offence complained of – and for damages. Section 3 would now enable the offender to be prosecuted, if the neighbour's health or safety was at risk – health, probably through disturbance of his sleep patterns; safety, perhaps through projecting buildings, obstruction of pavements, dangerous stacking of goods alongside public footways or overhanging pathways.

Again: Public Health Inspectors* have long had limited powers to curb excessive disturbance through (for example) the pouring of dust or fumes or smoke into the air through factory chimneys. Their hands are now strengthened by Section 5 of the Act, which provides:

1   That everyone must use 'the best practicable means' to avoid polluting the air with noxious or offensive fumes.
2   In so far as the best practicable means cannot prevent the polluting of the air, then all reasonably practicable steps must be taken to render the fumes harmless and inoffensive.

Strictly speaking, Section 3 as it affects neighbours and Section 5 as it covers 'emanations' into the air come outside the scope of employer's liability. Hence the sample letters in this Chapter are few.

Finally, note: Section 5 in any event deals with pollution of the air only and not with the pouring of filth onto the land or into lakes or rivers. That is the subject of other, more precise legislation.

*Prosecutions under Section 5 are rare. The Public Health Acts are more likely weapons – still.

391 Noise – kept to a minimum

I was sorry to receive your letter and to learn that the noise from our generator is disturbing you. As you know, we do our best to cause the least possible disturbance to our neighbours.

I think it fair to point out that yours is the only complaint we have received/it is really not possible for us to avoid a certain amount of noise/the noise is confined to normal working hours. But in any event, *without prejudice* and in view of our wish to maintain the best possible relations with you, we are arranging to insulate the room concerned/take steps to reduce the noise still further. We must ask you to exercise patience for about . . . weeks, while work is being carried out.

NOTE:

1 Never admit nuisance – and always remember to use the words 'without prejudice'.

2 Letters of this sort all too often end up before courts – so maintain a dignified, friendly, courteous attitude – however rude the letter you have received. Thus:

392 Offensive letter – reply to

I was sorry both to receive your letter and to note its very offensive tone. I am sure that on reconsideration you would have wished to phrase it differently – particularly as I could have told you – had you only asked me – that we have already arranged to take still further steps to deal with the matters referred to by you.

I can assure you that we are using the best practicable means to keep the disturbance to our neighbours to an absolute minimum – but I must respectfully point out to you that you live in a manufacturing district and that with the best will in the world, it is simply impossible to avoid the normal effects of manufacturing processes.

393 Solicitor's letter – answered

I acknowledge receipt of your letter dated . . . regarding

the alleged nuisance. This is denied. I am referring your letter
to the company's solicitors, Messrs . . . , of . . . , to whom any
further correspondence should be addressed.

We have always prided ourselves on our good relations
with our neighbours and we regard both the intervention
of solicitors and the tone of your letter as totally unwarranted.

394   Fumes not 'noxious'

We are sorry that you have received complaints from neighbours regarding fumes from our chimney. Our comments are
as follows:

1   We had wished to build the stack up by an additional . . .
feet — but these plans were vetoed by the Planning Authority.

2   We are already using the best practicable means to avoid
the emission of fumes and to render such fumes as are emitted
both harmless and inoffensive — but we are fully prepared to
discuss with you any suggestions which you might be able to
make in that regard.

3   Both from the viewpoint of Section 5 of the Act — and
because of our wish to maintain the highest standards of
management — we will continue to do everything in our
power to reduce disturbance to our neighbours to a minimum.
But I am sure that you will appreciate that we operate in a
factory neighbourhood; that if our processes are to continue,
a certain amount of disturbance is inevitable; and that we
cannot produce . . . without also producing some fumes. In
our view, the complaints you have received are unreasonable.

Please do call on me personally when you are next in our
neighbourhood, so that I can discuss this whole matter with
you.

With best wishes.

NOTE:
*These matters are best discussed — but it is wise to put your case firmly
on the written record.*

Chapter 47

Designers, manufacturers, importers, suppliers, erectors, installers — and product liability

Strictly speaking, product liability means the liability of manufacturers and others who put products into circulation for harm done if those products are defective. In practice, the term has come to mean: 'strict' or 'no fault' or 'absolute' liability.

If your company manufactures or sells a defective product, legal liability may arise in one of four ways:

1   In contract.
2   In the tort (or civil wrong) of negligence.
3   In crime — under Section 6 of the Health and Saftey at Work Act.
4   Under the various rules governing employers' liability to employees.

Contractual liability only applies to those who are parties to the contract or who benefit by a guarantee or warranty, designed to induce them to buy. But the liability is often strict. Normally, if goods are defective, the buyer may claim damages, irrespective of the cause of the defect.

Contracts are governed by their terms — they are agreements and the parties can make any deal they like. There are exceptions, though, under *The Supply of Goods (Implied Terms) Act, 1973,* and *The Unfair Contract Terms Act, 1977,* which (in broad terms):

1   Remove altogether the effect of exclusion clauses in contracts or in notices, in so far as they seek to exclude or restrict liability for negligence which causes death or personal injury.
2   Make totally void any clause which seeks to remove or restrict liability to private buyers ('consumers') in respect of merchantability or fitness for purpose, in contracts for the supply of goods.
3   Make such clauses impossible in contracts for the supply of goods to non-consumers of services or to consumers under business contracts under the seller's own standard written terms and conditions subject to the test of 'reasonableness'. In other words: they will only be enforceable if and in so far as they are reasonable in all the circumstances of the particular case.
4   Leave only exclusion clauses in commercial contracts for the supply of services, not on the supplier's own standard, written terms, to be as unreasonable as the supplier wishes.

If, then, the injured party has a contract with the supplier – or if (as in the case of guarantees or warranties supplied, for example, with vehicles or electrical appliances) the supplier induces purchase by a 'collateral warranty', then the contractual rules apply. But if the person injured is a stranger to the contract, he must rely upon the rules of negligence.

The Thalidomide children, for instance, could not sue the manufacturers in contract because there was no 'privity of contract' between them. So they sued for damages for negligence and therefore had to prove:

a That the goods were defective – which was no problem.

b That the defects had caused damage – again, alas, all too obvious; but also

c That the suppliers had failed to take all such steps as were reasonable – or had been careless in the steps they took, i.e. that they were 'negligent', which might well have proved impossible, because the suppliers maintained that they had taken all such precautions as the current state of medical and scientific knowledge would reasonably require.

Because negligence is so difficult to prove and ordinary people cannot finance expensive legal actions, the Royal Commission on Civil Liability (the Pearson Commission) as well as the English and Welsh, and the Scottish Law Commissions all recommend that liability for death or personal injury caused through defective products should be made 'strict', so that sufferers would get damages without proof of fault.

Strict liability exists in most parts of the United States; in West Germany; and in France – and the EEC has prepared a revised Draft Directive containing similar provisions. In due course, product liability will arrive in the UK. Meanwhile, business people should look to their insurance – for now and for the future.

It is a criminal offence under Section 6 of the Health and Safety at Work Act for any 'designer, manufacturer, importer or supplier' to fail to take such steps as are 'reasonably practicable' to protect – through research and testing – those who use their articles or substances at work. So those who put defective products into circulation in the UK may not only be sued in a civil court by those who suffer death or personal injury as a result. They may also be prosecuted – and to be acquitted, they must prove that they did that which was 'reasonably practicable'.

Defences:

1 That all reasonably practicable steps were taken to avoid the hazard.

2   That the accused reasonably relied upon research or testing done by others. Or

3   That the customer gave a written undertaking that he would himself carry out research and testing necessary for safety.

4   Finally: an employer must take reasonable care for the safety of his employees. If a defective product injures an employee, then the employer may be liable if he has been negligent or in breach of statutory duty, e.g. under the Factories Act; and if he has failed to take such steps as were reasonably practicable to protect employees in this respect, then he may be prosecuted under Section 2 of the Health and Safety at Work Act.

However: if the employer suffers death or personal injury due to a defect in plant or equipment supplied, then under *The Employers' Liability (Defective Equipment) Act, 1969,* the employer is *deemed* to have been negligent. In this area alone in our law, strict liability has arrived. Its extension to all products is only a question of time.

The product liability letters which follow are confined to the needs of employers.

395   Employee injured by sub-contractor

We thank you for your letter of . . . in which you refer us to a clause in our contract which seeks to exclude liability for death or personal injury caused to our employees by yours. Under the 1977 Unfair Contract Terms Act this clause is entirely void. So kindly refer this matter to your insurers without further delay.

396   Personal contract

On the . . . you supplied me with the following tool, namely a . . . . It was defective in the following respect: . . . . As a result, I suffered the following injury: . . . . You were therefore in breach of your contract with me in that the goods supplied were defective and unfit for the purpose for which you must have realised that they were intended to be used. As a result, I suffered personal injury, loss and damage and I now ask you to pass this matter over to your insurers. You will be hearing from my solicitors, Messrs . . . , very shortly.

397   Negligence

I write to you on behalf of our employee, Mr/Mrs/Ms . . . , of . . . , on . . . the . . . of . . . . He was . . . *(set out details of the circumstances of the injury).*

As a result, he suffered the following injuries: . . . .

His injuries were caused by your negligence and/or that of your servants or agents in that *(set out alleged nature of carelessness).*

I look forward to receiving an admission of liability on behalf of Mr . . . at an early date, together with an undertaking to provide adequate compensation for his personal injuries, loss and damage. *(Alternatively:* I am now passing this matter on to the company's solicitors, who will be acting on behalf of Mr . . . in this matter. Please refer this letter to your own solicitors and/or insurers.)

NOTE:
1   If in any doubt as to the nature of the negligence, just make the general application and leave it to your solicitors or other experts to specify the details.
2   If insurers are involved – on either side – then they should be informed at once and letters in general only written with their knowledge and consent or under the guidance of solicitors concerned.

398   Denial of liability

We are in receipt of your letter dated . . . . We greatly regret any injury, loss or damage which may have been suffered by Mr . . . . But it is denied that the same was caused by the alleged or any negligence on the part of the company, its servants or agents, as alleged or at all. And in the circumstances, I am passing this matter to the company's solicitors/insurers, namely Messrs . . . of . . . .

NOTE:
Be careful not to admit liability or you may lose any protection from your insurance policy. After all, it is your insurers who will have to

*foot the bill and therefore they are inevitably entitled to decide how,
when and what liability to accept.*

399   Accident admitted – liability denied

We greatly regret the accident which occurred to Mr . . .
on . . . at . . . . But liability is denied and we have passed the
correspondence and all details to our solicitors/insurers,
Messrs . . . of . . . . Kindly address all further communications
to them.

400   Accident not admitted

We acknowledge receipt of your letter of . . . containing
details of an alleged accident involving Mr . . . on . . . at
. . . . This is not admitted/is denied. We have passed your
letter to our solicitors/insurers, Messrs . . . of . . . and you
will no doubt be hearing from them in due course.

401   Letter passed to insurers

We thank you for your letter of . . . which we have passed
to our insurers, Messrs . . . of . . . . Kindly address all further
correspondence directly to them.

NOTE:
*If in doubt, say nothing – and let those responsible for meeting any
obligations deal directly with potential claimants.*

402   Allegation – faulty manufacture

We write to notify you that an accident occurred at our
above works on . . . , resulting in personal injuries. An investigation is to be undertaken by the Health and Safety Commission. No doubt you will be hearing from them. Meanwhile, we
must inform you that suspicion attaches to certain tools which
you have supplied to us. If you will contact our works manager, Mr . . . , at the above number, he will be pleased to provide you with details.

403   To designer – what testing done?

I have received a complaint about the design of . . . . This comes within the sphere of your responsibility and I would be grateful if you would let me have details of research and testing done to ensure, so far as is reasonably practicable, that the . . . is safe when properly used. Please be especially careful in the preparation of these details because I fear that we may run into difficulty under the Health and Safety at Work Act.

404   Designer – fault lies with materials

Thank you for your letter. I enclose a schedule of the research and testing done by us on the items concerned.

I note the alleged difficulties with the . . . . I suspect that these must have been caused by the materials used.

405   Research and testing by others

Thank you for your letter. I enclose herewith copies of documents received from our suppliers, Messrs . . . . You will see that they have carried out testing, examination and research as set out therein. Having regard to the high repute of those suppliers, we relied upon the results of their testing, examination and research, as provided for in Section 6(6) of the Health and Safety at Work Act.

As I expect that you will be contacting Messrs . . . , I am sending them copies of our correspondence.

NOTE:
You do not have to repeat research or testing that you reasonably understood to have been properly carried out by others.

406   Customer's written undertaking

I hereby undertake that we shall take the following steps to ensure, so far as is reasonably practicable, that the items supplied by you will be safe and without risk to health when properly used, as provided for by Section 6(8) of the Health and Safety at Work Act:

1 . . . .
2 . . . .
3 . . . .

In the circumstances, there will be no need for you to take those steps — so kindly supply the plant/machinery/equipment as ordered, as swiftly as possible and in accordance with our specifications.

NOTE:

It is a good defence to rely upon a customer's written undertaking, himself to carry out research and testing.

407   Reliance on customer's undertaking

I enclose herewith a copy of the undertaking received from our customers, Messrs . . . . As you will see, we were merely required to supply the plant/equipment/components in accordance with their specification and they undertook in writing to carry out all necessary examination, research and testing to ensure that the items were safe.

As no doubt you will be making further enquiries from them in accordance with Section 6(8) of the Health and Safety at Work Act, I am sending copies of this correspondence to their Sales Director.

408   Erectors and installers — reminder of responsibilities

Before you commence installing the vessel/plant/equipment on our premises at . . . , I am instructed to remind you of Section 6(3) of the Health and Safety at Work Act. As the article concerned is to be used by our employees at work, it will be for you to ensure so far as is reasonably practicable that nothing about the way in which it is erected or installed makes it unsafe or a risk to health when properly used.

For our part, we shall be pleased to co-operate with you — and we shall also be providing a copy of our works safety rules to each of your employees who work in our plant.

With best wishes.

409   Supplier's alternatives – guarding

All hydraulic guillotines must be fitted with effective operator guards or both the supplier and the customer may be guilty of a serious breach of the law which, as a result of the 1974 Health and Safety at Work Act, may lead to prosecution and to very heavy penalties. Front, side and rear guard must be provided and both front and side guards fitted as standard equipment.

You will note that the rear guarding is offered by us as an extra, which you may consider expensive. It may be that you can make or obtain this guarding more reasonably from a sheet metal works in your area. In addition, there are so many variables affecting the guarding of the rear of the machine – types of handling or lifting equipment; points of access; location in shop; and local factory inspectors' views – that we would not find it possible to make a guard which is universally acceptable.

In the circumstances, there are two alternatives. On the one hand, we would (as indicated) be pleased to supply the rear guarding, after discussions with you and your acceptance of our estimate. Alternatively, if you decide to procure the rear guarding independently of us, then we are only able to supply the machine to you upon receipt of a written undertaking from you that you will do so.

We look forward to hearing from you as to whether you wish us to provide the necessary guarding or whether you will yourselves do so and provide us with the necessary written undertaking.

410   Written undertaking – guarding

In the consideration of your supplying to us the equipment set out in Part 1 of the Schedule below, we . . . Ltd of . . . , hereby undertake to carry out the work specified in Part 2 of the Schedule below.

(Signed) . . . . . .   (Date) . . . .

*Schedule – Part 1 – Parts
and/or components to be supplied*

(1) . . .
(2) . . .
(3) . . .

*Schedule — Part 2 — steps to
be taken by customer*

(1) . . .
(2) . . .
(3) . . .

Chapter 48

Denial of liability

411   Manufacturer denies fault

The tools/equipment were in accordance with the contract and it is denied that they were unsafe or dangerous to health, as alleged. I am passing your letter to the company's solicitors for their attention.

NOTE:
When there is a potential threat of prosecution, call in the lawyers.

412   Research and examination adequate

Thank you for your letter. I note the allegations therein contained and deny that there was any lack of necessary research/or investigation or that the design of the goods was in any way defective, as alleged or at all. All reasonably practicable steps were taken to ensure the article was safe without risk to health when properly used, and under the circumstances liability is denied.

413   Sales letter

> *The Health and Safety at Work etc. Act, 1974*
> *Your Order No. . . . .*
> *Machine No. . . . .*

We thank you for your above order and confirm that the machinery concerned has been inspected by you or on your behalf.

For your protection, we must respectfully draw your attention to the Health and Safety at Work Act and in particular to the requirements of Section 2. The above machinery as purchased by you does not conform in all respects to the law. It is therefore necessary for us to obtain from you your written undertaking that you will, as discussed with us, fit all such safety features and interlocks that are necessary to ensure conformity not only with regulations but also with your local factory inspectorate.

It may be helpful to point out that we now fit necessary interlocks and key switches to all our new machinery and that we have found Messrs . . . very helpful in that regard.

We are sending this letter to you in duplicate. Please sign one copy and return it to us, so that we can then effect immediate despatch.

With our renewed thanks for your business.

We hereby undertake to take the steps specified above sufficient to ensure, so far as is reasonably practicable, that the machinery the subject matter of our above order will be safe and without risks to health when properly used.
(Signed) . . . . (Date) . . . .

NOTE:

The Act requires that (to provide protection) a written undertaking must be given in respect of 'specified steps'. If there are specific 'steps' which could and should be 'specified', then these should be incorporated in the body of the letter.

Chapter 49

The almighty inspector

The Health and Safety Executive holds sway over an integrated inspectorate – the factory inspectors, mines and quarries inspectors, alkali inspectors and the rest (including, since the Employment Protection Act, the agricultural inspectors) all come under the same aegis*. They have mighty powers.

The inspector may serve a 'prohibition notice', if he considers that a particular practice is likely to cause imminent risk of serious personal injuries. The recipient may appeal to an industrial tribunal, but the notice stays in effect.

The inspector may also serve an 'improvement notice', if he considers that the practice is unsafe but that there is no imminent risk of serious personal injury. Improvement notices generally give time to put matters right – rather than prohibiting the use of the machine, system or as the case may be. An appeal against an improvement notice suspends the operation of that notice until the tribunal has adjudicated on its necessity – or, more likely, in practice, on whether sufficient time has been given to put matters right.

In practice, thousands of these notices have been served, far more than originally expected. Many have been on the direct initiative of managers who could not induce their companies to spend money on putting matters right. Tip-offs are invariably oral and unprovable.

There have been few appeals against these notices and nearly all of those few have been against time given rather than against the notice as such – and most have failed.

The inspector decides whether or not to serve the notice. If he serves a prohibition notice which is not justified and which has been served negligently then – in theory at least – he may be personally sued for damages by the recipient who has suffered damage as a result. He will be indemnified against such claim by the Executive. Anyway, he must be careful before serving such a notice.

Equally, if he only serves an improvement notice and someone is killed or seriously injured while the process continues, then his misjudgement may be blamed for the tragedy. He has a narrow path to tread.

---

* Off-shore oil installations are still supervised by the Department of Energy.

Notices apart, the inspector decides: To prosecute or not to prosecute. If you receive a notice and fail to obey, then prosecution is almost inevitable. Otherwise, the inspector's discretion is fettered only by his good judgement.

There are no private prosecutions under the Act without the consent of the Director of Public Prosecutions — which means that, with the exception of a handful by local authorities, there are none at all. The inspector, then, decides what is or is not 'reasonable' or 'reasonably practicable' . . . whether there is a dangerous practice which warrants bringing you before the court . . . whether a warning or a notice will suffice or a prosecution (with all its potentially horrendous results) is warranted in the public interest.

If you do call in the inspector and get his advice, be prepared to follow it. Moreover: If you bring him into your premises and steer him, around the main hazards, and you are prosecuted for a dangerous practice, do not expect to rely on the inspector having been to your place and having said nothing.

There are now about a thousand inspectors covering the entire country. They cannot conceivably make as many calls as they should, nor supervise as effectively as the Executive would wish. The Act is to a large extent self-policing, relying upon managers, trade union officials and individual employers and employees for information — but, above all, hoping that the penalties provided and the personal liabilities imposed will induce people to give priority to health and safety, of their own accord.

The Act is working. The number of accidents, fatal and non-fatal, is dropping. Companies are giving time and sparing money for safety training. The inspectors are getting co-operation and help from all sides. Notices and prosecutions are multiplying. Adequate paper work is essential when dealing with the inspector.

414   Complaint — against contractors/sub-contractors

For . . . weeks/months, we have employed . . . Ltd to carry out contracting/sub-contracting work in our plant/premises at . . . . We are concerned at their failure to comply with what we regard as adequate safety standards and our efforts to induce them to do so have failed. You will appreciate that we have also had to be tactful, because we are anxious to have their work duly completed.

In the circumstances, would you be kind enough to make a call at our premises as soon as you can — preferably without indicating the source of the request. If you agree with us, then no doubt you will be able to induce them to mend their ways.

In our view, there is a danger not only to their own employees but also to ours. So your swift attention to this request would be very much appreciated.

415   Complaint against neighbours

We are sorry to trouble you again, but we have failed to induce our neighbours to take such steps as are reasonably practicable to avoid causing danger to our employees, through their undertaking. The matters complained of are as follows:

1 . . . .
2 . . . .
3 . . . .

We would be grateful if you would investigate these complaints and, if you take the same view as ourselves, if you would ensure — doubtless with co-operation of the local authority — that our neighbour's conduct is brought up to the appropriate standard.

With my thanks in anticipation of an early reply.

416   Complaint against own company — confidential

I would be obliged if you would treat this letter as entirely confidential. I write only because I can see no other way in which I can induce my company to take steps which are both necessary and reasonably practicable in order to avoid considerable danger to employees/contractors/sub-contractors/ visitors (*or as the case may be*). I have also attempted to reach you by telephone, but have failed.

The situation complained of is as follows:

1 . . . .
2 . . . .
3 . . . .

I would be very grateful if you could arrange to look into these matters at an early date — and, of course, it is vital that this letter be treated as strictly confidential.

NOTE:

1   This letter should be used only as a last resort – a complaint made orally may be just as devastating to your own position as one in writing, but writing is (as always) so much easier to prove. In general, proof is useful (or vital) – in this case, it could result (directly or indirectly) in the loss of your job.

2   Still, it may be necessary to write in order that danger may be dealt with – or even so as to protect your own position, if the danger which you fear gives rise to injury or death and you are blamed and wish to thrust the responsibility back where it belongs – on your superiors who are failing or refusing to carry out the safety measures which you recommend.

417   Complaint against inspector

I write with regret to complain of harassment suffered by my company at the hands of your inspector, Mr . . . . The facts are as follows:

   1 . . . .
   2 . . . .
   3 . . . .

I appreciate that the inspector has a job to do; our company prides itself on its health and safety practices and is, has been and always will be pleased to co-operate with your inspectorate; but we consider that on this occasion your inspector's behaviour has far exceeded the bounds of reasonableness or necessity. I am myself available to discuss the matter with you at any time, either at my office or at yours – and I look forward to hearing from you.

NOTE:

1   This letter may be addressed either to the inspector's immediate superior or to the Chairman of the Health and Safety Executive (Baynards House, Chepstow Place, London W2 4TF).

2   The letter should be written by the chairman or managing director – and, of course, care taken to get the facts absolutely right and, where possible, documented. If there has been a letter of complaint to the inspector himself (such as that which now follows) then a copy should be attached.

418   Complaint to inspector

My safety officer, Mr Jones, has referred to me a serious complaint regarding your behaviour when you visited our works on . . . . I appreciate that you have an important job to do, but before deciding what other steps ought to be taken (if any) in this regard, I would be grateful if you would call on me at your early convenience. The nature of the complaint is as follows:

  1 . . . .
  2 . . . .
  3 . . . .

I look forward to an early reply.

NOTE:

An inspector should carry out his job with firmness and determination – but with courtesy and restraint. Complaints against inspectors are rare – but occasionally serious.

419   Complaint to Health and Safety Executive – inconsistent decisions

We operate plants *inter alia* in the following places: (insert addresses and details).

On . . . , we installed machinery, particulars of which are appended hereto, in our . . . Works. This was duly approved by your local inspector, Mr . . . .

On . . . , we installed the identical machinery in our . . . Plant. Your local inspector, Mr . . . , has refused to approve the same, maintaining that it needs additional guarding (*or as the case may be*).

We consider that the machinery as installed at our . . . premises is safe and that the decision of your local inspector was correct in approving the same. We have now been placed in grave difficulty by the inconsistent decision in our other works – and would ask for this decision to be reviewed without delay. Our production is affected most adversely and may well lead to redundancies.

Your earliest attention would be most appreciated.

420   Complaint to MP

I enclose herewith correspondence in which complaints are raised against our local factory inspector, Mr . . ./in respect of the non-approval of machinery/systems/methods in our . . . works in your constituency. We consider this failure to be unreasonable, particularly as the same machinery/system/method has already been approved in our works/premises in . . . . Our production has been adversely affected; redundancies are now likely; we cannot get swift action from the inspector's superiors; and we would therefore be grateful if you would take up this matter on our behalf at your earliest convenience.

With my thanks in anticipation of your usual swift and helpful action on our behalf and on behalf of those of your constituents whom we employ.

NOTE:
For other correspondence with MPs, see Chapter 62.

421   Confirmation to inspector

My colleagues and I were grateful to you for sparing us so much of your time when you visited our works at . . . last . . . . We were particularly pleased to have had the opportunity of demonstrating to you our new . . . machine and were glad that you shared our view that it was well and safely guarded.

Do please call in on us whenever you are in our neighbourhood.

NOTE:
The importance of this letter is not so much to act as evidence or as an aide memoire for this inspector, but in case one of his colleagues comes next time and takes a different view.

422   Request for visit

I know that you are extremely busy, but as Factory Inspector for our neighbourhood, we would be most grateful if you would call and see us at your early convenience. We are especially concerned because:

      1 . . . .

423   Chaser to inspector

I refer to my letter of the . . . in which I asked you to be kind enough to call at our Works at your earliest convenience, because we have a particular safety problem in connection with . . . . We have neither heard from you nor have you been able to visit us. And while we fully appreciate the calls upon your time, we would be most obliged if you would now treat this as a matter of urgency.

With our thanks in anticipation of speedy action.

424   To inspector – notice complied with

I refer to the prohibition/improvement notice which you served upon me/my company on the . . . . I am pleased to inform you that the requirements of that notice have now been complied with. I would be obliged if you would return to our works/site at your earliest convenience, so as to confirm your satisfaction with the alterations/work carried out.

NOTE:

1   You are not bound to inform the inspector of your compliance with his notice; you are entitled to recommence operations or the use of the machine or system (or as the case may be), as soon as you have made the alterations or otherwise carried out the work specified in the notice.

2   However: If the inspector is informed and he is satisfied then you are sure of avoiding unwanted trouble with the law.

425   To inspector – thanks for confirmation

We appreciated the way in which you returned to our works/site at our request to inspect the alterations carried out as a result of the improvement/prohibition notice served upon us; and are glad to confirm that you informed us that you were satisfied that the notice had been fully complied with. We appreciated your courtesy.

NOTE:

This letter has two objects. It confirms your understanding of the inspector's approval; and it is a pleasant courtesy which should help to maintain future good relations with him.

426   To inspector — specifying further work to be done

We thank you for visiting our works/site yesterday and confirm that you consider that the following changes in our system/work/machine are still required to be made in order that we may comply with the improvement/prohibition notice dated the . . . . We estimate that the job will be completed by the . . . , and we will then immediately contact you in the hope that you will be able to return at the earliest possible moment in order to confirm your satisfaction — and so that full production may be resumed. We know that you do understand the importance of time for us — if we cannot get our assembly line/production/work/machine operating again with full efficiency very shortly, the survival of the company may be in jeopardy.

NOTE:
The final sentence must be adapted with special care to suit your circumstances. There is no reason why you should not emphasise the importance of prompt action, from your company's viewpoint.

Chapter 50

Protective clothing

The art of inducing employees to use protective clothing provided is the subject of Chapter 39. Its provision is dealt with in Section 9 of the Health and Safety at Work Act: 'No employer shall levy or permit to be levied on any employee . . . any charge in respect of anything done, or provided in pursuance of any specific requirement of the relevant statutory provisions'.

In other words: If there is a specific requirement that you provide the clothing or equipment, then you are not entitled to charge for it. Otherwise, a charge is a matter for you — for negotiation with your employees or their representatives.

The Protection of Eyes Regulations, for instance, require the provision of protective goggles or spectacles for certain processes. Even if you have to provide expensive, prescription lenses . . . or to replace spectacles, lost by the wearer . . . you must bear the full cost.

Similarly, specific regulations may force you to provide protective footwear, on pain of prosecution. You may not charge the wearers any part of the cost, even if you suspect that the boots are being used for gardening — or lost, through gross carelessness.

On the other hand, you may think it wise to provide glasses or boots when there is no 'specific requirement' that you do so. Whether or not you charge is a matter for you and not for the law.

* * *

427   Protective boots — employees to pay half

I am pleased to tell you that we have arranged for a large selection of protective footwear to be made available to all employees in the . . . workshop/plant. The Board has also agreed that the company will bear the full cost of one pair of footwear for each employee per year, provided that he undertakes to wear it at all times at work/to subsidise this footwear by paying half of the cost of each pair.

295

Please do encourage all concerned to acquire, use and take care of this footwear. There has in the past been too many accidents to people's feet — which have caused unnecessary suffering. The wearing of these shoes and boots should make a big difference and we are sure that you and your men will be pleased that this footwear is available.

If you have any queries about this letter, please do not hesitate to contact me.

428   Charge for replacements only

As you know, the company now provides free protective footwear for all who work in your department/works. However, I must remind you that we cannot provide free replacements. While employees may certainly take the footwear home, if they wish, or use it as they see fit, they must then accept the responsibility of acquiring and paying for all replacements.

Happily, even replacement footwear is provided by the company on a subsidised basis. The company urges you to use the footwear at all times when at work and to take care of it.

429   Catering department — footwear subsidised

We found from our accident book that a number of the ladies working in our kitchen and canteen have fallen and hurt themselves. In the circumstances, as the company places paramount importance on health and safety at work, I am pleased to tell you that we have decided to get in a large stock of non-slip footwear and to make this available to all those who work in our catering department, at half cost price.

Please do come and inspect this footwear which is both comfortable and as attractive as possible. We hope that you will take advantage of this arrangement as soon as possible — and so reduce the chances of your slipping and hurting yourself.

Chapter 51

Medical examinations

The Act does not require employers to submit employees to medical examinations. Regulations may in due course be made, requiring medical examinations — but sufficient unto the day are the examinations thereof. Note: this is an 'enabling statute', giving vast powers to make regulations — 'delegated legislation'.)

Meanwhile, though, how can you say that you are taking such steps as are 'reasonably practicable' to care for the health of your employees, if you do not even enquire as to their state of health?

So here is another area in which it is wise to be a step or two ahead of the oncoming law.

How can you achieve medical examinations when you have no doctor in the Works? Some companies have taken on full-time doctors and reckon that they make a profit — employees who previously took days off to visit their own GPs now come to work. Other employers take on part-time GP help in the area.

However: It is essential in any event to set up the arrangements with your employees, by letter.

430 Medical examinations now available

As you know, your company has always prided itself on its health and safety practices. But as a result of the Health and Safety at Work Act, it has now taken still additional measures for the welfare of all employees. In particular, it has made arrangements for medical examinations for employees (*or:* for the following categories of employees, in which you are included: . . .).

Please would you ensure that you take advantage of this new facility.

With best wishes.

431 Medical examinations — required

Now that medical examinations are available for all employees/for employees in your department/doing your job, we feel it right that full advantage should be taken of these facilities and we ask that you arrange for your examination at an early date. Please contact the nurse so as to fix a mutually convenient appointment.

NOTE:

You cannot force existing employees to submit to medical examinations – although it may possibly be 'fair' to dismiss an employee, in certain circumstances, if he refuses to be examined when he is at particular risk. New employees, though, may be required to submit to medical examination as a term of service – an example follows. But some trade unions retain archaic rules which forbid the inclusion of such terms in their members' contracts.

432   Term in contract – employee to be medically examined

I confirm that your terms of contract will contain our standard agreement that you will submit to medical examination, as and when required by the company.

Chapter 52

Passing the buck

433 Manager complains to superior

I am deeply concerned about the following unsafe practices
in my department:
>   1 . . . .
>   2 . . . .
>   3 . . . .

I have spoken to you about each of these matters on a
number of occasions and you have assured me that you would
do everything possible to have the complaints rectified — and
I am sure that you will have done so. But nothing has happened and I fear that any or all of these unsafe practices may lead
to accidents and/or prosecutions.

I will be very grateful if you would take urgent steps to put
matters right.

434 Manager — to subordinate

I am confirming in writing our numerous conversations
regarding the failure of operatives/men in your section/
workshop/gang to wear their protective spectacles/footwear
(*or as the case may be*).

As I explained to you, apart from the company's urgent
wish to ensure the safety of its employees, there is now a real
risk of a prosecution under the Health and Safety at Work
Act/Protection of Eyes Regulations *(or as the case may be)*.

In the circumstances, please use your best endeavours to
ensure that the safety rules are complied with, and note that
all infringements of the rules must now be reported to me.

435 Note of default — for file

Date: . . . .
Name: . . . .

Nature of Breach of Health and Safety Rules: . . . .
I said: . . . .
He/she replied: . . . .
Witness: . . . .

NOTE:

The above information can be put straight onto an employee's file without formality in any appropriate case. But the formalising of the system may make it easier to follow, particularly by line managers. Explain to them that this system is neither bureaucracy nor red tape but:

(a) *The knowledge that you are making a note should encourage the employee concerned to take the complaint seriously.*

(b) *The existence of the note will enable further disciplinary procedures to be taken, if necessary. And*

(c) *Production of the note will almost certainly free the manager concerned from criminal liability because it will help him show that he 'exercised all reasonable persuasion and propaganda' to avoid committing the offence.*

436   Request to Board for action

Please would you put the following matter onto the agenda of the next Board meeting:-

The need for additional guarding of . . . machines (*or as the case may be*).

In my view, it is vital that the above steps be taken, despite the expense. I am sure that if the fierceness of the Health and Safety at Work Act is explained to the Board — along with the personal liability placed on those who do not take such steps as are reasonably practicable to protect employees — they will approve my request for action.

NOTE:
If you have sought to induce the Board to take action and they (provably) refuse, you should be (criminally, if not morally) in the clear.

437   Instruction to managers

I write to you, along with all other top managers/plant managers (*or as the case may be*), to urge you to ensure that the company's (very carefully worked out and documented) safety measures are fully complied with. As a reminder, I enclose copies of some of those most relevant to you.

I must emphasise the heavy responsibility placed by the Health and Safety at Work Act on all managers at every level to ensure that all employees at every level fully comply with the company's rules. The company itself is taking all reasonably practicable steps to ensure the health and safety at work of its employees; but it must rely on every level of management to ensure enforcement of those rules.

Chapter 53

Safety representatives and committees

The rules on safety committees and representatives are contained in Regulations, Code and Guidance Notes. As always, the Regulations are requirements of law — and failure to comply is a criminal offence; the Code is guidance — failure to comply with which may be used in evidence in any relevant proceedings, civil or criminal; and the Guidance is just that — distilled and generally wise advice.

Any independent trade union may (but is not bound to) appoint safety representatives. The term 'safety representative' should be confined to union appointees and not used for other, non-union safety committee members (SCMs?).

The Regulations provide that if two or more safety representatives make a written request for a safety committee, the management must consult the unions; put up a notice, giving details of the proposals; and set up the committee within three months.

Guidance Notes suggest that a safety committee should not have a management majority nor be regarded as an arm of management. Its job is to achieve maximum cooperation from the workforce, so as to provide greater safety for them — and for all who are affected by their work. They should be run like any other important company committee — with proper minutes and agendas and with ordinary, sensible procedures.

438   To convenor — please appoint

In accordance with the Regulations — and in any event in line with the company's policy — we shall be most pleased to consult with the appointed representative of your union/ together with representatives of other recognised unions in our plant/company, on health and safety at work matters. I would be glad if you would appoint your representatives as soon as possible, so that we may establish the best possible arrangement, at the earliest possible date.

439   Confirmation – no personal liability on 'watchdogs'

Neither the Health and Safety at Work Act nor the Regulations made under it impose any civil or criminal liability whatsoever on union safety representatives in connection with their activities as such representatives. Having made that clear, I trust that you will now find it possible to appoint your representatives without further delay – and that you will have enough people who are not only prepared to do the job but who are genuinely interested in industrial safety matters.

440   Request for more frequent meetings

Both due to the absence of the works manager and to difficulties in fixing dates for other reasons, I am told by our safety officer that meetings of the safety committee have not been held on a regular or indeed on a frequent basis. We are sure that you will agree that this is regrettable, and I would appreciate your help in ensuring that a further meeting is held without delay – and that future meetings are held on a far more regular basis.

441   Agreement to safety committee recommendation

I am pleased to confirm that the Board has agreed to carry out the changes recommended by the Safety Committee at its meeting on . . . . In particular:
    1 . . . .
    2 . . . .
    3 . . . .
It will take a little time to put these changes into operation, but we expect the work to be carried out by . . .
With my best wishes and thanks for your co-operation.

442   Turning down committee's recommendation

The Board gave very careful consideration to the suggestion made by the safety committee, namely that: . . . .
We have regretfully come to the conclusion that it would

not be possible for us at the present time to comply with the
suggestion, for the following reasons:

    1 . . . .
    2 . . . .
    3 . . . .

I would emphasise that even though the cost of implementing the suggestion is very high, the Board would nevertheless have carried it into effect if we were satisfied that there would be a substantial improvement in the safety situation were we to do so, or that there was any substantial risk of injury or accident under the present arrangements [by continuing to use the machine as at present (*or as the case may be*)]. But we do not consider this to be the case and we cannot therefore justify the expenditure. Balancing the cost against the risk, we do not feel that — especially in the present economic circumstances — the expenditure would be justified.

I would add that we have also sought the best advice obtainable (give details, if desired), and our view has been confirmed.

We will, however, of course keep the matter strictly under review and please assure your committee that its concern is appreciated.

NOTE:

1 Cost is a consideration — but not the only one. It is important to get on record the fact that you give primary and paramount importance to life and limb.

2 The taking of expert advice is wise — and may enable blame to be passed on or avoided altogether. Do be sure, though, that the advice itself is, if necessary, provable.

443 Partial compliance with recommendation — safety shoes/boots

I am pleased to tell you that the Board has agreed to go a long way towards meeting the wishes of the safety committee/ trade union safety representatives, concerning the provision of safety shoes/boots in the . . . plant/stores/workshop/to engineers (*or as the case may be*). We would not feel justified, having regard to the enormous cost involved (probably exceeding £ . . .), in providing shoes or boots for everyone free of charge. But we are prepared to make a very heavy subsidy, to encourage people to buy their own shoes at a rate which will make them less expensive than the ordinary footwear which so many are wearing at the moment. This will also, of course, avoid the present situation where people who do spend their own money on safety footwear are, in effect, being financially penalised.

We hope that this decision will please you; that the facilities which we will now make available will be fully used; and that we will have your full support in inducing all employees concerned to wear the footwear made available.

I am arranging for the personnel manager/safety officer to obtain samples/catalogues of a wide range of footwear, so that each individual will have the opportunity to choose shoes/boots which are comfortable and which he will be pleased to wear.

With my renewed thanks for your co-operation.

NOTE:

1   It is wise to emphasise the positive – that you are going some distance towards meeting the recommendation – rather than the negative – namely that you have turned down the suggestion that boots be provided free of charge.

2   You should indeed give very careful thought before you turn down the request for safety footwear, fully paid by you. You recognise the danger of crushed or injured feet? Of course – that is why you are spending money on subsidising footwear. You realise that while some employees will take advantage of your offer, some will not because they will not be prepared to meet their share of the cost? Then are you really doing everything that is 'reasonably practicable' to meet the situation? The answer will be a question of degree, as always.

"IT WAS THE PERFECT BLACKMAIL LETTER — TROUBLE WAS,
I INCLUDED A STAMPED ADDRESSED ENVELOPE FOR THE REPLY!"

Part Six

CRIME AND SECURITY

Chapter 54

Introduction

Search

You are entitled to search the person or property of a suspect — employee, customer or anyone else — with (but only with) his consent. This may be obtained in two ways:

1 In the case of an employee, by including a term in his contract of service that he will agree to be searched at the request of the management.

2 Ask, at the time: 'Will you please empty your handbag/briefcase/pockets. . .', 'Open the boot of your car . . .', 'Let me see what you have in that box. . .'.

Even if you get permission from an employee in his contract, you should still seek consent at the time of the proposed search. To search without consent is an assault (a 'trespass to the person') or a 'trespass to goods'.

If the suspect refuses to be searched, then call in the police. If the suspect refuses to await the police, then arrest him.

Arrest

The private citizen is entitled to arrest if an arrestable offence, e.g. theft or other serious crime, has been committed and he reasonably suspects the person arrested of having committed that offence. If you put a constraint on a person's freedom to move, that is an arrest. But if a suspect refuses to submit to search, then you will almost certainly 'reasonably suspect' him of villainy.

Time for arrest

Theft is committed where a person dishonestly 'appropriates' someone else's property with the intention 'permanently to deprive him thereof'. *Note:* borrowing is not criminal — except in the case of motor vehicles and other conveyances.

A person 'appropriates' property as soon as he takes it into his possession. You do not have to wait until a suspected pilferer leaves your premises before you arrest him. In a recent case, a woman who had taken a bottle of whisky and put it inside her knickers was held to have been correctly convicted of theft even though she had not reached the pay-out counter.

Still: It is wise to wait as long as you reasonably can because the prosecution must prove guilt beyond all reasonable doubt. And where the suspect has left the premises he can hardly say that he was 'Looking for someone to pay'; 'Trying to find the supervisor, to get permission to take it away'; 'Only looking at the items in the light' — or any other spurious excuse.

Dealing with thieves

Once you have caught an offender, you may hand him over to the police — or you may exercise mercy, if you see fit. You may also do a deal and say: 'Give back everything that you have stolen and we will not report you'. Provided that you do not blackmail the offender, e.g. by demanding with menaces more than you are lawfully entitled to claim, deals of this sort with criminals are now legal.

Prosecution

If you hand the offender over to the police, they prosecute if — but only if — they wish to do so. They may decline, for one or more reasons:

1   Some police forces as a matter of policy leave prosecution of shoplifting or what they choose to call petty theft to the victims. And in any event

2   The prosecution must prove guilt — and the police will not sign the charge sheet unless they are satisfied that they have a good enough case.

If a citizen is *(a)* acquitted of the charge and *(b)* can show that it was brought out of 'malice', i.e. a desire to harm him rather than a wish to see justice done — then he can claim damages in a civil action for 'malicious prosecution'.

Private prosecutions

If the police invite you to sign the charge sheet, then take care before you agree. You, like the police, may face a malicious prosecution charge if you prosecute both maliciously and unsuccessfully.

You are entitled to hold the offender for a reasonable time while you seek advice on whether or not to hand him over to the police. And if you are in doubt as to whether or not to prosecute, consult your lawyer. Note:

1   While you can withdraw a civil action at any time on payment of the costs of both sides, a prosecution may only be withdrawn with the consent of the court – which will only be given for good reason.

2   Just as you cannot force the police to prosecute, they cannot require you to do so.

If you are to prosecute, make sure that you have sufficient evidence. And if you do suffer from theft, establish a system under which your staff know what steps to take if they spot a crook at work.

Costs and procedures

How, then, can you prepare for possible legal battle against the crooks? Here are some suggestions:

1   Remember that you will have to prove your case – so try to ensure that any observation is carried out by more than one employee – and that any accusation is made in the presence of a witness. Even if observation and accusation are initially effected by one person, a witness should always be present during any questioning – if only to ensure that the questioner is not accused of either blackmail or twisting the words of the suspect.

2   If you decide to sign the charge sheet – a very simple procedure – you should first call in the police and obtain their guidance. They will help you with your prosecution, even if they decide to leave the charging up to you.

3   An accused person may be convicted on the evidence of one witness and even without corroboration. If, for instance, you testify that you saw the culprit taking the goods from their proper place in a furtive manner and hiding them in his brief case and you are given an unsatisfactory explanation and if the court believes you – then you will win your case. But (as an example) over 60 per cent of women who plead not guilty to shoplifting charges and are tried by jury are acquitted. Corroboration is sensible if not essential.

4   The better prepared your evidence, the swifter and more satisfactory the procedure is likely to be. If you have prepared a case which a court is almost certain to accept, then the accused will probably plead guilty before the Magistrates' Court and not trouble to elect for trial by jury — in which case the entire business may be over very swiftly. If the accused elects for trial by jury, though, it may be many months before the case is heard. If the accused is an employee, then you must also consider whether or not you have enough evidence of misconduct to warrant dismissing the person 'fairly'. If in doubt, discuss proposals with your solicitor.

5   If you do the prosecuting, you may not have to pay the costs. If the prosecution was properly brought, in many cases the costs should be paid out of public funds. Once again: talk to your solicitor.

*   *   *

Security companies and the police often warn that it is cheaper and quicker to prevent theft than to go to law. Unfortunately, though, thieves cannot be banned and the law must frequently be mobilised — if only to discourage other crooks from following the same expensive path. Follow the above rules, though, and you should avoid producing more trouble for yourself than you do for the villain. No one can guarantee that the accused will be convicted — in a recent case, the Court of Appeal emphasised that however common the defence raised, e.g.: 'I wasn't thinking . . . I did not realise what I was doing . . .'), a court must avoid the temptation to treat it with cynicism — the defence must be considered on its merits.

However: A properly prepared case should not produce a civil action for malicious prosecution. Consider the facts, the evidence and the tactics before you launch into any prosecution. You are entitled to make your decision. Do so with your eyes well open.

Chapter 55

Search and prosecution

444 Confirming agreement to search*

I confirm that you — like all other members of our staff —
have agreed that the management may search your person or
property at any time when you are on the company's premises. Having regard to the recent spate of stealing — and
especially to the unfortunate suspicion which this has tended
to cast on the innocent, along with the guilty — we are convinced that the spot checks which will be arranged from now
on will be of benefit not only to the company but to all
concerned — and we are grateful to you for your co-operation.

445 To trade union — re search

I must ask you to reconsider your union's decision to refuse
to agree to the inclusion of a search clause in the contracts of
employment of your members. I would emphasise that there
is no intention whatsoever on the part of the management to
victimise any individual or group — but only to take such
steps as are reasonable to avoid the heavy losses which are at
present caused through pilferage. This stealing not only causes
vast problems for the company but also suspicion and unnecessary ill-will as between employees.

I shall be pleased to discuss this matter again with you at
any mutually convenient time, and look forward to hearing
from you.

446 Allegation of wrongful search

I protest at the series of searches of my person and property during the past three weeks. I am being victimised in a
most unpleasant and improper fashion and hereby give you
notice that I shall not in future agree to be searched other
than at your personal request.

*More 'search' precedents are in Part 1.

NOTE:

The employee who refuses to be searched, in breach of a term in his contract of service, may or may not have 'repudiated' the contract. If an employee is being victimised through the use of the search procedures, then it would certainly be 'unfair' to dismiss him as a result.

447   Why police were called

I greatly regret yesterday's incident in which you refused to be searched and we called in the police. Because the company is suffering so greatly from pilferage/theft, these spot checks are vital. You were in breach of your contract of service in refusing to agree to search; and in the circumstances, the security officer followed our normal procedures in calling in the police.

While regretting the unpleasantness caused as a result, this was entirely due to your own breach of contract/refusal to comply with the reasonable request of our security officer, in the exercise of his duty. I trust that in future you will remove the need for such procedures by co-operating with our security measures. And because of their importance, I must warn you that any future refusal may be grounds for dismissal.

448   Arrest − unreasonable refusal to be searched

Your refusal to agree to empty your pockets/open the boot of your car was wholly unreasonable. In view of the major losses through theft from which the company is suffering, our security officers had instructions to restrain any employees − from shop floor to board level − who refused to comply with requests to undergo a search of person or property. The resultant unpleasantness in your case was entirely the result of your own behaviour and I must warn you that this procedure will remain unchanged in future and that a most serious view will be taken of any cases in which an employee causes unnecessary difficulty to our security men in their already difficult job.

449   Instructions to security officers

Please convey the following instructions to your men, regarding future search and arrest arrangements:-

1   Neither the persons nor the property of employees are to be searched without their permission.

2   Most employees have by now accepted terms of service which include agreement to be searched at the request of the management. However, such request must always be renewed, prior to the carrying out of any search of person or property.

3   If it is not possible to obtain consent – either because the individual has refused or because he is not available or for any other reason, the co-operation of the police must be sought and obtained.

Any employee who refuses to agree to search of his person or property is to be asked to remain in the gatehouse/security room/office while the police are called. If he refuses to remain voluntarily, then the minimum force reasonably necessary to restrain him shall be used. He must not be permitted to leave until the search has been carried out. As all searches will be required because of the commission of theft (which is, of course, an 'arrestable offence') and as any individual who refuses to agree to the search of his person or property would inevitably reasonably be suspected of having committed that offence, the arrest of such person would be lawful.

5   However: I repeat that as any forcible search of person is an assault (a 'trespass to the person') and any laying hold of the property of another without his consent would be a 'trespass' to that property, the police should be called upon to co-operate where consent is unobtainable or unavailable.

6   All steps must be taken promptly. In particular, there should be no delay in contacting the police after an arrest.

7   If a suspected thief (whether or not an employee of the company) is arrested, then the company's procedures on enquiries and prosecution must be carefully followed. I must

emphasise that the law permits a suspect to be held for a reasonable time while instructions are sought or a decision taken as to future action. But this delay should be kept to the unavoidable minimum.

If you have any queries in this regard, please contact me at once.

450   Procedures for enquiries and prosecutions

The following are the company's procedures which will in future be followed by all security officers, where a suspect is arrested and a prosecution is contemplated:

1   Wherever possible, the suspect's behaviour should be observed by more than one person — and in the event of the observation producing results, these should be recorded by each such person in his notebook at the earliest opportunity. 'Contemporaneous records' may be referred to by witnesses in court — those that are not 'contemporaneous' will be excluded from the witness box.

2   Wherever possible, all enquiries should be carried out by more than one person. Where an employee is to be questioned as to his behaviour, then such questioning should be carried out, wherever possible, in the presence of a staff/trade union representative. Once again, details of questions and answers should be recorded.

3   Where it is decided that the person concerned may be prosecuted, he should be informed that he is not bound to answer questions and that any answer given will be taken down and may be used in evidence. Note: It should not be stated that such statements 'will' be used in evidence nor that they will be used in evidence 'against' the person concerned.

4   If it is felt that there is enough evidence for a prosecution, in normal circumstances the police should be informed and invited to prosecute. If they refuse so to do, then (and only then) should the question arise of a prosecution by the company.

5 A charge sheet should be only signed on behalf of the company by .../with the authority of .... Before such signature or authority is given, the company officer must be satisfied as to the following:

(a) That there is sufficient evidence against the accused to warrant a prosecution.

(b) That the prosecution is in the interests both of justice and of the company. And

(c) That a fair and reasonable opportunity has been given to the proposed accused to explain his behaviour – and that the explanation is unacceptable.

Please note the following:-

1 The company is not bound either to hand the suspect over to the police nor (still less) to initiate a prosecution.

2 The prosecution may only be withdrawn with the consent of the court.

3 If a prosecution is both unsuccessful and proved to have been brought out of 'malice' – that is, a desire to harm the person prosecuted, rather than to see justice done – both the company and the individual prosecutor may be faced with a civil claim for damages for 'malicious prosecution'.

4 No criminal prosecution may be dropped without the consent of the court – which will only be given for some very good reason.

If you have any queries regarding the above, please contact me without delay. And please ensure that these instructions are both received and understood by all security men under your control and/or supervision.

451 Company policy – prosecute

Having regard to the intolerable level of 'shrinkage' suffered by the company during the past year as a result of thefts by both employees and customers, the Board has decided that all offenders who are apprehended will be prosecuted. Naturally, if there is any reasonable doubt as to the guilt of the person concerned, the company's usual procedures will be followed – including, where necessary, consultation with the company's solicitor. But both employees and customers should be informed that in future security officers have no discretion in matters of prosecution, where a culprit is caught red-handed.

452   Without prejudice apology to innocent suspect

I have carefully considered your letter concerning your recent arrest by the company's security officer. Without prejudice to my view that this arrest was entirely brought about by your own behaviour, the incident is of course greatly regretted. I hope that in future you will agree to be searched/not take home the company's tools without written permission from your foreman/supervisor/that you will comply with the company's security procedures, so that no such action by our security men will be necessary.

453   Referral of complaint to solicitors

I am in receipt of your letter complaining about your detention by the company's security officers/prosecution for theft. It is denied that the arrest was unlawful, unjustified or caused otherwise than as a reasonable response to your own conduct; it is further denied that the prosecution was malicious or improper in any way; and I am passing your letter to the company's solicitors, Messrs . . . , to whom all future correspondence on this matter should be addressed.

454   Denial of defamation

Thank you for your letter.

I have consulted the company's solicitors concerning your allegation that you were defamed through being asked to empty your pockets/questioned regarding the theft of . . ./ challenged by the company's security officers regarding the presence of . . . in your car/bag. I am told that the occasion was privileged — the company's officers were taking proper steps/making appropriate enquiries/. . . for the protection of the company. Further and in any event, if (which is denied) you were defamed, there was no 'publication' of such defamation.

Without prejudice to the foregoing and in any event, the security officers were carrying out their job in a proper manner — and their job was not made any easier by your unreasonable and unwarranted refusal to co-operate with them.

455   Confirming deal with culprit

I confirm our conversation in which you admitted that you
had wrongfully appropriated the following items of the company's property, to a total value of £ . . .:

    (a) . . . .

    (b) . . . .

    (c) . . . .

I further confirm that provided you repay to the company
by . . . the above full amount [*Note:* do not demand more
than was wrongfully appropriated], I shall not inform the
police or take any other steps against you. However, as I
further informed you, it is not possible for the company to
retain you in its service and you will be paid your full remuneration up to the . . . .

I greatly regret that our association has to come to an end
in such an unhappy manner. I trust, however, that you will
repay the company as agreed and so avoid our having to take
other steps against you.

456   Warning – but no prosecution

I am sure that you will be pleased to learn that the Board
has instructed me to inform you that they do not intend to
take any further steps regarding your admitted misconduct
in connection with . . . . This means that the company will
not prosecute; that the police will not be informed; and that
the matter is now regarded as closed.

I trust that you will not regard this exceptional clemency
as a sign of weakness. If there should be any recurrence, however minor, not only will you be dismissed forthwith from
the company's service but a prosecution will almost inevitably
result.

The reasons why the Board have decided to take no such
steps on the present occasion are the following:

1   Your lengthy and loyal service to the company.
2   The excellence of your work.
3   The exceptional strains which were placed upon you at
    the time in question by your/your wife's/your child's
    illness/by the death of . . . (*or as the case may be*).

NOTE:

The above letter should be marked 'Personal – Private and Confidential' – and should preferably be handed personally to the individual concerned and a receipt or acknowledgement obtained from him. If this is done at the time when the culprit is informed of the company's kindness, there should be no difficulty in obtaining such a signature. This letter, of course, will also serve as a written warning of possible dismissal.

Chapter 56

Theft

It is a crime wrongfully to appropriate property belonging to another person, with the intent at the time of taking 'permanently to deprive him thereof'. It is not normally a crime to borrow — anything other than a motor vehicle or other convenyance which must not be taken away without the owner's consent or other lawful excuse. *Exception:* it may be a crime *dishonestly* to borrow your employee's money from the till.

In practice, most large scale employers are plagued by theft, by employees and others. Security arrangements are, of course, essential — but so are letters making the situation and the rules abundantly clear to all. The following letters explain those rules, as well as the law which lies behind them.

457 Warning – no 'perks'

I am writing to you and to all other supervisors to ask you to make plain to everyone under your supervision or control that the following conduct is absolutely forbidden:

1   The taking home of tools or equipment, for whatever purposes.
2   The removal from the premises of off-cuts/leftovers/ stationery/office supplies/. . . or any other property belonging to the company, without the prior, express, written consent of . . . or . . . .
3   The borrowing of money from petty cash or till, whether or not an IOU is left.
4   The use of company telephones for private calls.

I understand that some employees have removed company property and when challenged said that they understood that they were entitled to do so as a 'perk'. There are no such 'perks'; breach of these rules will be treated extremely seriously and may lead to dismissal; and employees found with company property in their cars or homes may be prosecuted.

I ask for your cooperation both for the protection of the

company — which has been suffering from theft on an unprecedented scale — and from that of the employees concerned, who must know the position so as to avoid risk to their jobs and, potentially, to their freedom.

458   When to challenge and arrest

I have been asked to explain when suspected thieves/shoplifters should be challenged and/or arrested. The law is that a person is guilty of theft as soon as he removes an article from its proper place, with the necessary dishonest intent. So there is dishonest 'appropriation' the moment that goods are taken from a shelf/store/counter/display by a person who intends to steal them.

On the other hand, it is often difficult to prove intent. The employee may maintain that he was looking for someone from whom to ask for permission to remove the item/the customer may allege that he was merely seeking somewhere to look at the article in the light. It follows that the further away the article is from its proper place, the less likely these excuses are to be effective. You are therefore asked to allow the suspect to take the article as far as possible away from its proper place before you challenge. Naturally, you must not wait so long that the suspect may escape — but patience is important.

With many thanks for your co-operation.

459   Instructions on 'finding'

To avoid misunderstandings about goods found on the company's premises, the position is as follows:

1   All goods found belong to their owners, i.e. to the losers. Failure to take reasonable steps to trace the owner may lead to a prosecution for theft.

2   Steps must therefore be taken in all cases to trace the owner — unless the goods have been obviously abandoned. All employees who find goods should hand them in to . . . . A careful note will be taken of the date, time and place of such finding and of the finder. Equally, any person other

than an employee who finds goods should be asked to hand them in.

3   Where goods are of little value, they will be kept for six months when they will be handed over to the finder. In law, where an employee finds property in the course of his employment, that property belongs — if the true owner does not turn up — to the company. However, as a matter of policy, the company wishes to encourage the handing over of lost property and will not assert its claim as against employees who find and hand in.

4   In the case of valuable property, e.g. rings or other jewellery left in the wash room, such steps will be taken as the personnel manager/ . . . considers reasonable in the circumstances in an attempt to trace the owner.

460   Borrowing — and theft

I note your complaint that your . . . was borrowed by a colleague. Borrowing anything other than a motor vehicle or other conveyance is not normally illegal, even if the consent of the owner is not obtained. Nor is it a breach of the employee's contract of service. In the circumstances, I have asked the personnel manager to have a word with Mr . . . , to avoid any recurrence — for the sake of good relations among employees. But it is not proposed to take legal action in this sort of case.

461   Warning — motor vehicles

There seems to be a peculiar and incorrect idea in our transport department that the borrowing of the company's motor vehicles without consent is permitted.

1   The borrowing of a motor vehicle without the owner's consent or other lawful excuse is a criminal offence. Please warn employees that no vehicle may be used without the company's consent — so that there can be no question of any employee who is caught borrowing successfully alleging that he thought that the company's permission would have been

available, if sought. The use of company vehicles without prior consent is expressly forbidden.

2   Further, the taking of company vehicles without consent will be regarded in future as a most serious breach of an employee's contract of service, rendering him liable to be dismissed. Please warn all drivers and others employed in your section that the current practice or borrowing company vehicles for private purposes without prior consent must cease forthwith.

462   Suspension – suspected of stealing

I confirm that you are suspended (on full pay/without pay) as from today's date, because you have been found with property belonging to the company/another employee in your possession. You told me that you had no intention permanently to deprive the company/your colleague of this property, but whether or not it is decided to report this matter to the police and whether or not they prosecute, you have absolutely no right to behave as you did.

I expect to be in touch with you again within the course of the next few days, after a full inquiry has been made, during which time I suggest that you remain available.

NOTE:
1   If you suspend an employee without pay, then by definition you are refusing to pay the employee his wage or salary and are therefore in serious breach of his contract of employment. He may therefore regard himself as constructively dismissed.

2   If the employee agrees to a suspension without pay, while his case is being investigated, then that is a matter for him.

3   If in doubt, suspend with pay. Most procedure agreements provide for suspension without loss of remuneration or rights, so as to enable a complaint against an employee to be investigated fully and with care.

4   When unfair dismissal may be so costly, suspension arrangements may grow in importance. Use them, where appropriate, in accordance with union agreements and consultation with their officials.

Chapter 57

Bribery and corruption

It is a crime to give or to receive, to attempt to give or to seek to obtain any consideration for the giving of a favour. Whether in cash or in kind . . . however small or large the gift . . . if the intent is 'corrupt', the gift is illegal — and could lead to prosecution, conviction and heavy penalties.

Note: The prosecution must normally prove intent. But where the bribe concerns an official of a local or public authority, there is a presumption of guilt which the accused (giver or receiver, as the case may be — or both) must attempt to shift.

The test of 'corruption'? Usually: secrecy. That which is done or given openly and above board is seldom 'corrupt'. That which is given or received under the counter . . . furtively . . . is usually bribery, 'the drop', 'dropsy', 'greasing the palm', 'payola' — in a word: Bribery.

Here are some letters designed to show that honest, business gifts must not and cannot be interpreted as criminal bribes.

463   Christmas gift — to customer

I have today arranged for the despatch to you of a crate of whisky/a crate of wine/a box of cigars — which I hope that you will accept as a small token of our great appreciation for your many kindnesses. It has been a pleasure working with you and we all appreciate that you have gone out of your way on many occasions to be kind and accommodating.

We wish you a most happy Christmas — and health and prosperity in the coming year.

464   Commission — consult the boss

I write to confirm that my company will be pleased to pay you commission on any orders placed by your company with mine on the following basis:

(a) . . . .
(b) . . . .
(c) . . . .

I understand that no objection will be taken to this arrangement by your company — and I would be grateful if you would let me have your written confirmation, or that of your managing director, at an early date.

NOTE:

There is nothing improper in the giving or acceptance of commission — and many people rely upon it for at least a substantial part of their livelihood. It is the dishonest, corrupt, hidden giving or receipt of a pay-off, rake-off or other hand-out which is a criminal offence.

465   Requirement to staff — gifts to be returned

Kindly inform all employees — and in particular, all buyers/ catering managers — that under no circumstances are any gifts to be accepted from suppliers, at any time. Reasonable hospitality may be accepted — but only if the company has full knowledge of that hospitality, so that the person able to place orders on behalf of the company will be under no personal obligation to the giver of the largess.

Kindly confirm that you have received and understood this letter and that all concerned personnel will be duly informed. Any breach of this rule must lead to immediate disciplinary action, its nature and extent depending upon the circumstances

466   Gifts to be reported

The Board has carefully considered the question of gifts to buyers. It has agreed that these need not be returned, provided that full details of each gift are provided to the appropriate manager, without delay. Any failure to report gifts will lead to the immediate dismissal of the buyer concerned.

467   Food and drink — for canteen or party

The Board has decided that gifts of drink received at

Christmas need not be returned, but should be reported.
In normal circumstances, these will be put into the pool for
the staff party/canteen Christmas celebrations.

Other gifts — whether in cash or in kind — must be returned
to the senders, in future as in the past.

468 Covering letter with returned gift

It was extremely kind of you to think of me and to send
such a generous gift. However, we have an absolute and un-
shakeable company policy that no gifts must be accepted by
staff, however senior, on pain of the most severe penalties!
In the circumstances, I hope that you will not be offended
that I have arranged for your gift to be returned to you.

Nonetheless, I heartily reciprocate your Christmas greetings.

469 To supplier — protest at gifts to buyers

I understand that you have persisted in sending Christmas
gifts to buyers, in spite of protests from my company. I hereby warn you that any future gift will lead to the placing of no
further orders by my company with yours — a result which
both I and my Board would regret but which we would regard as inevitable. It is firm and absolute company policy that
no gifts must be accepted by any employee at any level — and
I would ask for your co-operation in this regard.

470 Dismissal — for gifts

You have been warned — both orally and in my letter to
you of . . . — that you are not permitted to accept any gift
of any sort, in cash or in kind, from any supplier or his
representative. It has now come to my attention that you
have once again flouted this rule. In the circumstances, your
further presence at the company's premises will not be required; kindly return all samples forthwith — and deliver up
the company car to our garage at . . . , without delay. Upon
receipt of the samples and of the car, you will be paid all outstanding money due to you.

"WE HAVE A WELL DEVELOPED WRITTEN COMPLAINT PROCEDURE!"

Part Seven

DISPUTES AND
DISAGREEMENTS

Chapter 58

Picketing, secondary action and industrial disputes

The individual employee is weak. If he takes action, he normally loses his job. But those who act collectively have the strength given to them by numbers — as well, of course, as by the organisation which their union makes available through and to them.

When an individual withdraws his labour, he inevitably acts in breach of his contract of service. The law provides him with no protection and if he does not do the work for which he is paid, then he has normally repudiated his contract and may be dismissed.

The same rule would apply to group action, but for the law which recognises that unions, their officials and members need to be protected when they act 'in contemplation or furtherance of trade disputes'. This protection is vital not only because the individual union member is in breach of his contract of service, but because together they inevitably induce breaches of other contracts by their employers and even by third parties.

When employees take action against their own employers, this action is 'primary'. So 'primary picketing' means making efforts outside your own working premises, in attempts to induce others to help you to make your action effective.

When employees picket, 'black' or engage in sympathy strikes, outside or in connection with premises or businesses other than their own, then such action is 'secondary'. The 1980 Act is aimed mainly at restricting 'secondary' or other non-primary industrial action.

The theory is the same as that laid down by the Court of Appeal in a series of actions following the long, hard winter — and the lorry drivers' strike — of 1978/79. These decisions were overruled by the House of Lords, but the 1980 Act has restored their effect. Action other than *(i)* primary or *(ii)* aimed at blocking supplies to the people actually in dispute, is generally 'too remote' to enable the people concerned to be protected by law.

Unfortunately, the 1980 Act itself is obsure in its wording and the Code does no more than to explain what the Government considers that the Act means. So if you run into actual difficulty in this area, take expert and up-to-date advice. The actual, practical effect of the new rules is to give an employer who is adversely affected by secondary action the power to go to a civil court, to claim an injunction against those who are disrupting his business. That is fine in theory. But in practice, it may well be worse to win than it is to lose.

Suppose that you apply for an injunction and you do lose. Obviously, you would have been better not to have sued in the first place.

Now suppose you win. If the strikers (like the famous Pentonville Five) refuse to obey the order of the Court, they are then in contempt of Court. The punishment for contempt is normally: imprisonment — so consider: what good would it do you if the union strikers went to jail?

In practice, wise employers will keep as far away from these new powers as they do from industrial disputes. Meanwhile, the matching powers of the police remain identical. No one pickets without the consent of the local police. After all, anyone who pickets on the pavement or on the road obstructs that pavement or highway. And if a police officer asks him to 'move along' and he refuses, then he 'obstructs' the policeman in the execution of his duty.

In practice, then, good industrial relations still depend upon good personal relations. The law now provides less protection for unions, their officials and their members than it has done. But the dislike of unions for Courts, lawyers and Judges should be matched by the employers' realisation that to use the law to solve industrial disputes is to wield a two-edged sword.

As with the law, so with letters — in general, the best rule in industrial disputes is: keep away — at least until the dispute is settled. But at that stage, put the terms of the settlement into writing, immediately — and get them signed by both sides. If you pack up your negotiations in the early hours of the morning and leave documentation until the next day, you will almost certainly find that your work force is well misinformed of the outcome, long before you arrive, smilingly back to work.

471   Employer to unions — trouble protest

I was pleased to meet your colleagues and yourself regarding your dispute over . . . . At the very least, our discussion cleared the air and I will now discuss your proposals with my colleagues and I know that you will put ours to your committee. I hope that as a result we shall reach some amicable conclusion. I am sure that you all appreciate that any break

in production could prove disastrous to the company – and
hence, of course, to employment prospects.

With best wishes.

NOTE:

Unions must do the best they can for their members – and must strike a
balance between obtaining top terms and not killing the goose that lays
the wage packet. If the company is having troubled times and if
redundancies are a real possibility if production is interrupted, then
reference to this misery is fair and sensible. Stronger terms, even, may
be necessary – thus:

472   Beware of redundancies

When we met, I made a full disclosure to you of the current
situation in the company. You now know just how important it is to keep production moving. For our part, we will
make every effort to settle the current dispute in an amicable
fashion – and I do hope that you and your colleagues will
do the same. The Board is most anxious to avoid any unnecessary redundancies – but a stoppage would certainly
mean a permanent reduction in our work force.

When you and your colleagues have had time to consider
the management's latest – and, I am afraid, final – offer,
please do not hesitate to contact me personally.

With my best wishes.

473   Offer accepted

My Board has carefully considered the proposition which
you have put forward on behalf of the Union and on the
whole it is considered fair. So I am pleased to tell you that
it is accepted – and I confirm its terms as follows:

1 . . . .
2 . . . .
3 . . . .

474   Acceptance – with reservations

Your offer is accepted – but I must point out that under

no circumstances can the company consider any further improvement in pay until productivity substantially improves. We are now stretched to the absolute limit — certainly with our present work force.

475   Terms agreed — as in letter

Thank you for your letter dated . . . . I confirm that the terms agreed between your Union and the Company are correctly set out. I hope that this agreement signals a permanent end to the unfortunate animosity between your Union and the Company — and the start of happy co-operation between us, both individually and on behalf of the management and the Union respectively.

With kind regards.

476   Counter-offer — all terms not agreed

Thank you for your letter, setting out proposed terms of agreement. These are accepted, with the exception of paragraph . . . . The company cannot agree for the following reasons:

      1 . . . .
      2 . . . .
      3 . . . .

Instead, we propose that . . . .
I look forward to hearing from you.

477   Agreement not correctly set out

Thank you for your letter in which you refer to the agreement which we arrived at in my office this morning. There appears to be a misunderstanding on two points:-

      1 . . . .
      2 . . . .

I have a clear recollection — and also, incidentally, a note — that as to (1), we agreed . . . , and as to (2), we agreed . . . .

I am sorry that I cannot accept the terms as set out in your letter — and I hope that on reflection, you will agree that my recollection and note are correct. I look forward to hearing from you, so that the new arrangement can be put into immediate effect – for the benefit of your members, and, I hope, for that of our company.

With best wishes.

NOTE:
If terms of agreement are set out in a letter, it is vital that you check these through with the greatest of care. If you do not agree with any term as specified, you must say so – otherwise you are asking for trouble. If there is a dispute and a letter has been written setting out the terms and you have failed to challenge any which are in dispute, you are unlikely to be believed. The union representatives will be fully entitled to say: 'If you did not agree with the terms as I set them out, then obviously you would have said so. You are now – a long time afterwards – trying to pull a fast one.' Maybe you are not – but appearances are against you.

478   Let us meet again

I am sure that since our meeting on Monday we must both have had second thoughts. Rather than allow the situation to cascade into chaos, causing infinite harm both to the company and to your members – why do we not meet again?

Perhaps you would telephone me to arrange a mutually convenient appointment?

With best wishes.

479   The ever-open door

Our efforts seem doomed to failure, but my door is always open to you if you have second thoughts. It would be a great pity if we cannot reach an agreement – for the benefit of your members, as well as that of the company.

480   Must you strike?

I was perturbed to learn that you feel that the circumstances are now so serious that you propose taking industrial action. Naturally, this would cause grave harm to the company – but I am sure that you will appreciate that it will prevent our retaining the present high level of employment — and make eventual short time working absolutely inevitable. If you would care to discuss the matter with me, even at this eleventh hour, please do not hesitate to contact me.

481   Complaint at vituperation

I am surprised at the way in which you have seen fit to write to me. I hope that, on reflection, you will regret the intemperate language you have used — and the accusations which you have seen fit to make against my company and myself. These are totally without foundation.

I appreciate that you are working under considerable stress at the moment and in the circumstances, I shall not reply in kind. However, I wish to deal with certain specific allegations of fact:-

   (a) . . . .
   (b) . . . .
   (c) . . . .

Despite the nature of your letter, we are still prepared to meet with you and your colleagues — and to attempt to re-establish the sort of atmosphere within which good industrial relations may prevail, to the benefit of your members as well as that of the company.

482   Negotiations at an end

I have read your letter with care. I have already dealt with your allegations, many times — I would refer you in particular to my letters of the . . . , the . . . and the . . . .

No useful purpose would be served by prolonging this correspondence. It is simply impossible for the company to improve its offer — which I hope that you and your colleagues will, on reflection, appreciate goes a very long way to meeting your wishes, and if accepted, would provide considerable benefits for your members.

483   The door re-opened

My door will always be open to you — and you will be

welcome to come in for a chat – in the future, as in the past. There must be some way out of this horrible mess – for the sake of your people, as well as mine.

484   Why strike must end

As a result of the current industrial dispute, the company has lost . . . days' production and your members . . . days' pay and as a result we will almost certainly have to create redundancies. This situation suits no one – and I cannot believe that – with goodwill and the understanding of the damage caused to all concerned, on both sides – we cannot find an answer.

If you agree that our talks resume, then please let me know.

485   Company in trouble through strike – notices given

We have struggled to keep the company afloat and the workforce intact – but this strike has meant the downfall of our efforts. If it continues beyond . . . , we shall have no alternative other than to terminate the contract of employment of our entire workforce/all those employees engaged in . . ./all those employees still on strike.

My colleagues and I would deeply regret having to take this step, but we do hope that you will not leave us with no other alternative.

486   Industrial agreement

We, the undersigned representatives of the . . . Company and the . . . Union, respectively, hereby record on behalf of the company and on behalf of the union, the following agreement:

1   Mr X, Mrs Y and Miss Z to be reinstated in their jobs forthwith and on the same terms as previously.
2   All employees to return to work from the first shift on the morning of . . . .
3   No employee to be victimised for taking part in the industrial action.
4   The parties agree to a pay and productivity arrangement

as specified in the Schedule hereto; and the . . . Union hereby agrees to recommend acceptance to its members.

SCHEDULE

1 . . . .
2 . . . .
3 . . . .

(Signed) . . . .

NOTE:

In the absence of some clear and specific agreement to the contrary, collective bargains are not intended to have legally binding effect. So neither the above agreement nor almost any other collective bargain – whether in settlement of a dispute or otherwise – can thereafter be the subject of enforcement through the powers of the Courts. However, collective bargains normally are adhered to by both sides and they have powerful moral effect.

487   Dispute at an end

Just a note – to express the pleasure of my colleagues and myself that the dispute between your union and our company has now come to an end. I hope that in future we shall manage to resolve our differences in amicable fashion. And I look forward to seeing you, with a view to seeing how we can make up some of the lost production – and pay – resulting from the strike.

488   Personal appreciation

I write on behalf of my colleagues and myself to say how glad we are that the dispute affecting the company and your members has been settled. On a personal basis, we have all appreciated your patience and restraint and we hope that the agreement now arrived at will enable us to work together for the benefit of the company's business and hence to ensure that we can preserve and if possible expand our work force, despite these difficult times.

NOTE:
A private word of appreciation seldom goes amiss. As usual, it is the intelligent personal touch that ensures good industrial relations.

Chapter 59

Replies to threats of legal action

Once a dispute — whether with an individual employer or employee, union, firm or anyone else — has reached the stage when the contestants are threatening court proceedings, letters must be written with consummate care. They may well be placed before a Court — unless they contain 'without prejudice' negotiations.

When replying to threats of litigation, the following drafts should be useful.

489   Employers to unions — troubled protest

Thank you for your letter. I was extremely perturbed to learn that you feel that the circumstances are now so serious that you wish to take the dispute over the meaning of our agreement, to a court of law for interpretation. Surely we can sort matters out between ourselves, with a little more patience and goodwill? I would be pleased to see you, if you would like to contact me.

NOTE:
Unions do (a) *dislike Courts, but* (b) *on occasion, sue on their own behalf or on behalf of a member.*

490   Management to union — calling the bluff

If you wish to go to court, we cannot stop you.

491   Management to union — please think again

Before you plunge into litigation, may I respectfully suggest that you and your colleagues might reconsider the following points?
(a) . . .
(b) . . .
(c) . . .

492   Suggested meeting outside door of Court

The only people who are absolutely certain to emerge victorious from our current battle are the lawyers. We are bound to meet inside the Court tomorrow morning. I shall be there half an hour early, just in case you might care to meet me outside.

I assure you that in spite of what has happened – and without prejudice to our views as to the merits – there is a fund of goodwill in the company, for your union in general and for yourself in particular.

NOTE:
1   Few laymen really approve of lawyers – until they need them. So if you cannot join with your opposition in mutual love, perhaps mutual dislike of lawyers might do the trick! Even if you are fond of men of law, no one enjoys paying legal costs.

2   Even the most unreasonable of men sometimes turn friendly, when they are actually within sight of the witness box. Only a few exhibitionists really enjoy being cross-examined. And anyway, there is something salutory about hanging around in draughty court corridors – with the prospects of useless, aggravating, boring, protracted further hours of (extremely expensive) misery, in precisely the same place.

3   Even if you decide not to write a letter of this sort, you might bear in mind that a vast majority of cases which actually reach the door of the court are settled without adjudication by the judge.

493   Denial of justification for complaint

There is a misunderstanding. Your complaint is unjustified, for the following reasons:
   (a) . . .
   (b) . . .
   (c) . . .
If you see fit to proceed with your case, then it will be most strenuously opposed.

Without prejudice to our views, we are perfectly prepared to meet you to see whether some compromise arrangement can be arrived at. We maintain our view that this form of litigation is of no use to anyone – except, perhaps, to the lawyers.

I shall telephone your office, tomorrow morning, to see whether you and I cannot hammer out some sensible arrangement.

With my best wishes to you personally.

NOTE:

1   Litigants are always afraid of 'showing weakness' by apparently seeking a settlement. So olive branches are usually waved rather gently.

2   On the other hand, hostility and aggression tend to breed a like response. So moderate letters are normally sensible, when industrial relations are concerned – even in reply to thoroughly aggressive outbursts. Such letters show maturity as well as restraint – and are far more likely to lead to satisfactory results than the venting of steam. This may make you feel better to 'get it off your chest', but aggressive responses are bad medicine, in almost every case.

3   Letters like the above – which make it plain that there is no ill-will between the writer of the letter and its recipient – may pave the way to future good relations. It is important, where possible, to distinguish between a man's views and his personality. One of the joys of both Parliament and the Courts, from the viewpoint of Parliamentarians and lawyers, is the comradeship and friendliness which exist outside political or legal battle (as the case may be). Life is sufficiently short and unpleasant without forming personal animosities against opponents. And the same should also apply in the world of industrial relations.

If you say something unkind, stupid, aggressive or hurtful, then it may be forgotten – or, perhaps, explained away as a misunderstanding. Or the hearer may even convince himself that he has misheard. Not so if you put your remark into writing. It is then available to be mulled over – not only by the recipient but also by others.

4   There are colleagues who have to see the letter – and if you humble the recipient, you will do so in the eyes of others – and make it harder for him to lift his head and hence to compromise. And you will also do so in the eyes of the Court – unless the letter is marked 'without prejudice'. When dealing with complaints made to an Industrial Tribunal, precisely the same principles apply when you put pen to paper as they do when you are coping with ordinary litigation. The effect which your letter has on its immediate reader is doubtless important – but you should have your sights fixed on the future – and in particular on the effect which the letter is likely to have on the Court, i.e. on the individual or people who will eventually decide your case, one way or the other. Thus:

494 Letter will be referred to the Court

I really am surprised at the way in which you have seen fit to write to me. I hope that on reflection, you will regret the intemperate language you have used — and the accusations which you have seen fit to make against my company and myself. These are completely without foundation.

Your letter, of course, will be brought to the attention of the Court, in due course. I am sure that it will make as bad an impression upon the judge as it has done upon me and my colleagues.

I do appreciate, though, that you are working under considerable stress at the moment. In the circumstances, I shall not reply in kind. However, I wish to deal with certain specific allegations of fact:

(a) ....
(b) ....
(c) ....

Despite the nature of your letter, we are still prepared to meet with you and your colleagues — and to attempt to re-establish the sort of atmosphere within which good industrial relations may prevail, to the benefit of your members as well as that of the company.

495 When negotiations are at an end

I have read your letter with care. I have already dealt with your allegations, many times — I would refer you in particular to my letters of the ..., the ... and the ....

No useful purpose would be served by prolonging this correspondence. Unfortunately, it appears that this matter will now have to be decided by the Court.

Chapter 60

Industrial tribunals

New Industrial Tribunal Regulations came into force in October 1980. These had three main objects:

1   To *consolidate* and to emphasise existing Tribunal procedures — such as the power of the chairman to decide how to conduct his Tribunal; and the Tribunal's power to ignore normal court rules of evidence, e.g. the 'hearsay' rule.

2   To introduce a *'pre-hearing assessment'*. This is the Government's attempt to sieve out some of the hopeless cases which form part of the 72 per cent or so of claims which are heard and which fail. It usually costs employers between £600 and £6,000 *to win* an Industrial Tribunal hearing. So the 'pre-hearing assessment' gives the employer — and, in theory, the employee — the right to ask for assessment prior to the hearing. A Tribunal may also set up a pre-hearing assessment of its own volition.

Although there is no law requiring the hearing to be held in private, in practice the public are not invited in. The Tribunal of three considers documents and any oral representations which the parties may wish to make — but it does not hear evidence.

If it decides that the case really does look hopeless, then the applicant is advised not to proceed. Otherwise, the case goes fórward — and, of course, the employer has then had two cases for the price of one.

Note that a 'pre-hearing assessment' is not the same as a 'preliminary hearing' — at which evidence is normally taken on a preliminary point, such as: Does the tribunal have the power to hear the case? Or was the claim brought 'out of time', i.e. more than three months after the termination of the employment; when it was 'reasonably practicable' to bring it within that time?

3   To award *costs* against a party who has proceeded 'reasonably'. An order for costs could only have been made against a party who proceeded 'frivolously' or 'vexatiously' — but now the Tribunal considers 'reasonableness'. It would, for instance, normally be 'unreasonable' to proceed after a pre-hearing assessment at which the Tribunal has advised the claimant that he has no real prospects of success.

496   Application for pre-hearing assessment

We, . . . Ltd of . . . , respondents to the claim numbered
. . . , brought against us in the . . . Industrial Tribunal by
. . . , hereby apply to the Tribunal for a pre-hearing assessment.

Chapter 61

Misunderstandings and apologies

If only people knew how to say 'Sorry' — how many disputes would never occur? Some battles are necessary. Many could be avoided, were it not for pride, feasting upon misunderstandings.

To apologise, though, is not easy. The following letters are designed to make the written apology less hurtful, more dignified — and even, on occasion, to turn it to good account.

*   *   *

497   Misunderstanding — on your part

I have heard that you believe that the management will . . . .

I cannot conceive where this idea came from. It is totally without foundation.

If the fault was mine because I failed to express myself sufficiently clearly — or if I said something which could have been misinterpreted in that way — then I apologise.

The management's position is in fact as follows: . . .

With that misunderstanding out of the way, I hope that we can now get together and see whether we cannot sort out our disagreements. Do please contact me.

498   Misunderstanding — your fault

Forgive me if I have misunderstood — but I have been told that you have informed your members that we agreed that they would be paid at the rate of . . . .

There is clearly a misunderstanding here — and the sooner we meet and talk about it, the better. I repeat: Whatever the basis of that misunderstanding, it is very real and if I caused it by anything that I said, I am sorry.

However, I suspect that someone has simply given you incorrect information which you have passed on and I am now anxious that we should meet so as to prevent the situation from getting out of hand. I look forward to hearing from you.

With best wishes.

499 Agreement – misunderstood

I expect it was because we did not finish arguing until the early hours of the morning – but I have now seen a copy of the Minute which you have sent round your members regarding our agreement. Unfortunately, there are several matters contained in it which differ totally from my note and also from my recollection.

It is therefore essential that we meet again so as to sort out this misunderstanding – can you please contact me immediately?

I think that we will both have to learn a lesson from this – that however late at night we finish our labours, it would be worth staying on just a little longer so as to put our agreement onto paper – together!

With best wishes.

500 Apology – without frills

The fault is entirely mine – and I apologise. I should not have lost my temper – and I did not mean what I said.

There are, I am afraid, times when one is under great strain – this was just such a time. I was also extremely tired. My apologies to you. I understand that you were insulted – that was not my intention.

I trust that you will accept this apology in the spirit in which it is offered – and that you will join me for a drink this evening at . . . . For the sake of your members as well as that of the management, it is obviously disastrous that you and I should fall out – and I am very sorry that my words should have caused the unnecessary breach.

Looking forward to seeing you and with all best wishes.

Chapter 62

Your Member of Parliament

The services of an MP are free, unique and, in most cases, readily available. Because the local Member is concerned to preserve and where possible to increase employment in his constituency and for his constituents, he will rarely refuse to help local employers.

Exception: most MPs keep the maximum distance from industrial disputes, recognising that they are best solved by management and unions, if necessary with the help of ACAS.

To contact an MP, you could ask to see him in his constituency, where he probably holds frequent 'surgeries'; or at Westminster. Better still, write – to the House of Commons, London, SW1.

* * *

501   Invitation to MP to visit

We employ a large number of your constituents and would be delighted to welcome you to our works at . . . . We would be happy to show you around; to introduce you to our workforce and to the leaders of their union; and to entertain you to lunch.

If you are agreeable in principle to accepting this then would you kindly let me have some alternative dates?

With best wishes,

NOTE:
1   Invite your Member before *you need him.*

2   Always include the workforce and unions in your invitation and in your plans. It is a grave error to show an MP around the place and then to whisk him off to a private, directors' lunch – without at least introducing him to the trade union team. Even better: why not set up a meeting for him with trade union representatives?

3   If you have a specific problem to discuss with him, then prior indication does no harm, thus:

502 Invitation – to discuss problem

We are deeply concerned with the increased dumping of . . . , manufactured by very cheap labour (and/or with the help of substantial government subsidies). This unfair competition is driving our business to the wall – and we may have to make a substantial number of your constituents redundant.

In the circumstances, we would be grateful if you would spare time to see us, either in your constituency or in the Commons. Alternatively, would you care to visit our works, where we would be very pleased to introduce you to our trade union leaders, as well as to members of our management team and to discuss these and other problems with you at our leisure and your own.

Looking forward to hearing from you and with best wishes,

503 Thanks to MP

We read with interest and with appreciation of your efforts to assist our industry and in particular your speech/ question in the House last week. Thank you! We are working hard to keep the business afloat in these very difficult times and your encouragement and help is greatly appreciated.

We look forward to seeing you again at our works at any time you would be free to call on us.

504 Appreciation for MP's services

We thank you most sincerely for your intervention with the Minister. As a direct result, he has now agreed to . . . .

With renewed thanks and kind regards,

"WHAT DO YOU MEAN COMMA MY MIND IS ALWAYS ON MY WORK QUESTION MARK "

Part Eight

APPENDICES

Employment law— and the 1980 Act: your guide and summary

The Employment Act, 1980, is in full force. So are the new Codes on picketing and closed shops. How, then, do the changes leave the law on personal and trade union protection? How do they affect your rights, if you are dismissed – or your protection, if you are engaged in trade union duties? Or if you are a manager, what are the main rules on individual and trade union protection in the 1980s, if you need to know them?

Here is your practical guide and summary of some of the most important rules – reflecting the Government's attempted new balance between employers and employees and managements and trade unions respectively.

* * *

Appointment

Every employee works under a contract of employment. He is entitled to written particulars of the main terms within 13 weeks of the start of the employment or 4 weeks of any change. If he is dismissed, then his contract is terminated.

Notice – and wrongful dismissal

An employee is entitled to agreed notice; in the absence of agreement, to such period as is reasonable in all the circumstances of the case; and in any event to not less than the statutory minimum – one week after four weeks; two weeks after two years; then adding a week a year, up to twelve weeks after twelve years' service. Unless he is lawfully, summarily dismissed for 'repudiating' or 'smashing' his contract of service, if he does not get his proper notice or pay in lieu, he is said to be dismissed 'wrongfully', He may claim damages in the County Court (usually, up to £2,000) or in the High Court. The Government has power to shift wrongful dismissal claims to industrial tribunals — but has not done so.

Unfair dismissal

An employee who is dismissed 'unfairly' may get his remedy from an industrial tribunal. He must show that he was 'dismissed' — 'actually' or 'constructively' (by being forced out of his job) — as opposed to resigning voluntarily. And he must be qualified for protection by (in general) 52 weeks' employment (instead of 26 weeks as before); by not being a part-timer (working less than 16 hours a week or 8 hours after 5 years' continuous service); a pensioner or a person normally working outside the UK.

Once a claimant has shown that he was 'dismissed', his employer must show the reason for the dismissal. But under the 1980 Act, the burden of proving 'fairness' no longer rests on the boss. The tribunal must look at all the circumstances of the case, including the employer's size and administrative resources.

A successful claimant may now get a **compensatory award of up to £6,250** (to compensate him for his actual loss); a basic award (equal to his lost redundancy entitlement) — maximum £3,900 after 20 years; but a basic award of up to two weeks' pay for an employee who is unfairly dismissed but suffers no loss has now been repealed. The 'additional award' for an unfairly dismissed employee whose employers unreasonably refuse to obey a tribunal order for his reinstatement or re-engagement is extremely rare.

An employee can only successfully contract out of his right to go to a tribunal if he has come to an agreement with his employer which has been recorded by a conciliation officer; or if he has a fixed-term contract for 12 months or more containing a contracting-out clause. Until the new Act, this period was two years.

Maternity rights

A woman who has been continuously employed for at least two years as at the beginning of the eleventh week before the date of her expected confinement and (normally) who stays at work until that date, is still entitled to maternity pay — six weeks at 9/10ths of her normal rate, minus the maximum current maternity allowance. But she must now give notice to her employer that she will be absent due to pregnancy or confinement, where reasonably practicable, at least 21 days before leaving.

A mother's right to return to her job if she is qualified (as above) remains unchanged — but the Act has created a series of important new notices:

1 Where reasonably practicable, i.e. where she knows she has rights, the mother must give written notice of her intention to return, at least 21 days before she leaves.

2 Not less than 49 days after the confinement, the employer may give notice to the mother, asking her to confirm if she still intends to return; she must do so in writing within 14 days or lose her rights.

3 At least 21 days before returning, the mother must now give written notice of her intended date of return.

In addition, if an employer offers the mother reasonably suitable alternative employment which she either accepts or unreasonably refuses, the rights disappear.

Small businesses

Firms employing less than five people no longer have to give maternity leave. And the qualifying period for unfair dismissal protection for an employee of the business employing not more than 20 people is now two years.

New Tribunal regulations

Under new Industrial Tribunal Regulations effective from 1 October 1980, a tribunal may order a 'prehearing assessment' to look at the documents and other evidence to see whether the case should proceed to a full-scale hearing. A tribunal also has new powers to award costs, not only where the claim is 'frivolous' or 'vexatious', but also where the claimant has proceeded 'unreasonably'.

In practice, these Regulations are likely to be more effective in producing less tribunal cases than the Employment Act changes — which are unlikely to be greatly felt as 72 per cent of all claims which come to a hearing already fail — and the effect of extending the period of required employment for unfair dismissal protection from 6 to 12 months has been to reduce the number of applications by about 26 per cent.

Closed shops

An employee may now contract out of a closed shop if he has a genuine, conscientious objection – or a deeply held personal belief – which prevents him from belonging. And to enforce a future (as opposed to an existing) closed-shop agreement, the employer or union will have to show that it has been 'approved' by a secret ballot in which over 80 per cent of those eligible to vote did so in favour. And any union which 'unreasonably excludes or expels' a person may be taken to a tribunal – and if an employer (including a sub-contractor) can prove that he has been forced unlawfully to dismiss an employee in a closed-shop situation due to union pressure, he may join the union as a party to the action and claim an indemnity.

Picketing and secondary action

Trade unions and their officers are protected against civil and criminal suits if they act 'in contemplation or futherance of a trade dispute'. In brief, the new rules remove that protection where (in general) that action is directed against people not directly involved in the dispute. These sections are highly complicated and if you run into them, you should take expert advice.

The Codes explain and to a small extent expand the rules. Failure to comply with their terms is neither a civil nor a criminal offence but may be used in evidence in any proceedings to which it is relevant.

Trade union rules

Unions continue to have secret ballots if, but only if, they so desire. No changes are required in their rules, but in most cases, they may apply for repayment of the cost of secret ballots from public funds.

In conclusion

Most of the new rules – for unfair dismissal and closed shops in particular – are unlikely to be of great individual effect. But the Act itself, taken as a whole, will have a powerful impact on industrial relations – already made difficult through recession, inflation and unemployment. Naturally, the unions will do what they can to prevent the curbing of their rights and powers. In practice, time and court interpretation will tell how the new employment scene will develop in the rough 1980s.

Small businesses

Believing that smaller businesses would take on more employees if their proprietors did not believe that employees were over-protected, the Government set about lessening that protection in the following ways:

1 By increasing the qualifying period for unfair dismissal protection. Employees must now be continuously employed for 12 months (as defined) instead of the previous 26 weeks. But where a business has at no time during the employee's employment had more than 20 people on its books, that qualifying period is now 104 weeks.

2 When assessing fairness or otherwise of a dismissal, the tribunal is now required to take into account 'the size and administrative resources of the employer's business'. But in the past, the tribunal always did have to take into account all the circumstances of the case — which always did include the size and strength of the employer's business. So this change is more cosmetic than real. What matters to the small business is that it may now be as unfair as it wishes for twice as long when dismissing an unwanted employee (see 1 above).

3 While any-sized firm may now offer a returning mother 'reasonably suitable alternative employment, which she accepts or unreasonably refuses on pain of losing her maternity rights, when a firm employs less than five people and it is not reasonably practicable to give the returning mother her job back, she will lose her rights.

4 Finally (but of little practical importance) employers of not more than 20 people are not bound to provide facilities for secret ballots.

Unqualified protection

Your employment with this company began on the . . . and terminated on . . . . At no time during this period did the company employ more than 20 people. In the circumstances, as your employment with the company lasted less than 104 weeks, you are not protected against unfair dismissal. It follows that if you see fit to pursue your unfair dismissal claim, we shall ask for either a prehearing assessment or a preliminary hearing, because in the circumstances you are clearly unqualified for protection.

NOTE:

See Chapter 60 for new rules on industrial tribunal hearings, designed to avoid the wasting of time and costs through the pursuit to trial of hopeless cases.

Maternity – no return

Thank you for your letter dated . . . , saying that you intend to return on the . . . . . Unfortunately, it was not possible for us to keep your job vacant during your absence. It would not now be reasonably practicable or fair to dismiss your replacement. In the circumstances and as we have no other employment which we can offer you, we very much regret that it will not be possible for us to take you back, as you and we had both hoped.

NOTE:
For remaining maternity letters, see Chapter 22.

Contracts of Employment — in perspective

Every employer and personnel manager or executive has two perspectives on a contract of employment — that of the company, firm or authority which employs him, and his own. Either way, it is the contract that decides the rights of the parties, while the employment continues and even after its termination.

So for your own protection as well as that of your employers, consider the rules — and whom they protect.

* * *

Every employee, however mighty or however miniscule, works thanks to a contract of employment. Its main terms should be in writing, so as to comply with *The Employment Protection (Consolidation) Act, 1978* — and for the avoidance of doubt and dispute. But employment contracts which are wholly or partly oral are far too common, especially for longer-serving employees whose terms have changed along with their work and status. But although the law sometimes interferes by establishing minimum rights for the employee, the main terms of the agreement are those made between the parties — expressly or by implication.

So every employer or personnel manager should give careful attention at and from the beginning of the employment to the terms of the contract — in the professional and executive fields even more than in others. You do not enter marriage with a view to divorce — but to create a contract of employment without an eye on dismissal, redundancy or retirement is a grave error. If you fail to consider the terms of subordinates' contracts properly, then your own position is unlikely to be strengthened. Conversely: fail to put and to keep your own terms in sensible order and you risk losing most of the protection which the law can give you.

From the start, take notice. Until an employee has been on the books for 52 weeks (as defined — which may be a little less), notice is his only hedge against the sack. And as most redundancies are 'fair', the importance of his notice period will re-emerge, if his job goes along with him.

An employee is entitled to such period of notice as is agreed. Only in the absence of agreement is he entitled to 'reasonable notice' – or anyway, to *not less than* the statutory minimum of seven days after four weeks; two weeks after two years; and then adding a week a year until 12 weeks after 12 years.

Dismiss an employee without his proper notice or pay in lieu and that dismissal is 'wrongful'. Even if he is off work ill and his sick pay entitlement has expired, his right to normal pay revives during his period of notice.

Or suppose that you make an employee redundant. He will be entitled to such redundancy pay as may be agreed by you at the time – and if he is represented by a strong union, you may pay him far more than his minimum entitlement. Once again, the law provides only a minimum – and then only beginning after he has served at least two years after reaching the age of 18 and rising to a new maximum (as from 1 February 1981) of £3,900 after 20 years' service at the appropriate age and pay. Even today, no employment contract contains redundancy provisions. But in addition to his redundancy rights, the employee must get his proper notice or pay in lieu. And its amount is – or at least should be – built into the original contract.

Again: the contract should state the employee's 'job title', as well as his place and hours of work. If you are closing a department or a unit and you want to move your employee to some other place or position, look at the contract. Does it contain a mobility clause? If it is inflexible, then you have no right to require the employee to change from the agreed terms, merely because of what courts call 'the exigencies of your business'. Also if you insist on a change and are not prepared to keep him on upon the old terms, then he may leave and regard himself as dismissed constructively. You have forced him out of his job by refusing to keep him on, doing the same work at the same place or time.

If the employee is qualified for unfair dismissal protection (in general, by serving at least 12 months and not being a part-timer or pensioner), then he may claim that he was unfairly made redundant – that you unreasonably chose him for the chop.

Equally, the recession may require you to change your system of shift-working – perhaps using new machinery round the clock – or stopping your night shift because your order book empties. Your right to require your employees to change their hours depends upon their contracts.

Conversely: if your employers wish to move your work, in terms of time or space, then your contract will determine their right to do so – with or without compensation. So the moral is clear: if you are trying to do the best for your company or firm, you should ensure wherever possible that all contracts have maximum flexibility. But you should keep your own terms of service as *in*flexible as you can manage.

Or suppose that you are trying to cut your workforce with the minimum misery so you decide to invite your older employees to retire early. Are they bound to do so? As always – look at the contract. If the agreement is silent on retirement, then would a term be implied, through your invariable custom? Or, more likely, do women retire at 60 and men at 65?

If you wish to retire someone early, there are only two possibilities. Either you have or you have not got his agreement. Assuming that the agreement is not contained in his contract, then you must get it at the time – if you can. If he is willing to leave early and to accept his pension (again, on agreed terms – subject to statutory arrangements), then so be it. Not only will the law decline to interfere but the Department of Employment will almost certainly cooperate by accepting a redundancy situation and paying over the Revenue's 41 per cent share of the statutory redundancy money – leaving the employer, of course, to pay 100 per cent of any sum over and above the statutory minimum which he may agree to pay out.

Assume, then, that you get an employee's agreement to retire early – or, for that matter, to accept voluntary redundancy. Beware! There are only two circumstances in which the law will allow an employee to contract out of his right to make a claim for unfair dismissal or for redundancy pay to an industrial tribunal. Normally, any such term will be void, whether it is contained in the original contract, or in a later deal under which the employee agrees to 'go quietly'. So unless one of those two circumstances apply, he may take your money . . . sign that he has accepted it 'in full and final settlement' of all claims against you – and still go to a tribunal and ask for more.

The first exception to the general rule: fixed-term contracts for one year or more may contain effective 'contracting out' clauses. *The Employment Act, 1980,* reduced the period from two years. But remember that an appeal court has held that an employee taken on to do a fixed *job* is not 'dismissed' when that job terminates and the employer does not provide him with further work.

So even if you actually employ someone to do a fixed job for you – maybe an O&M study or a research project, computer installation or building maintenance or repair – that person is now totally unprotected against unfair dismissal or redundancy.

If, though, you employ an apprentice – or, for that matter, a senior executive or a professional expert – on a fixed-term contract which is to last for one year or more, then a 'contracting-out clause' is both proper and effective.

Second: an agreement to compromise a potential unfair dismissal or redundancy claim will be enforced if – but only if – it has been recorded by a conciliation officer. The ACAS man will tell the parties their rights but has no power to rule on the merits of the agreement. His job is merely to record it on his form COT3.

Still, any agreement in any employment contract other than one for a fixed term of a year or more is void, in so far as it tries to remove an employee's statutory rights. The same applies to most terms giving employers rights to employees' inventions.

The Patents Act, 1977, provides that any invention made by an employee belongs to him. There are two exceptions: first, if a person is employed to invent, then his employer will own any invention which he makes in the course of his employment and which may reasonably be expected to arise from it. Second: an employer may buy from his employee either a patent or licence to use that invention. But in either case, the employee may apply to the court or to the Comptroller of Patents for a further payment, if he considers that his employers have taken an unfair advantage of him and that it would be 'just and equitable' for him to get more.

Note: these rules apply whatever may be in the contract of employment. In general, and subject to statutory minimum rights, you may make whatever deal you like with your own employers – or on their behalf with their employees. But you cannot generally take away either an employee's rights to go to a tribunal or to keep his patentable inventions as his own.

Still, there is a much wider area left to agreement. For instance: with the exception of employees to whom Wages Council Regulations apply, no employee has any statutory right to sick pay or (with the additional exception of women and young persons in factories) to holidays. The law requires employers to put into the terms of service what sick pay or holiday entitlement *if any* the employee is to receive.

Precisely because the law is so weak, you should ensure for yourself that *your own* rights are clearly recorded. You may say: 'My company are very decent. They look after their executives.' No doubt they do – unless and until times get really rough – or the company gets taken over by other, less kindly businessmen, determined to get the return on their purchase price.

Nor should you rely on any 'gentlemen's agreement'. Either there is a contract or there is none. In business, the only 'gentlemen' are people doing well – so the number of 'gentlemen' with industrial and commercial power in the UK is dwindling rapidly.

Again: suppose that you are asked to give up part of your holiday because of pressures on your department . . . shortages of staff . . . or (hopefully) a sudden burst of business activity. You can only insist on your lost time or pay 'rolling over' to some future date if your contract so provides or if you can induce your employers to agree to give you this right, when they ask for your assistance. Then confirm the agreement in writing and keep a copy – for your protection.

So contracts of employment matter – from their inception to their end. For the sake of everyone concerned – your company or authority, your employees or yourself – remember: care with contracts today avoids unnecessary misery and expense tomorrow – and sometimes, for ever after.

Health and Safety Commission: guidance notes on employers' policy statements for health and safety at work

These preliminary guidance notes are given in two parts: Part 1 answers some basic questions on the statutory duty of employers under Section 2(3) of The Health and Safety at Work etc. Act, 1974, which came into operation on 1 April 1975; Part 2 gives general guidelines to the preparation of a written statement.

The written policy statement – blueprint for greater safety and better health at work.

The Health and Safety Commission attaches the greatest importance to this requirement of the Act. For each employer it is the blueprint on which his entire health and safety at work policy, organisation and activity are based. It should therefore be drafted clearly so that the entire labour force, management and employed, understands it and knows what its responsibilities are.

The Commission issues this pamphlet to give employers preliminary guidance on the preparation of their written policy statements. In the light of experience the Commission will decide what additional guidance is necessary, and whether at any time codes of practice on written policy statements should be prepared to cover particular industries or circumstances.

Part 1   Some basic questions

What is the law?

Section 2(3) of *The Health and Safety at Work etc. Act, 1974*, says:
'Except in such cases as may be prescribed, it shall be the duty of every employer to prepare and as often as may be appropriate revise a written statement of his general policy with respect to the health and safety at work of his employees and the organisation and arrangements for the time being in force for carrying out that policy, and to bring that statement and any revision of it to the notice of all his employees.'
The Act places on employers the statutory duty to ensure so far as is reasonably practicable the safety and health and welfare of their employees at work. Section 2(3) of the Act requires every employer (except those prescribed in regulations) to prepare, revise and bring to the notice of his employees, a written statement covering two distinct aspects: (1) his general policy with respect to the health and safety at work of his employees; (2) the organisation and arrangements for carrying out that policy.
Note: In the larger companies or undertakings it might be necessary to deal separately with matters of organisation and with the arrangements for carrying out the general policy.

What is meant by 'employee' and 'employer'?

The Act defines 'employee' as an individual who works under a contract of employment and adds that related expressions shall be construed accordingly. Although the Act does not specifically define an 'employer' it can be taken to mean that an employer is any person, partnership, corporate body or unincorporated association which employs one or more individuals under a contract of employment. All such employers (with the exception of those prescribed in regulations) are to have written policy statements. Where the structure of an enterprise or service is such that a number of subsidiaries (e.g. in a local authority) under its overall policy or financial control are themselves employers, it may be possible for a common policy statement to be applied, but in such cases each individual employer would need to promulgate it under his own authority as part of his written statement.

Can the employer pass on his responsibility to employees, their appointed/elected safety representatives or to safety committees?

No. The employer cannot pass on his responsibility to his employees or their representatives. It will be sensible for an employer to consult his employees, through their safety representatives and to heed to the advice of the safety committees, where these exist, in order to ensure that the best arrangements and organisations for safety and health are evolved and maintained. Such consultation does not diminish his responsibility; it is clearly part of his greater responsibility under the Health and Safety at Work etc Act. The Commission will issue separate guidance and draw up the necessary codes of practice concerning safety representatives and safety committees.

Will all written policy statements look alike?

No. The length and content of each written policy statement, like any blueprint, must be specifically prepared to meet the situation of the particular employer. He must thoroughly assess the possible hazards to the health and safety of his employees which might arise in connection with the activities on which they are employed and in the premises or other working area in which they are required to work.

Cannot the Health and Safety Commission draw up a model policy statement?

Although it might be possible to produce some sample statements, it is unlikely that these would suit any individual employer. To provide a model might cause some employers to overlook important health and safety measures which their particular activities and premises demanded. Nevertheless, the Commission feel that certain general guidelines might be helpful and these are set out and discussed in Part 2 of this leaflet. In addition, the Executive and its staff will be prepared to advise individual employers on the compilation of written policy statements. Some employers' organisations, industry associations, professional bodies and similar groupings have already issued their own guidance directly related to the activities with which they are concerned, and others may wish to do so.

What needs to be done about existing written policy statements?

They should be examined against the requirements of Section 2(3) of the Act and considered in the light of the advice given in this leaflet as well as that issued by the employer organisations, etc. Some existing written policy statements might be found to meet all these requirements, others might need some adjustment. The re-writing of policy statements should do nothing to disturb satisfactory arrangements already existing between the employer and employees.

Will the written policy statement be all that is required to be communicated to employees?

No. Under Section 2(2)(c) of the Act there is an obligation on every employer to provide such information, instruction, training and supervision as is necessary to ensure, so far as is reasonably practicable, the health and safety at work of his employees. This means, particularly where there are large labour forces and the more complex and potentially dangerous industrial processes, that there is an additional need to publish detailed rules and regulations for particular activities. The written policy statement is not, for instance, the appropriate way of covering detailed rules for the handling of toxic substances, although it would be appropriate for it to refer to the fact that such additional detailed rules were to be maintained and followed. The Commission will issue separate guidance or codes of practice on these additional responsibilities.

How should the written policy statement be brought to the notice of employees?

There may already be adequate methods of written communication between the employer and all individual employees. Otherwise the way in which the statement is brought to their notice might be a suitable point for discussion with workers' representatives. A suitable channel for ensuring adequate communication might be the joint safety committee or any other existing joint consultative arrangement in the firm. Nevertheless the employer must ensure that it is brought to the notice of every employee.

How should the statement be kept up-to-date?

Every employer must recognise his statutory obligation for keeping up-to-date both parts of the written statement. Where, for instance, those named in the second part as responsible for the various aspects of health and safety are replaced, amendments must be published without delay and brought to the notice of all employees. Then as joint safety committees are developed, these should provide the impetus for improving the existing arrangements and such improvements must then be incorporated into the written policy statements. Other improvements will stem from new regulations, codes of practice, guidance issued by the Commission, research into health and safety at work, from accident analysis and investigation, and from developments in the design and safeguarding of machinery. Wherever such improvements or changes affect the written policy of an employer, they should be reflected in its periodic revision.

Part 2   Guidelines to drafting

Structure of written statement

1   Although no model layout could possibly suit all situations, all written policy statements should cover both the essential parts referred to in Section 2(3) of the Act, i.e.

a   the general policy

b   the organisation and arrangements for carrying it out. (In larger undertakings these two subjects may best be dealt with in separate sections.)

In some larger or more complex undertakings it may also be better to produce the policy statement in the form of two documents:

a   a concise statement of the general policy, organisation and arrangements in a single document which could be distributed to all employees and which would make reference to;

b   a more detailed document or collection of documents (e.g. including manuals of rules and procedures) which could be held in a central position in each location for all to see on request, or posted where it could be seen by all employees.

Detailing the levels of responsibility

2   The general policy statement should be a declaration of the employer's intent to seek to provide the safest and healthiest working conditions possible and to enlist the support of his employees towards achieving these ends.

3   In the case of employers engaged in a number of different activities

or where the operations are geographically widespread, the policy may require formulation at more than one level. The highest management level should lay down in writing the principles of the policy whilst the sub-groups or operational units interpret that policy in a realistic written form to suit the identified needs at the lower levels.

4 The policy statement should give the name and where necessary business address of the Director, Secretary, Manager or Senior Executive who is responsible for fulfilling the policy, or designate the appointment wherein that responsibility lies. In the case of mines and quarries, reference should be made to the holders of statutory appointments.

5 Whilst the overall policy responsibility for health and safety rests at the highest management level, all individuals at every level will have to accept degrees of responsibility for carrying out that policy. Wherever appropriate key individuals or their appointments should be named and their responsibilities defined. In addition there should be adequate arrangements to cover the absence of personnel with key safety functions.

6 Where functional expertise exists to advise line management, then the relationship of these functions, e.g. safety adviser, chemist, etc. should be made clear and the extent of their functions defined in relation to safety and health.

7 The policy statement should make it clear that the final level of responsibility is that of each and every individual employee.

Safety representatives and joint safety committees

8 Where appropriate, the organisation for joint consultation on health and safety (e.g. joint safety committees) should be described and should be accompanied by a list of persons responsible within the safety organisation, including employees' safety representatives or inspectors (which must be kept up-to-date).

The employer's policy on training and supervision

9 The written statement should ensure that all who are at risk are well aware of the hazards, the reasons for control in working practices and the part they as individuals have to play in maintaining a safe and healthy

working environment.

10   However adequate these written statements, etc. are in themselves the aim will not be achieved without good training and thorough supervision. Employers' policy statements should reflect their determination in these areas. It is, for instance, vital to spell out the supervisor's key role as he is the person on the spot who knows how the job is done. It is equally important for management to consider, and then set down, the positive steps which are to be taken to train and equip supervisors for this responsibility.

Detailing the hazards

11   Many accidents occur because workpeople do not understand the hazards involved and the precautions that have to be taken. The main hazards should be identified and reference made in the statement to additional rules and regulations which must be observed. It should be quite specific about the employer's policy in respect of certain fairly common hazards, such as the dangers of untidy working areas, the failure to use guards or to wear protective clothing, the introduction of new machinery or substances, maintenance work, etc.

12   Procedures should be laid down for accidents, particularly those involving any personal injury, to be systematically recorded by an employer. Also any information, based on expert analyses of accidents or dangerous occurrences, published by employers' federations, safety organisations of the HSC itself, should be monitored by the employer and relevant extracts made pertaining to his particular activity. The employer should regularly present such records and information to all management levels and his safety committee with a view to identifying and providing against new, or hitherto unidentified, hazards and checking on the frequency of occurrence of known hazards.

Model policies

The Health and Safety Commission Executive do not favour 'model' or 'specimen' policies — and they do not intend to produce any such publication.

Disciplinary procedures

Written particulars of terms of service must either set out disciplinary procedures or state where they are easily accessible to the employee. Brief samples appear in the appropriate places in the book. Here are three good, representative samples of disciplinary procedures currently in use.

Example 1

In the case of a misdemeanour or unsatisfactory behaviour on the part of an employee a verbal warning may be given by the employee's immediate supervisor or above and it will be recorded on his/her personal file on the recommendation of his/her Departmental Executive.

If there is no improvement in the behaviour which necessitated the first verbal warning the employee will be interviewed by his/her Departmental Executive who, in conjunction with the Personnel Manager or Deputy, will hear the complaint and issue a second warning as necessary.

Should there still be no improvement in the employee's performance or behaviour a final written warning will be issued by the Departmental Executive and the Personnel Manager.

If at any stage the employee considers that he/she has been unfairly or unjustly disciplined he/she should as soon as possible after the incident approach the person who administered the discipline and request a meeting to discuss the matter with his/her Departmental Executive or the Personnel Manager.

If the employee's behaviour continues to be unsatisfactory no further warning need be given to effect dismissal should this be considered necessary by the Departmental Executive.

If an employee feels he/she has been unfairly or unjustly dismissed he/she may appeal in writing to the Personnel Manager within one week of receiving notice.

The Personnel Manager will arrange an interview within one week to determine the matter finally.

The following are Departmental Executives: . . . .

Example 2

THERE CAN BE NO PRECISE RULES AS TO THE APPROACH FOR DISCIPLINARY PROCEDURE.

Normally, a verbal reprimand between a Manager and an individual, is adequate. However, a persistent offender will be aware that he will be called to task officially at some time. There may be occasions where a member of staff, who does not normally err, finds himself in the position of an official warning due to the degree of his misdemeanour.

Stages of Disciplinary Procedure
In essence there are three stages:
1 Verbal warning (1a — verbal warning and letter).
2 Final warning in writing.
3 Letter of dismissal.

Stage 1: verbal warning   A reprimand for misconduct will be administered to the offender in the presence of his Chapel Officer and a Management Representative. In the event of no Manager being available from own department as a witness, a Manager will be requested from Central Production or another Production Department.

A detailed report must be made to the Production Manager; copied to Personnel Department and departmental files. The offender must be informed that the facts of the incident will be noted in his personnel record.

It may be felt necessary that at Stage 1 the offender is issued with a letter confirming that any further problems will result in a final warning letter. This is a useful device when the offender is taken to task on a matter not quite so obvious, such as performance at his work. It may also serve a useful purpose when there are some special circumstances surrounding an incident.

Stage 2: final warning   In the event of an individual, previously dealt with above, again being disciplined for misconduct he will be advised verbally that a letter, from his Department Manager, will be sent to him concerning this reprimand and advising him that any further serious misconduct will result in dismissal.

The interview will again take place before the individual, his Chapel Official and a Management Representative.

The Department Manager will write the letter, copies of which will be sent to the Production Manager, Chapel Official and Personnel Department. He will also advise the individual that the letter of warning will be included in his personnel record.

Furthermore, a detailed report of the incident which necessitated the letter will be made to the Production Manager, copied to Personnel Department and departmental files.

Deputy Managers   If the Deputy Manager is unacquainted with the previous record of the offender and does not at the time have access to the written information on the offender, he may, before committing the Company, advise the individual that the incident will be fully reported to the Department Manager.

Stage 3: letter of dismissal   Any further misconduct will result in confrontation as before; dismissal verbally, followed by dismissal letter from Department Manager, copied to Production Manager, Chapel Official, Branch Secretary and Personnel Department.

As previously a detailed report will be prepared.

It is imperative that the man dismissed is advised that he has the right of appeal, to the Production Manager, and may be accompanied by a Chapel Official if he wishes. Time must be allowed for him to properly prepare his case. At least three working days is recommended.

Deputy Managers   Procedure as far as the Deputy Manager is concerned must vary. The Deputy Manager could carry out the verbal dismissal, before the witnesses previously mentioned, and instruct the dismissed that a letter confirming the dismissal will be sent by the Department Manager. There could be a situation whereby the offender is sent home by the Deputy Manager and told to report to the Department Manager the following day. Again this action would take place before the normal witnesses.

The Deputy Manager, if not fully acquainted with the previous history of the offender, should call Central Production for advice.

Having quoted the broad lines of Disciplinary Procedure to be followed in three stages, it must be borne in mind that the action to be taken will at all times depend on the circumstances and nature of the misconduct.

Full documentation is essential in order to establish the basis of a dismissal at all times. Deputy Managers must be able to have access to all relevant information.

Note: a further point concerning proof of delivery of Final Warnings and Letter of Dismissal is to post such correspondence by Recorded Delivery.

Federated Chapel

It should be noted that the Federated House Chapel have made representations to the Company that letters of warning should have a specific life and that disciplinary measures should not be based on a historical misdemeanour of long standing.

The Company has replied to the Federated House Chapel that although no formal arrangement will be made for automatic destruction of warning letters after a given period of time, the Company has no wish to be unreasonable and will obviously take into account the age of previous warnings issued to a member of staff. If the employee has for example worked well and normally over the last three years then it is possible that the previous warnings will be ignored by the Departmental Manager.

DISMISSAL: *Date...*

Dear Mr...

Last night you were (circumstances – witnesses etc.).

You were previously reprimanded verbally in the presence of etc., etc., for your conduct on (date) and my subsequent letter to you dated ... is quite explicit as to the Company's attitude.

You have clearly chosen to ignore the verbal and written warnings previously given and I therefore have to advise you that you are dismissed from the Company as from the date of this letter.

As stated to you in the presence of your Chapel Official, you are entitled to make representations concerning my decision to the Production Manager within three working days, when you may, if you wish, be accompanied by a Chapel Official.

Your appropriate documents and holiday entitlement, less any deduction due by you to the Company, will be forwarded immediately. You will also be advised of your pension entitlement within the next few weeks.

Yours sincerely

Example 3

Should it be necessary for the Company to take disciplinary action against any employee, the normal procedure will be:

Recorded verbal warnings.

Final warning in writing.

Dismissal.

This procedure will not apply where an employee is guilty of breach of contract or gross misconduct.

Employees who are members of a trade union or staff organisation recognised by the Company may be accompanied by a representative of that body whenever a disciplinary interview is taking place.

At the request of the employee, the Company will provide a written statement of the reason for the dismissal.

Any dismissed employee who wishes to appeal against dismissal, may do so within two working days, by applying to his Manager. The appeal will be considered by the Managing Director of the Operating Company concerned, unless he has been involved in the decision to dismiss. In this case the appeal will be considered by the Chairman of the Operating Company.

"HOW DO YOU SPELL 'DEAR SIR'... ? "

Index

letters concerning, specimens
of suitable, 313-20
police, must you report to?
310
property, restitution of, 310
prosecutions, 310-12
company policy and, 316-18
search, power of, 309
security officers (within
company), 315
theft explained and discussed,
321-4
borrowing distinguished,
323
warning in lieu of prosecution,
319

Danger to others, 245
Defamation, 40-1
Demotion, 45
where dismissal follows,
107-10
Design fault, 281
Disagreements, *see* Disputes
Disciplinary procedures, 11-12,
101-6, 371-5
Discrimination, 145-62
complaint to ACAS, 149
complaints to Equal Opportunities Commission,
148, 150
equal pay, 147-8, 151-2
married man, 152
sex as essential qualification,
149
Dismissal:
categories of, explained, 59-61
constructive, what constitutes,
62-5
definitions, 59-61
disciplinary procedure and,
373-5
due to illness, 53-4
effected with notice, 72-84
aptitude, lacking necessary,
75-6
insufficiency of skill, 73-4
kindness, exercising, 79,81
misconduct and holiday
accrual, 73
of director, 73

payments made 'without
prejudice', 77
qualifications, lack of, 74-5
typical reasons for fair,
78-84
Employment Act, 1980,
provisions of, 353-5
fairness of, 72-84
of executives, *see* Executives
reasons for (in writing), 101-6
unfair, employees excluded,
96-100
provisions of *Employment
Act, 1980,* respecting,
354
warnings on intended, 66-71
where demotion involved,
107-10
see also Redundancy
Disputes and disagreements:
apologies, how to make, 346-7
industrial, 331-9
industrial tribunals, 344-5
legal action, letters dealing
with threats of, 340-3
Members of Parliament,
approaches to, 348-9
misunderstandings, 346-7
picketing, 331-9
secondary pickets, 331-9
tribunals, 334-5

Employment:
applications for, reasons for
rejecting, 24
fixed-term contracts of, 36-41
for apprenticeships, 38-41
variations in, 42-4
probationary period of, 32-3
trial periods of, 32-5
Employment Act, 1980, 153-9,
177, 361
provisions summarised, 353-6
Employment Appeal Tribunal,
address of, 190
*Employment Protection Act,
1975,* 167, 173, 191,
207
*Employment Protection
(consolidation) Act,
1978,* 3, 210, 359-63

380 *Janner's Letters of Employment Law*